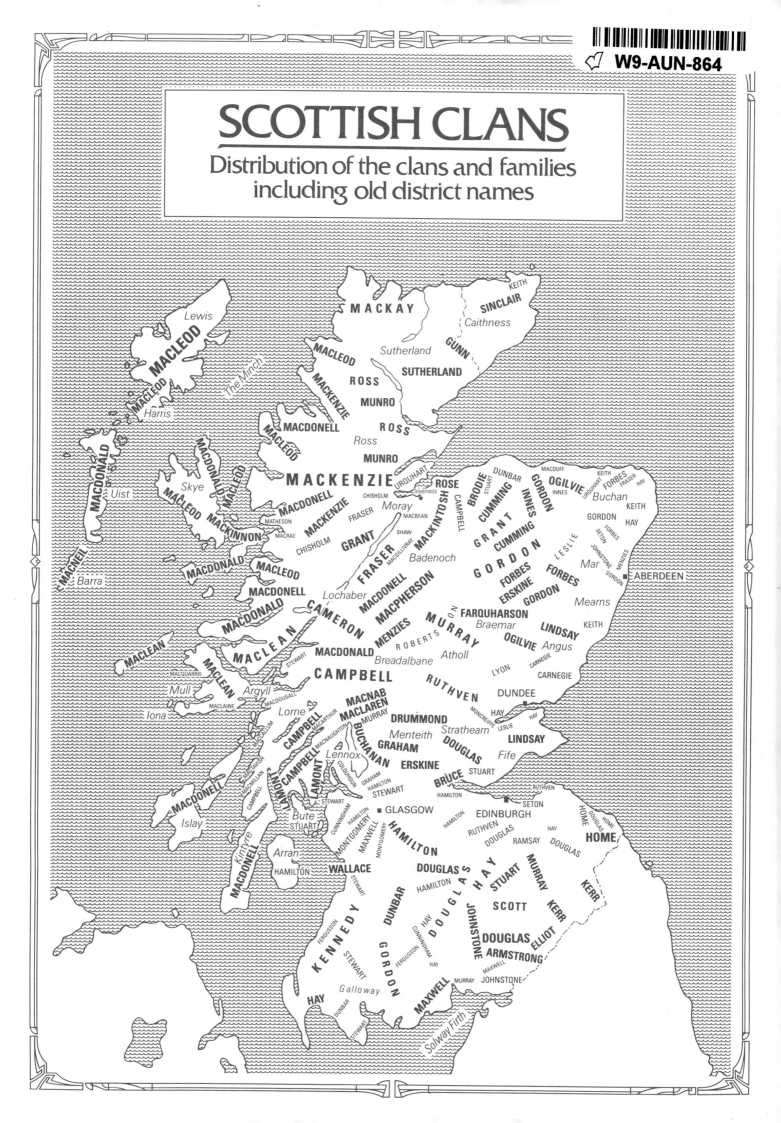

SCOTTISH CLANS

Distribution of the clans and families including old district names

SCOTTISH CLANS & TARTANS

SCOTTISH CLANS & TARTANS

Neil Grant

CRESCENT BOOKS
NEW YORK

ACKNOWLEDGMENTS

Sincere thanks are due to Rennie McOwan and Ronald Black who kindly read the book in typescript and made many invaluable suggestions and corrections. Remaining errors are the responsibility of the author alone.

Photographs
Reproduced by gracious permission of Her Majesty The Queen 24, 40-1, 43, 44-5 (Windsor Castle, Royal Library. © 1986 Her Majesty The Queen), 174-5; Ken Andrew 54-5, 69, 76-7, 94-5, 136, 178, 179 left, 198-9; The Commanding Officer of the Black Watch 62; by permission of the Trustees of Blairs College, Aberdeen 17; reproduced by courtesy of the Trustees of the British Museum, London 19; Dr J. G. Burgess 226; The Master and Fellows of Corpus Christi College, Cambridge 13; W. F. Davidson 24-5, 172, 212, 233, 246; reproduced with permission of John Dewar & Sons Ltd, Scotch Whisky Distillers 200; John Dewar Studios (by permission of John MacLeod of MacLeod) 193 bottom; Mary Evans Picture Library, London 50; Derek Forss 2-3, 60-1, 130 left, 146, 149, 168, 185, 207; Great Scot! Pictures, Edinburgh 8, 11, 251 bottom; John Green 180-1; V. K. Guy 106-7; The Hamlyn Group, Twickenham - Peter Davenport (reproduced by courtesy of the Scottish Tartans Museum, Comrie) 30, 34 left; The Hamlyn Group - Robb Campbell Harper (reproduced by courtesy of Daniel Shackleton's Art Gallery, Edinburgh) 89; The Hamlyn Group - Hector Innes (reproduced by courtesy of the Duke of Roxburghe) 25; The Hamlyn Group -

Michael Warren 144; The Hamlyn Group - West Highland News Agency (reproduced by courtesy of Donald Cameron) 71; A. G. Ingram Ltd (reproduced by courtesy of the Regimental Trustees of the Queen's Own Highlanders) 74-5; Jarrold & Sons Ltd, Norwich 20-1, 82-3, 102-3, 126-7, 191; A. F. Kersting 79, 104; National Galleries of Scotland, Edinburgh 15, 16, 18, 26-7, 28-9 (by courtesy of the Trustees of the late Mrs Magdalene Sharpe Erskine, on loan to the National Gallery of Scotland), 35, 39, 122, 163, 167, 216, 234, 237, 247 bottom; National Library of Scotland, Edinburgh 1, 6-7, 10 right (reproduced by courtesy of the Duke of Roxburghe) 32, 33, 219, 238; National Museums of Scotland, Edinburgh 36, 51, 113, 179 right; National Trust for Scotland, Edinburgh 66; Perthshire Tourist Board, Perth 105; The Photo Source/ Colour Library International, London 12-13, 22-3, 46, 52-3, 64, 72-3, 84-5, 86-7, 90-1, 98-9, 109, 114-15, 124-5, 132-3, 140, 153, 159, 160-1, 162-3, 164, 165, 171, 182, 197, 204-5, 209, 221, 232, 240-1, 242, 249; James Pringle Woollen Mills Ltd, Edinburgh 42 top, 121, 147, 152, 176, 183; Tom Scott (by permission of the Duke of Atholl) 223; Tom Scott (reproduced by courtesy of the Royal Company of Archers) 252; Tom Scott (reproduced by courtesy of the Scottish Tartans Museum, Comrie) 31, 34 right, 42 bottom; The Scottish Tartans Museum, Comrie (reproduced by courtesy of Inverness Museum and Art Gallery) 119; Scottish Tourist Board, Edinburgh 48, 49, 111, 128, 243, 251 top; Bob and Sheila Thomlinson 14, 80-1, 116, 154, 158 bottom, 193 top, 194, 196, 229, 235, 247 top; Judy Todd 9, 138, 156, 186, 202, 218, 239; Werkgroep Loevesteyn, Utrecht 38 (all four); by courtesy of the Dean and Chapter of Westminster 10 left; George Young 130 right, 142, 158 top.

Half-title page: Highland chiefs dressed in the Stewart and Gordon tartans.

Title page: Kilchurn castle and Loch Awe

Designer: Karel Feuerstein

This edition published 1987 by
Crescent Books and distributed by
Crown Publishers Inc.

First English edition
published 1987 by Country Life Books
an imprint of
The Hamlyn Publishing Group Limited,
Bridge House, 69 London Road
Twickenham, Middlesex TW1 3SB, England

© The Hamlyn Publishing Group 1987

hgfedcba

ISBN 0-517-49901-0

Printed in Spain

CONTENTS

The figures in the corners of the map of Scotland by John Speed show Highland dress as it was developing during the 17th century. At bottom left is what appears to be an early version of the belted plaid. The female figure (bottom right) also wears a plaid. The female equivalent of the belted plaid was the *arisaig,* which stretched from neck to heels and had plenty left over to form a hood.

The Yles of Orknay

A Scale of Miles

THE GERMANE

SEA

PART OF ENGLAND

A Scotch Woman

A Highland woman

Performed by Iohn Speed and are
to be sold by Roger Rea y Elder &
younger at y Golden Crosse in
Cornhill against the Exchange

A HISTORY

In the notes on individual clans which make up the bulk of this book various events of wider significance are mentioned out of their historical context. This section, therefore, is intended to provide a brief background to those events. For a history of the Scots and an account of the social and economic life of the Highlands there are many excellent books available.

The Origins of the Scots

The Scots came from Northern Ireland and settled in Argyll in Roman times. In about AD 500 a fresh influx from Ulster established a separate kingdom which is called Dalriada after them, 'the tribe of Riada'. They made their capital, such as it was, at Dunadd.

The dominant race in Scotland at this time were the Picts, a Celtic people of diverse origins who inhabited roughly the north. Strathclyde in the south-west was a kingdom of the Celtic Britons, while most of the south-east, from the Forth to the Tweed, was Anglo-Saxon.

The initial expansion of the Scots, or Gaels, could be achieved only at the expense of the Picts, a much more powerful, though divided, people. For some time the fate of Dalriada looked highly insecure, and after a sweeping Pictish victory in 559 the Scots appeared to be on the verge of expulsion.

However, they survived. The decisive factor seems to have been the mission of St Columba, who must have been a man of tremendous force of character. He arrived at Iona from Ireland in 563 and found favour among the Picts as well as the Scots. He re-established the Scots monarchy, converted the northern Picts to Christianity, saw off the Loch Ness monster (it must have been a great deal smaller then), and probably dissuaded the Picts from completing the reconquest of Dalriada.

Thereafter the Scots expanded steadily, both north and east. There was probably some intermingling with the Picts, although the two nations remained generally hostile to each other.

During the late 8th century a new power appeared on the scene: the Norsemen. They moved steadily southward on the western side of the country and at the beginning of the 9th century attacked Iona.

It seems probable that the Picts suffered more than the Scots from the Norsemen's raids. At any rate, the threat posed by the Scandinavian invaders was a spur to union, and in 843 Kenneth MacAlpin, king of the Scots of Dalriada, made himself by a mixture of force

Left: Relics of the Picts include many stone relief sculptures, often of scenes of hunting or battle, as in this sophisticated example from about 800.
Right: The first Christian church in Iona was established in the 6th century and St Columba, who made Iona his base, arrived 15 years later. Several freestanding crosses survive at Iona which date from the 8th and 9th centuries, when this type of monument was common throughout northern Britain and Ireland.

and treachery king of the Picts as well. He had in fact a claim to the Pictish crown, which he reinforced by eliminating other claimants.

Kenneth MacAlpin is regarded as the first king of a united nation, although his kingdom of Scotland, known as Alba, or Alban, was a relatively small one. It extended no farther south than Forth and Clyde, not much farther north than the Moray Firth, and did not include the Western Isles or parts of the western coast. His own attempts to incorporate Lothian were unsuccessful, and the task of extending the kingdom to its natural boundaries was to occupy his successors for many generations. Lothian was not conquered until King Malcolm II's victory over the Anglo-Saxons in 1018.

In that same year Malcolm's grandson Duncan inherited the throne of Strathclyde, the kingdom of the Celtic Britons (they were sometimes called 'Welsh'), when the last of its independent kings died without a male heir. Malcolm also regained the northern mainland and the Hebrides from Norway, so that when Duncan succeeded him as king of Scots in 1034 the kingdom was roughly equivalent to modern Scotland – larger, in fact, for although it

lacked the Northern Isles it included a sizable swathe of Cumbria.

The following period in Scottish history is the earliest with which most people have any familiarity. However, their knowledge is derived from Shakespeare's *Macbeth*, which gives a very misleading picture. Far from being a hated usurper, Macbeth appears to have been a successful monarch and his death an unfortunate event for the Scots. King Malcolm III, known as Canmore or *Ceann Mór* (Great Head), who regained the Crown from Macbeth in 1057, introduces a new era.

The Clans

Significantly, Malcolm was the last king of Scots to bear a Gaelic nickname. He had been brought up in England, was sympathetic to English customs, and married as his second wife a strong-willed Anglo-Saxon/Hungarian princess, Margaret, who with other Anglo-Saxon notables had taken refuge in Scotland after the Norman Conquest. His reign marks the beginnings of the future divide between the Gaelic-speaking Highlands and the English-speaking Lowlands. An event symbolic of this trend was Malcolm's decision to move his capital south, into Anglo-Saxon Lothian.

In this reign the foundations of feudalism were laid, and Malcolm's Queen Margaret took the lead in attempting to reorganise the Church on more 'Roman' lines, with celibacy of priests and government by bishops. These reforms had little effect in the Highlands, where some of the more liberal customs of the old Celtic Church were to persist into Reformation times.

Malcolm's sympathies for English ways did not affect his territorial ambitions, and his defeat by William the Conqueror at Abernethy (1071), when he was forced to swear fealty to the king of England, did not restore peaceful relations in the Borders, which were to remain a turbulent area into the 17th century. During a pre-emptive raid into Northumbria Malcolm and his heir were killed (1093), ushering in one of those long periods of weak royal government which so gravely hindered the nation's development.

In the early 12th century the king of Scots ruled a territory scarcely larger than that held by Kenneth MacAlpin. The Norse King Magnus Barefoot regained the Hebrides, although after his death the Norse position steadily weakened until the defeat of King Haakon at Largs (1263) which resulted in the reduction of Norse holdings to the Northern Isles alone.

There are still many signs of the Norse influence in the west, but on the whole it is surprising that they are not more plentiful. In many respects the culture of the

Gaels was the more advanced, and after the removal of Norse overlordship it was Gaelic culture that predominated in the Hebrides.

More significant for Scotland generally was the Norman takeover in England. The immediate result was the increase of English (i.e. Anglo-Saxon) influence with the immigration of political exiles, like St Margaret (she was canonised for her religious work), but more important was the ensuing influx of Anglo-Norman barons, especially under King David I (1124-53) who, besides being king of Scots, was also the premier English baron, prince of Cumbria, and brother-in-law of the English king. When he returned to Scotland to take up the Crown he brought many Anglo-Norman magnates with him. From such men

sprang future dynasties: Bruce, Stewart (named after the office of Steward held by the Breton Walter fitzAlan under King David I) and future clans: Chisholm, Fraser, Grant, Sinclair are among those of Anglo-Norman origin.

Feudalism on the Anglo-Norman pattern became firmly established in the Lowlands, with French-speaking landholders and Celtic, Gaelic-speaking tenants, although a form of English was already standard in the south and east.

The Highlands were remote and inaccessible; growing differences in custom and language accentuated the separateness of the Highlanders.

The feudal system and the clan system in Scotland were established at roughly the same time (it would be difficult to ascribe dates to either). Under the feudal system land was held of a lord, or directly of the king, in return for loyalty and service (i.e. in the case of the barons, military service). In the tribal Highlands land was held by the chief of the clan, a group united, in theory at least, by blood, all claiming descent from a common ancestor (*clann* – means children). The chiefship depended to some extent on popular consent and at one time the land was held on behalf of the clan; in practice the chiefship eventually came to reside in the one landholding family. Although clans sometimes moved, by choice or compulsion, to another district, it was the land as well as the kinship bond which cemented the clan.

There was an old belief, certainly older than

Left: The Stone of Scone under the Coronation Chair in Westminster Abbey. It is an ordinary chunk of stone and possibly not the original, for Edward I, it is suggested, may have been tricked by the Scots.
Above: A miniature from a charter of 1159 to Kelso Abbey showing King David I and his son Malcolm IV, 'the Maiden'.
Right: St Margaret's Chapel at the summit of Edinburgh Castle rock, one of the oldest (and smallest) ecclesiastical buildings, in Scotland. It was possibly founded by King David I after Queen Margaret's death, though some say it was built on the Queen's instructions in 1080.

feudalism, in the right of 'kindness', the right to remain in occupation – though not ownership – of land through long-standing habitation alone. Though occasionally acknowledged in legal documents, this was a dangerously vague concept. Nevertheless, it was deeply entrenched and is far from dead even now. There was no generally recognised, clearly defined, legal concept of the right to own land until feudalism was established under Anglo-Norman influence. In parts of the Highlands this had little immediate effect, but where it did it assisted rather than diminished the development of the clan system ('but for Feudalism', wrote Sir Thomas Innes of Learney, 'we should have had no Clans . . .'). The founders of many clans were vassals of the Crown, with their landholdings authorised by royal charters. In Argyll and some other parts long-established landholders were confirmed in possession. Elsewhere, however, the absence of clear feudal rights could lead in later times to the loss of the land and the ensuing disintegration of the clan.

The Wars of Independence

In 1290 the royal line came to an end with the death of Alexander III's granddaughter, the four-year-old Maid of Norway, who had been promised in marriage to the son of the English king, Edward I. Numerous claimants now asserted their right to the Crown, the most prominent being Robert Bruce and John Balliol, a pair of Anglo-Norman nobles with lands on both sides of the border. To avoid a civil war, Edward I was

invited to preside over an assembly to decide whose head should wear the Crown. Edward's choice was Balliol, who besides having the better claim was also thought to be more amenable to English direction. However, even Balliol was not prepared to accept a position as Edward's decidedly humble vassal, and in 1296 he rose against the English. Edward promptly invaded Scotland in crushing force. At Berwick the bulk of the chief Scottish landholders (including Bruce) paid reluctant homage to him, and Balliol was swept into history's dustbag.

Edward's conquest of Scotland appeared to have settled the future of the country as a subordinate kingdom, but in fact the long wars of independence had only just begun. In 1297 William Wallace led a popular rising against the English, defeating a superior English army at Stirling Bridge. Edward, 'the Hammer of the Scots', returned to crush Wallace, who was nevertheless not captured until 1305. Soon afterwards Robert Bruce (son of Balliol's rival of the 1290s) took up the cause of Scottish independence and had himself crowned king of Scots (1306). Though roundly defeated at Methven, he escaped and

recouped his forces. The death of Edward I in 1307 removed the chief menace to the independence of the Scots, and within a few years Bruce was not only in command of virtually all Scotland but was also able to raid northern England. A great expedition was launched against him in the manner of Edward I, but without that formidable monarch's leadership it was utterly smashed in the greatest of all Scottish victories against the English, at Bannockburn, near Stirling, in 1314.

The Scottish forces included the fighting men of about twenty 'clans' though perhaps most of them should be more accurately regarded at that early date as merely the tenants of certain Highland barons.

Like all Scottish kings', Bruce's main concern, after defeating the English, was to unify the kingdom under the authority of the Crown. Lands were confiscated from opponents and bestowed on supporters, though Bruce tried to ensure that the new landlords were kin to the old, or had at least some link with their newly acquired territories which would make them acceptable to their tenants. The rise of the Campbells can be dated from the rewards they

The first of the great Scottish clans was Clan Donald, descended from Somerled, who despite his Norse name was himself descended from the ancient High Kings of Ireland. Somerled built up a large dominion in Argyll and the southern Hebrides before his death in 1164. His sons were the ancestors of the MacDougall lords of Lorne and the MacDonald lords of the Isles (*Mac* means son of) whose power at its height rivalled that of the king of Scots. Clan Donald became subdivided into a number of branches which, after the end of the lordship of the Isles of 1493, became independent clans.

Other clans traced their descent from equally venerable ancestors, and although the old Celtic genealogies cannot be taken too literally – they were sometimes manipulated for family advantage – where hard evidence can be adduced it often tends to confirm clan legends.

Their origins were varied. Some were of largely Pictish descent, some like the MacLeods were of Norse origin, some stemmed from the earliest Scottish settlers in Dalriada. In the east and north many clan chiefs were descended from Anglo-Norman feudal landlords, who had soon become thorough Highlanders. (Most of their clansmen, who adopted their chief's name when surnames came into general use in the late Middle Ages, would naturally have had older native origins.) It is necessary only to look at a number of Highland people today to become aware of their disparate racial origins.

Clan names generally derived from an ancestor

Above: Melrose Abbey. The 12th-century Cistercian successor to the original 7th-century Columban monastery was virtually destroyed by the English in 1322 and 1385. The Abbey ruins were neglected during the post-Reformation period. The Church forms the major part of what can be seen today. Here, and not in the Holy Land as he wished, the heart of Bruce is believed to rest.

Right: At Bannockburn (the illustration comes from a 15th-century manuscript) the Scots were heavily outnumbered but as in many other medieval battles, they drew a decisive advantage from the weight of an armoured knight on a heavy horse and the prevailing lack of drainage, for the English cavalry was bogged down in the marshes beside the bush.

received for their support, while the MacDougalls, Bruce's opponents, suffered correspondingly.

Even Bruce made little serious effort to bring the Western Highlands under royal control, and the lack of strong leadership after his death in 1329 was reflected in the general lawlessness of the country. The prime example of this political failure is the career of the notorious Wolf of Badenoch, Alexander Stewart, Earl of Buchan (died 1405), an illegitimate son of King Robert II, who combined the office of justiciary with the career of bandit.

The absence of national order and justice tended to strengthen the growth of clanship.

considerably later than the alleged founder who was responsible for occupying the land and thus establishing the clan more or less permanently. The Campbells are called Clan *Diarmaid* and may or may not be descended from that legendary Ossianic hero; but their chief is called *Mac Cailein Mór* (Great son of Colin), a historical figure who established their fortunes in the 13th century. Moreover, lands were usually built up gradually over a period of time, by marriage, conquest, royal grant or other means. Although as a rule they were held by the chiefly family with some legal title, the most important assurance of landholding was the ability to protect the land by force. Thus clan chiefs were eager to acquire not only land, but men as well.

The military aspect of the clan, combined with devotion to the homeland, reinforced the spirit of clanship, the strength of which it would be hard to exaggerate. Because all clansmen claimed, rightly or wrongly, a common descent, there was a much closer bond between clansman and chief than between feudal landlord and tenant. Clanship involved mutual respect: an 18th-century Englishman was amazed to see a Highland chief unaffectedly shaking hands with the humblest of his men. There were no 'servile yokels' in the glens.

The practice of fostering was common among the clans. Thus a chief's son would be brought up by another family, usually one of his tacksmen (i.e. leaseholders, generally fairly close relatives) and the bond between the child and his foster parents was as strong as the bond with his real parents.

Some clans prospered and expanded; others blossomed briefly and disappeared. The more powerful the clan, the larger the number of branches, septs and dependants. Smaller clans often lived on the lands of great chiefs, and there were numerous examples of the intense loyalty shown by such dependants to their benefactors in times of conflict.

The clans varied so much in size and composition that any generalisation stumbles over exceptions. Even within well-defined clan districts people with different names would be found. In some areas there was no dominant clan. In others, especially fertile agricultural districts, different chiefs conflicted over feudal superiority, often as a result of contradictory charters issued by an inefficient (or malignant) government.

It is also difficult to distinguish between what was indisputably a clan and what was really a powerful family backed by feudal tenants, the Gordons being a prime example of the latter. Moreover, though the clan system was essentially a Highland development, the great Border families are usually included. The major Border clans will be found in this book along with many of the great families who were not in a strict sense the leaders of a clan.

Raiding for cattle and other booty was a major occupation among the clans. From this heritage the Highlanders derived their well-deserved reputation for military prowess, though also their tendency to put everything into their initial charge. Because of commitments at home it was difficult to maintain a force in the field over a long period of time.

Although they did not like long campaigns the clans were addicted to long-standing quarrels, and the blood feuds that were the bane of the clan system could last literally for centuries. They coloured the many engagements in which Highlanders fought on both sides.

The Stewart Age

Gaelic culture probably reached its height under the lordship of the Isles, but such a power could scarcely have co-existed for long with the Scottish monarchy as it developed under the Stewarts (or Stuarts), the first of whom was King Robert II (1371-90).

The power wielded by the Lord of the Isles was exemplified in 1411, when he set out in pursuit of his more or less justified claim to the great earldom of Ross with a huge Highland host (probably over 10,000 men) which included most of the western clans. He sacked Inverness and would have given Aberdeen the same treatment had he not been checked – scarcely defeated – at the battle of Harlaw by the forces of the Regent, the Duke of Albany.

The earldom of Ross did later pass to the Lord of the Isles, but meanwhile the accession of King James I in 1424 brought to the throne a monarch determined to assert royal control and none too particular as to the means he employed. Thus in 1427 Highland chiefs were summoned to a parliament at Inverness, but on their arrival some were thrown into prison and a few lesser chiefs were hanged.

James was assassinated in 1437, when his son, James II, was six. King James II was killed during Border warfare with the English in 1460 when his son, James III, was nine. These unfortunate minorities naturally had a dire effect on central government and encouraged the great barons, north and south, to seek their own advantage. The Lord of the Isles and the Earl of Douglas formed an alliance with the English, yet more evidence of the incompatibility of the

Above: King James II (reigned 1437-60) by an unknown artist.

Left: Highland cattle beside Loch Quoich. The breed has changed considerably since the days when they were described as small and black. Agricultural reformers in the 18th and 19th centuries bred out their original black colouring and increased their size and length of coat, but eventually turned them into ornaments for rich men's parks. Their chief commercial drawback was (and is) their slow growth: hence the preference for Aberdeen Angus and other breeds.

monarchy and the lordship, and this unsuccessful venture led to the forfeiture of the lordship in 1493.

The immediate results were unfortunate for the western clans: the vacuum of power exacerbated inter-clan rivalry, and a series of vain revolts broke out on behalf of the son and grandson of the last Lord of the Isles. It is one of history's sadder ironies that a similar sequence was to be enacted 300 years later on behalf of the Stewart dynasty against which the men of the Isles had rebelled.

James III, though he did gain the Northern Isles by marrying a Norwegian princess, was unable to control the noble factions, and disorder reigned in the Highlands and the Borders. In 1488 his son, James IV, was proclaimed king in his place; James III was assassinated after the battle of Sauchieburn and once again the king was a minor – though at 15 he was soon able to take control.

Moreover, James IV proved perhaps the most successful – and most attractive – of his line. Though his efforts to pacify the Highlands were not always

Above: John Knox, leader of the Scottish Reformation, a zealous and implacable Calvinist.
Right: Mary Queen of Scots whose sex and religion were both repugnant to the austere Scottish form of Protestantism practised by Knox. This is the Memorial Portrait of Mary probably painted after 1603.

honourable, he was at least prepared to use conciliation as well as force. He had the tact to wear Highland dress when in the Highlands, and he spoke Gaelic, the last king of Scots to do so. James also pursued a generally more sensible, i.e. more conciliatory, policy towards England, marrying Margaret Tudor, Henry VIII's sister and sealing a treaty of peace and friendship 'to endure for ever'. However, the 'auld alliance' with France, which had so often squeezed the English in the past, was to endure rather longer. In 1512, when Henry VIII joined a massive European coalition, the 'Holy League', against the French, James attempted to preserve the balance of European power, first by mediation and when that failed, by war. In 1513 the Scots army crossed the Tweed and, after taking various strongpoints, met an English army at Flodden where it suffered a terrible slaughter, the king, the cream of the Scots nobility and many Highland chiefs being killed.

Perilous times ensued. Not only was James V a baby, but most of the natural leaders of the country had also been swept from the scene. In many parts of the Highlands anarchy reigned: this was the time of the bloodiest feuds in the north, of civil wars in Clan Chattan (the ancient confederation of clans generally led by the Mackintosh) and Clan Ranald (MacDonald), involving the Frasers and many other clans. Barbarous deeds were committed.

As usual in times of weakness, the English showed unwelcome interest in Scottish affairs, seeking a marriage alliance first with the young James V, later with his infant daughter Mary, who was a week old when her father died in despair after his defeat by the English at Solway Moss (1542). Henry VIII's 'rough wooing' continued with invasions of the Lowlands, and after his death the English inflicted a severe defeat on the Scots at Pinkie (1547).

Mary was despatched to France to marry the Dauphin, but on his early death in 1561 she returned to reign as Queen of Scots. The 'auld alliance' was still strong, but the Protestant Reformation had complicated matters. The Lowlands were now largely Protestant, like the English, and also spoke the same language as their southerly neighbours. The Highlands remained relatively untouched by the Reformation. Mary herself was a Catholic, though it was not her religion so much as her favours to undesirable persons that largely provoked her downfall. Following the defeat of her supporters at Langside (1568) she fled to England, where she became the centre of Catholic plots against the English Queen Elizabeth I and ended under the executioner's axe.

The infant King James VI had already been crowned, but the country was again rent by civil war, exacerbated in the Highlands by clan feuds. By the time James VI was old enough to take up the reins, the runaway horses were going at a gallop he could scarcely restrain. Indeed, sometimes it was hard to say who was driving. On one occasion the king was captured by one noble faction and held prisoner for a year. In 1589 a group of northern Catholic earls plotted first to invade England with Spanish help, then rose against James himself. Led by the (Gordon) Earl of Huntly and the (Hay) Earl of Erroll, they defeated government forces under the (Campbell) Earl of Argyll at Glenlivet (1594), though they later surrendered to the king himself.

The 17th Century
In 1603 James VI succeeded Elizabeth to the English throne as James I of England, an event which brought great changes to Scotland. One immediate benefit was the end of the incessant warfare in the Borders. After 1603 the great Border plunderers – Armstrongs, Elliotts, Johnstons, Kerrs, etc. – rapidly faded from the scene.

One of James's last acts before leaving for London was to proscribe Clan Gregor, recently involved in a particularly bloody massacre of the Colquhouns, but on the whole perhaps sinned against as much as

PROMISSI FIDEM CAPTIVA RETENTA, POST CAPTI
VITATIS AN. 19, RELIGIONIS ERGÔ, EIVSDEM ELIZ.
PERFIDIA ET SENATVS ANGLICI CRVDELITATE,
HORRENDA CAPITIS LATA SENTENTIA NECI
TRADITVR, AC 12 CAL. MARTII 1587 IN
PITE TRVNCATA EST. ANNO ÆTATIS
REGNIQVE 45
IOANNA KENNETHIE.
ELIZABETHA CVRLE.
AVLA FODRINGHAMII,
REGINAM SERENISS. REGVM FILIAM,
VXOREM ET MATREM, ASTANTIBVS
COMMISSARIIS ET MINISTRIS R.
ELIZABETHÆ CARNIFEX SECVRI
PERCVTIT ATQ. VNO ET ALTERO
ICTV TRVCVLENTER SAVCIATÆ
TERTIO EI CAPVT ABSCINDIT,

sinning. This savage act was symptomatic of the growing tendency to regard the Highlanders as a barbaric race fit only to be forcibly suppressed, an attitude which prevailed throughout the 17th century – not a tolerant era – and was finally expressed in the deliberate destruction of clan society after the Jacobite defeat at Culloden in 1746.

Of course, the government had its friends and agents in the Highlands, most notably the Campbells of Argyll, one of the first Highland districts to be thoroughly feudalised (to the long-standing benefit of the wise – or crafty – Campbell chiefs), and the Gordon Earl of Huntly, whose role in the east was similar to that of Argyll in the west. The moral principles of Campbell and Gordon were no better, and no worse, than those of their neighbours, and not surprisingly they were often guilty of employing government commissions for private ends. The MacGregors were arguably the victims of Campbell ruthlessness (in the boyhood home of Alasdair Alpin MacGregor the name Campbell was never spoken, and perhaps this attitude, Highlanders having notoriously long memories, is not entirely dead now).

One way of pacifying the Highlands was by infiltrating Lowlanders into the area. For example, the government of James VI granted powers to a commercial company in Fife to the Isle of Lewis, as if it were some distant colony of recent acquisition. It was, however, inhabited by the MacLeods, who threw the Fife Adventurers out. That was not the end of the story, since the Adventurers sold their interests to the Mackenzies, enabling them eventually to extend their large dominions to Lewis.

In 1609 the Statutes of Iona were promulgated. Ostensibly they were directed towards the improvement of living standards in the Highlands and Isles; in reality, they were intended to destroy the Highland way of life. One of their provisions stated that gentlemen's sons must be educated in the Lowlands, to learn English. The suppression of the Gaelic language, the vehicle of Highland culture, was the clear aim of the government throughout the 17th and 18th centuries.

A number of chiefs were forced into agreeing to the Statutes, though in practice they were widely ignored. One clause had a contrary effect to that intended, since it banned the import of *aqua vitae*. Whisky had been made in the Highlands probably since the 15th century, though it was not widespread and was not drunk by gentlemen, who preferred claret. The attempt to ban strong spirits probably gave an impetus to whisky distilling, which was to become the one really successful Highland industry.

It was at this time too that the forests began to disappear at an increasing rate. Wood was scarce in

Above: When the revised *Book of Common Prayer . . . for the use of the Church of Scotland* was first read in the churches, it caused riots. In St Giles's, Edinburgh, tradition says, the missiles were propelled chiefly by women, led by one Jenny Geddes. From an etching by Wenceslaus Hollar.
Left: King James VI/I (1566-1625), by De Critz.

England, and the first ironworks in Scotland were built by Loch Maree as early as 1607. It was not until at least a century later, however, that the smelting furnaces began to make serious inroads, domestic fuel being no doubt a much larger consumer in the 17th century. Afforestation in recent years has aroused strong criticism, sometimes from people unaware that those gloriously stark hills once supported forests. However, the forests then did not consist of large plantations of Sitka spruce, Lodgepole pine and other boring though profitable aliens.

The efforts of Charles I to impose an Anglican form of religion on Scotland united the Scottish Presbyterians in resistance expressed in the National Covenant (1638). The ensuing Bishops' Wars proved to be a prelude to the English civil war, in which the Covenanters joined on the side of the English parliamentarians, in the Solemn League and Covenant (1643). The leading Covenanter in Scotland was the Earl of Argyll: otherwise, neither Covenant had much support in the Highlands. Another Covenanter was the Earl (later Marquess or, more correctly, Marquis) of Montrose who, however, fearing that Argyll meant to substitute 'King Campbell' for King Charles, offered his services to the king.

Montrose's campaign of 1644-45 is one of the most sensational episodes in Highland history, in the course of which he gained control of virtually the whole of Scotland with a small and irregular force of Highlanders formed around the nucleus of a thousand or so Irish MacDonalds, who had seized the opportunity to launch an attack on the hated Campbells.

However, when the Scottish army returned after assisting in the final defeat of the royalists in England, Montrose's diminished force, having attracted little support from the big Border and Lowland families and lacking the genius of Alasdair MacColla, the Clan Donald war leader, who was campaigning in the west, was crushed at Philiphaugh. The long-term effect of this campaign was to deepen the rift between Highlanders and Lowlanders, who became the more determined to prevent future Highland raids.

The Scots, including the Covenanters, had never been anti-monarchist, and the execution of Charles I by the English in 1649 provoked a sharp reaction. Charles II, having reluctantly signed the Covenant, was acknowledged as king of Scots, and a national rebellion mounted in his support. Montrose returned from exile but was betrayed and executed in Edinburgh under the malign squint of his old enemy, the Marquess of Argyll. Though several of the clans fought alongside the Covenanters (MacLean of Duart was a casualty at Inverkeithing), they were no match for Cromwell's highly professional army, and their invasion of England ended in defeat at the Battle of Worcester in 1651.

With Cromwellian efficiency General Monk undertook the suppression of the Highlands. Some chiefs, like Cameron of Lochiel, did not submit easily, but the fact must be admitted that under Monk the Highlands enjoyed seven years of relatively untroubled calm.

This was not the natural state of affairs, however, even then. The restoration of the monarchy with Charles II in England (1660) did nothing to ease the mutual suspicion and hostility between Lowlands and Highlands and the Covenanters, now out of favour, were driven deeper into resentment by the 'Highland Host' which was billeted on them under the dukes of Atholl and Perth in 1678. The Earl of Argyll (son of the opponent of Montrose) joined Monmouth's rebellion against James VII/II, Charles II's brother and successor, in 1685. This was a rare case of *Mac Cailein Mór* choosing the wrong side, and he was subsequently executed, like his father before him. (The Campbells made no such errors again.)

Three years later King James VII/II was deposed. He had considerable support in the kingdom north and south, but he squandered it by dithering. Still, Graham of Claverhouse, Viscount Dundee, led resistance to James's successor William III in the Highlands and won a striking victory at Killiecrankie (1689). Unfortunately, he was killed in the battle and succeeded by a less effective leader, imposed by James (inept to the last). Resistance was soon quelled.

The grand but grim Pass of Glencoe, scene of the notorious massacre of 1692. Like other morally evil acts of government, it was a disastrous mistake even from the purely political point of view, as it failed to destroy the clan and terminated any chance of reconciliation between William's government and the Jacobite clans.

The new government promised a free pardon to all Highland chiefs who took an oath to the Crown before a certain date. MacDonald of Glencoe was, through no fault of his own, some days late in signing, and the government made this the excuse for the notorious episode known as the Massacre of Glencoe (1692). Massacres were not rare in the Highlands and in terms of casualties Glencoe was not one of the worst. However, this extraordinary act of attempted genocide on the part of the government, executed with Campbell troops, approved (knowingly or not) by the king, still excites horror and revulsion. The alienation of the Highlands grew the more intense.

Jacobitism

Strictly speaking the Stewart dynasty did not end with James VII/II. His joint successors were his daughter Mary and her husband William III who had a claim in his own right as grandson of Charles I, and they were succeeded by another of James's daughters, Anne. Her death with no living heir in 1714 brought the Hanoverians to the throne and simultaneously fuelled Jacobite resistance.

There had been Jacobite revolts before. The Act of Union (1707), which united England and Scotland by ending Scottish independence, had been very unpopular throughout the country. The support for the union by the Duke of Argyll and the Campbells did nothing to alleviate the hostility of the Highlands generally, and in 1708 'James VIII' ('the Old Pretender' as the English call him) arrived in the Firth of Forth with a substantial French force. The moment was opportune, but the English navy prevented him landing (the French captains overrode his desire to make the attempt) and he withdrew again to France.

Had James Edward been prepared to abandon his religion and conciliate the English ministers he might have regained the throne in 1714. As it was, he had to rely on force, with French help no longer likely in view of the recently concluded Peace of Utrecht (1713). The Earl of Mar, formerly a supporter of the union, raised the clans in the Highlands and easily captured Perth (1715). But he hesitated over advancing south and at a time when decisive action was vital he lingered while the government forces built up. Mackintosh of Borlum made a dash as far as Preston in Lancashire, but received little of the expected help from English Jacobites and was compelled to surrender. The Frasers took Inverness for George I, and Mar's army began to disintegrate. Eventually he moved towards Stirling and encountered Argyll at Sheriffmuir. The military action was indecisive, but for the Jacobites anything less than total victory was a defeat. Whig clans like the Mackays, Rosses and Munroes commanded the

north; government forces steadily expanded in the south. By the time James Edward arrived at Peterhead in December, the cause was lost. In little more than a month he was on his way back to France, accompanied by his diffident general.

Despite this discouraging example the Jacobites rose again in 1719, this time with backing from Spain. A small force led by the earl marischal (an office hereditary in the Keith family) took Eilean Donan Castle on Loch Alsh but was swiftly defeated at the Battle of Glenshiel.

The Highlands were, of course, never solid for the Jacobites; nor was the Hanoverian dynasty the sole or

The monument at Glenfinnan at the head of Loch Shiel, where Prince Charles Edward raised his standard in August 1745. On that day his followers probably numbered about one thousand, mainly Camerons and MacDonalds.

even the primary object of Highland hostility. On the field of Sheriffmuir MacLean of Duart had addressed his men: 'Gentlemen, this is a day we have long wished to see. Yonder stands *Mac Cailein Mór* [i.e. Argyll] for King George. Here stands MacLean for King James. God bless MacLean and King James! Gentlemen, charge!'

The clans were indeed fighting for their culture and their very existence – against the government, against the encompassing power of the Campbells, and, unwittingly but surely, against the tide of history. While Culloden is generally regarded as marking the end of the clan system, modern historians see it in slow but inexorable decline several generations earlier.

Wealth and power in the Highlands were measured by cattle and men. Fighting and cattle-raiding were far from being the sole pursuits of clansmen as many accounts tend to suggest, and agriculture, though primitive, was widely practised (signs of

disarm the Highlanders. General Wade, the government's commander-in-chief in Scotland, embarked on a road-building programme designed to make the Highlands more accessible to government troops (in fact, the General's second-in-command was chiefly responsible for the construction). Some companies were formed from loyal Whig clans for policing duties, and the Kirk sent ministers into the Highlands in an effort to instil the 'true religion' in Highland hearts.

Culloden

The French planned to support a Jacobite rising in 1744 but were thwarted by the weather and the British navy. Nevertheless, Prince Charles Edward, son of James VIII (called the 'Young Pretender' by the English and 'Bonnie Prince Charlie' by romantics everywhere), decided to go ahead with a landing in Scotland the following year ('the Forty-five'). He

agricultural activity on land since abandoned can occasionally be found today). The crafts were by no means absent, and visitors sometimes commented on the Highlander's ability to turn his hand to a variety of trades (a trait also still evident).

However, the social system encouraged over-population. Food shortages led to more raids on neighbours; raids made the ability to defend clan territory the more vital; defence demanded more men.

After the Jacobite rising of 1715 ('the Fifteen') the government took measures to prevent a future outbreak. Many Jacobites were transported, two of the leaders were executed in London, while the titles and estates of others who had escaped to the continent were forfeited, though most of these were later restored. Attempts were made, with limited success, to 'root out the Irish language' (i.e. Gaelic), and to slipped past the British warships and landed in the Outer Hebrides with fewer than a dozen companions, most of them foreigners. Jacobite sympathisers were almost universally appalled at this ill-considered and unsupported act. However, with the fact of the prince's presence and the influence of his personality, many of the clans rallied to him when he set up his standard at Glenfinnan. Probably most people, like Lord George Murray, the chief Jacobite strategist and one of the few Jacobite leaders with military experience, did so out of a sense of duty and with some foreboding.

The battle of Prestonpans, in the manner of Highland victories, was over in a matter of minutes, and apart from a few isolated fortresses, including Edinburgh Castle, the Jacobites were soon in control of Scotland. Nevertheless, many of the clans, including the MacLeods and MacDonalds of Skye, did not rally to Bonnie Prince Charlie.

Left: Memorial to the fallen at Culloden.

Above: Detail of a portrait of James Drummond, third Duke of Perth (1713-47), a Jacobite leader during the Forty-five by Allan Ramsay. Perth died while escaping to France after Culloden.

Opposite: **Bonnie Prince Charlie entering Holyrood House** by Pettie.

It was a remarkable beginning, but after Prestonpans the prince's fortunes turned. Once again England failed to provide the expected support, and at Derby the prince was in danger of being caught between two much larger forces. Despite his own desire to make a dash to London, his advisers, notably Murray, persuaded him to withdraw to Scotland in the hope of making it secure by taking the remaining Hanoverian strongholds. Inept English generalship gave the Jacobites one more victory at Falkirk early in 1746, but it was practically their last. Their strength began to dwindle; pay, supplies and weapons were all scarce. Under the capable, if limited, generalship of the royal Duke of Cumberland, the government forces advanced northward.

Against the advice of Murray, whom he now groundlessly mistrusted, Prince Charles decided on a surprise attack on Drummossie Moor, near Culloden, coincidentally the home of the leading Whig Highlander, Forbes of Culloden. The Jacobite army was cold and tired, after an abortive attempt to launch a night attack, and also unorganised and outnumbered. Despite some charges of characteristic gallantry, they were decimated, losing about 1,200 men in the battle, about four times the number of Hanoverian casualties. The Hanoverian reaction to victory was savage reprisal against their defeated opponents, earning Cumberland his nickname of Butcher. The prince, after a series of romantic adventures, escaped to France along with a few Jacobite leaders.

The aftermath of the battle is one of the most hideous episodes in modern British history. Plunder and violence were let loose on the clans, often regardless of their allegiance. The atrocious details are given in John Prebble's well-known modern account *Culloden* (1967).

The campaign of terror was designed to annihilate the clans as units of independent action. To the same end an act was passed which forbade the wearing of Highland dress, including the tartan. No doubt, if such legislation had been practicable, the government would have outlawed the Gaelic language too.

The End of the Clans

There is no end to the clans, yet Culloden and its aftermath surely marked the end of the clan system. The chiefs, perhaps not before time, lost their old powers of 'pit and gallows' and became no different from other landholders in relation to their tenants. That the old bonds of kinship often survived, and strongly, many years afterwards, was demonstrated by the attraction of chiefly names in the raising of Highland regiments and by the unquestioning way in which many clansmen followed the dictates of leaders no longer committed to their welfare.

The influx of sheep had already begun before the rising of 1745, and it gathered pace thereafter. Highlanders were dispossessed in large numbers to make sheep pastures and sportsmen's estates, and the Highland Clearances are often linked with the heavy emigration, mainly to North America, that began about the same time. But the facts of the matter are not simple. Emigration, particularly to North Carolina, began as early as the 1730s; subsequently many of the Scots settlers in North America were ex-soldiers of Highland regiments, raised in surprising numbers after the Forty-five, who received land

grants in the colonies. Rising rents and agrarian poverty encouraged more to leave. Eviction was probably the direct cause of only a minority of emigrations in the late 18th century, and emigration was not encouraged by all landlords by any means. Nevertheless, accounts of the more savage Clearances make grim reading.

The Clearances and the simultaneous emigrations appear to have had remarkably little effect on overall population in the Highlands, which is thought to have been not significantly smaller in the 1820s than it was a century earlier. Rising health standards and the introduction of the potato, contributing to lower death rates, were partly responsible for the maintenance of numbers, but it is hard to reconcile the judgment of social historians that the population did not decrease significantly during the century of emigration with the numerous remarks about depopulated settlements and vanished congregations made by visitors to and residents of the Highlands in the late 18th and early 19th centuries. No doubt it was the more striking examples that caught people's attention.

The new landlords, many of them Lowlanders or Englishmen, were 'improvers', and although 'improvement' really meant larger profits for the landowners, not better living conditions for the tenants, naturally not all improvements were deleterious. New towns and villages – Inveraray, Grantown – were built and new industries started. An 18th-century Lord Breadalbane introduced spinning and built miles of roads and bridges, though his 19th-century successor was one of the worst of the evicting landlords.

Most industrial enterprises had disappointing results. Lord Breadalbane's spinning wheels were soon put out of business by power looms; the kelp industry which briefly became almost the only source of income in parts of the western coasts and isles collapsed disastrously after 1825 with the repeal of duties on imported alkaline barilla. Whisky (then spelt 'whiskey') was distilled throughout the Highlands during the 18th century, but until 1823 it was all quite illegal because the licensing arrangements were impossibly harsh. Roads and canals, including Telford's great Caledonian Canal, on the whole failed

Above: Rent Day in the Wilderness by Sir Edwin Landseer, whose romantic pictures of the Highlands in the mid-19th century were painted with considerable care for detail.

Overleaf: Detail of *A Highland Wedding* at the end of the 18th century, by David Allan.

to generate as much commercial traffic as expected.

Perhaps almost the last occasion when it was still possible to see Highland chiefs and clansfolk living naturally in the manner of their ancestors was when that famous English traveller Dr Samuel Johnson took his tour to the Hebrides accompanied by his friend James Boswell, the Lowland lawyer, in 1773. Johnson, no admirer of the Scots, was with difficulty persuaded that he would not need to tuck a pair of dags (pistols) in his ample belt. Though some of his comments on the Highlanders ('crushed by the heavy hand of a vindictive conqueror') were more perceptive than those of other visitors of more enduring ignorance, his experience of a quite different culture left him unenlightened on the whole. Nor was he entirely immune to the myths which only a generation after Culloden were already gathering in the glens.

TARTANS

The origins of tartan are obscure and controversial. Cynics maintain that the whole business was dreamed up by 19th-century romantics, encouraged by textile manufacturers, hoteliers and others with an eye to commercial potential. At the other extreme it is said that many tartans are as old as the clan system itself. Both opinions can be confidently rejected, but it is much more difficult to decide where between the two the truth lies. We scarcely know enough yet, and perhaps never shall, to make any final statement on the matter, although we must acknowledge that some evidence can be found to support even these extreme views. No reasonable person would deny that tartan was worn in the Highlands before the end of the Middle Ages or that the evidence for tartan being a generally accepted symbol of clan identity before 1745 is rather slight.

The original meaning of the word tartan, which probably comes from the French *tartaine* and was introduced into Scotland in Norman times, refers to the pattern. In Gaelic, the word *breac* means speckled or particoloured and a *breacan* is literally a particoloured thing, i.e. a tartan plaid. In earlier times, the word 'tartan' was sometimes used in a broader sense than its modern meaning, a cloth woven in a regular pattern of coloured stripes and checks.

Chequered cloth is of course not exclusive to the Gaels and has been made in many societies far removed in time and place. Tartan, it has been

Very few physical remains of tartan before the Forty-five exist today. This is one of the oldest surviving remnants, known as the Glen Affric tartan and possibly dating from before 1700.

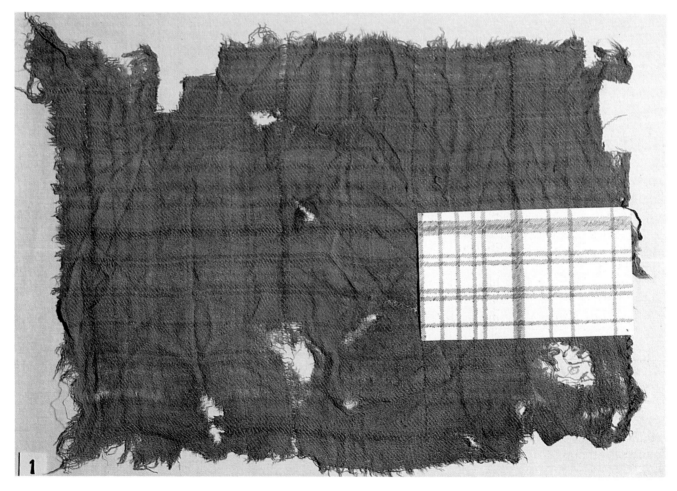

1

A reconstructed loom at the Scottish Tartan Museum, Comrie, Perthshire.

pointed out, occurs in paintings of 15th-century Siena and 18th-century Japan.

Some rather desperate attempts have been made to establish a dubious antiquity for Scottish tartan. One writer claimed that Julius Caesar's mention of woad referred to a practice of painting coloured stripes on the leg to denote the family or sept to which the subject belonged. A phrase in the *Aeneid* translated variously as cloaks 'chequered and bright', or 'striped and shining', has been identified as Virgil's attempt to describe tartan.

Serious historians of Highland dress usually begin with the Saga of Magnus Barefoot in 1093. Magnus III of Norway, returning from one of his expeditions to the 'western lands' (i.e. Ireland and the Hebrides), adopted the manner of dress of those parts. He went about bare-legged (thus acquiring his nickname), 'having short kyrtles and upper garments'. Despite some claims, a kilt cannot be detected here, nor of course tartan. What Magnus actually wore was almost certainly the garment, common to Ireland and Scotland at that date, which was called in Gaelic *léine*, a kind of shift reaching to the knee and usually described by English writers as a 'saffron shirt'. Any image of the Old Highlanders dashing about in the garb of Buddhist monks should be instantly suppressed. The material was probably a yellowish linen – it is unlikely that it was always dyed with saffron.

In Ireland the *léine* was marked in coloured stripes which denoted the ranks of the wearer, but there is no evidence that this practice was continued in Scotland.

The 'saffron shirt' was still normal – and one would think rather inadequate – wear in the 16th century, but at that time we also hear of 'woollen coverings of several colours'. This was a description of the clothes worn by the Highlanders at the battle of Haddinton in 1548, and ten years before that King James V, during a period when he was trying to establish his authority in the Highlands by conciliation rather than force, himself ordered a Highland costume in tartan.

Although the saffron shirt continued to be worn in at least some parts of the Highlands into the 17th century, it had generally been supplanted by the belted plaid, encouraged by the easier availability of woollen cloths. This was not a very radical development from the simple rug or shawl of earlier times. It consisted of a simple rectangle of cloth, at least 15 feet long and 5 feet wide.

On the hand looms then in use, this garment had to be made in two separate lengths which were sewn

Right: This engraving shows ways of wearing the belted plaid about the middle of the 18th century. It comes from Captain Burt's *Letters from a Gentleman in the North of Scotland*, published in 1754 but describing events 20 years earlier. Among the advantages of Highland dress, Burt mentioned the ability 'to skip over the rocks and bogs' without wetting the clothes.

together. As the shuttle was thrown by hand, the weaver had to reach both sides of the web – to throw with one hand and catch with the other. This limited the width of the material to 30 inches at the most.

No doubt people were adept at donning the belted plaid in various ways, but the method usually described as typical does seem rather cumbersome, especially as the state of the Highlands must have frequently required hurried dressing. In this method the plaid was laid out flat on the ground with the belt beneath. The lower part was folded in pleats and the wearer then lay down on top of it and gathered it with the belt around his waist. When he stood up the greater part of the plaid trailed behind. Having donned his jacket or tunic he looped the long end of the plaid over his shoulder. By that time, one feels, his cattle might have been spirited far away. However, in such an emergency he would have been prepared to defend them in his shirt. In battle Highlanders customarily discarded their plaids before the charge, to be picked up after victory had been secured. If they lost the battle they lost their plaids too.

The belted plaid was a highly versatile garment. It could be worn as a cloak when the weather was cold, as a cape when it was raining, and of course it could be rolled around the body as a blanket at night. It is said that a group of – say – five men forced to sleep out with no shelter would lay out one plaid on the ground. Four of them would lie down on it, leaving a space in the middle. The fifth man spread a second plaid on top of them, piled heather on top of that, and covered the lot with the three remaining plaids before creeping into the space left for him.

The functions of the belted plaid, though numerous, did not include that of an ideal riding habit, and although it is possible to ride a horse in a kilt or a skirt, it is not very comfortable: this may explain why gentlemen more often wore trews.

That name sometimes causes confusion because it is now given to the tartan trousers worn by certain Highland regiments, whereas trews were originally tights. They incorporate hose and breeches in one piece and are tailored to fit skin-tight.

King James V's Highland suit included trews but not a plaid, and one early authority on Highland dress always claimed that trews predated the belted plaid. They were worn in Ireland as early as the 10th century, but in Scotland they seem to be roughly contemporary with the belted plaid.

The kilt, *féile beag* (little kilt) or philabeg is the skirt section of a plaid with the pleats sewn in and it has been seen as an evolution in the less unruly times of the 18th century when the Highlander was less likely to be sleeping out in all weathers. Alternatively, the inconvenience of the belted plaid on the battlefield may have had something to do with the change; military motives have often played a part in the evolution of tartan.

An alleged English inventor of the kilt must not be ignored. His name was Thomas Rawlinson, 'a man of genius and quick parts' and he was the manager of an iron foundry in Glengarry some years after the Fifteen. Among his acquaintances were an English regimental tailor named Parkinson and the local laird, Alasdair MacDonell of Glengarry. On one occasion the tailor was astonished to discover that the belted plaid of a visiting Highlander was a single garment which its wearer was unable to discard despite the warmth of the room. He conceived the idea of dividing it more conveniently into two, and Rawlinson persuaded him to make him an outfit of this kind. MacDonell of Glengarry was so impressed that he adopted it too.

We have good authority for this story, although its popularity is due to the besetting sin of Scottish historiography of preferring English sources. Gaelic sources provide evidence of the kilt much earlier than this. Moreover, we do not know what other experiments were going on at the same time, or indeed earlier. The scanty pictorial evidence is sufficient to show that plaids were worn in innumerable different ways, as far back as these scanty sources can take us.

Whether kilt or plaid, tartan has a long history in the Highlands. The question remains, what significance did the pattern or 'sett' of the tartan have in relation to those who wore it?

Most modern tartans, including those labelled ancient, would undoubtedly be unrecognisable to the clans now associated with them before the Forty-five. This is partly due to the banning of tartan in the late 18th century and does not necessarily imply that clan tartans did not exist earlier.

There is plenty of evidence of a certain uniformity of tartans at an early period. When Martin Martin, a native of Skye and factor to MacLeod of Dunvegan, toured the Western Isles at the beginning of the 18th century he reported that 'Every Isle differs from each other in their Fancy of making Plads, as to the Stripes in Breadth, and Colours. This Humour is as different thro the main Land of the Highlands, in-so-far that they who have seen those Places are able, at the first view of a Man's Plad, to guess the Place of his Residence.' As has often been pointed out, this argues only for the existence of 'district' tartans. However, in the Highlands and in the Western Isles particularly, a 'district' was often much the same as a 'clan'. From the late 16th century, the ground rent due to the Crown on Islay was paid in cloth of black, green and white. The predominant clan in Islay was MacLean, and the MacLean tartan today is made up of the same three colours. This can hardly be coincidence, although such connections can be made with few other clans.

There are obvious reasons why some uniformity should exist in particular districts. A local weaver

Right: A tartan suit, with plaid, in Robertson of Struan tartan, probably worn in 1822, in the Scottish Tartan Museum, Comrie, Perthshire.

Opposite: Detail of a fine early portrait of *A Highland Chieftain* by Michael Wright, painted about 1660. The painting is in the Scottish National Portrait Gallery, Edinburgh. The subject may be Lord Breadalbane, or it may be a contemporary 'comedian' named Lacy who, according to the English diarist John Evelyn, was painted in this guise by Wright. The tartan bears no relation to any modern one.

This piece of tartan dates from 1726 and comes from a plaid worn at Culloden by Thomas Arbuthnot, a naval officer who deserted to join Bonnie Prince Charlie in 1745. It is a prize piece in the John Telfer Dunbar collection now held by the Scottish Tartans Society and to be seen in the museum at Comrie, Perthshire.

would tend to reproduce his own patterns, and would find it an advantage to run off a large quantity in the same pattern, which might well be offered at a lower price than an individual order. Chiefs, for whom cost would be less important, are said to have often worn a different tartan. Sometimes, too, chiefs would equip their men for a particular purpose, and in that case would presumably order one pattern only. Military motives may have been at work here again. Another factor was the local availability of dyes.

The fact that people of a certain district, or indeed clan, wore the same tartan does not mean that it had any significance in a tribal or heraldic sense. The attitude of the chiefs would be of interest in this connection. Did they encourage uniformity of tartan or not? Dubious evidence comes from a now lost and possibly forged letter written on behalf of the Earl of Sutherland to Murray of Pulrossie in 1618 requesting him to 'remove the red and white lines from the plaids of his men so as to bring their dress into harmony with that of the other septs'.

There is sounder evidence from Clan Grant about a century later, when the Chief of Grant issued an order commanding his tenants to wear coats, trews and short hose of 'red and greine set dyce all broad springed'. Similar orders were issued on several occasions. However, that such orders had to be issued at all proves that the Grants were not all wearing the same tartan earlier. The description, though the colours are the same, does not sound much like the modern Grant tartan either. And, finally, there can be little doubt that (not for the only time) the laird's orders were ignored, since a number of portraits, formerly at Castle Grant, survive from this period which show that even the closest relatives of the chief wore tartans which have no resemblance either to each other or to the present clan sett.

As part of the government's programme of pacification of the Highlands after the Fifteen six local companies or watches were raised in the Highlands to police their own districts under the command of reliable Whigs such as Campbell, Grant and Munro. They were known from the beginning as the Black Watch after the dark tartan they wore to distinguish them from the red-uniformed soldiers of the regular army. In 1739 it was decided to make them the basis of a new regiment, the 43rd (later 42nd), under the

command of the Earl of Crawford, a professional soldier who was a protegé of the Campbell chief, himself a former lieutenant of Marlborough in the French wars, the Duke of Argyll.

The regiment continued to be called the Black Watch. Its uniform was the belted plaid, to which its members were long accustomed, plus red jacket and waistcoat. The philabeg was worn off duty. It was also necessary to choose a tartan, and the sett which was adopted by the regiment then and now is known as the Black Watch tartan. It is probably the most influential – and most exploited – of all tartans, the first to be known by a specific name and to have an indisputably authentic heritage.

Some older authorities, following the researches of Stewart of Garth in the early 19th century, say the Black Watch tartan was based on the old 'Royal' tartan, but today it is generally agreed that this Royal tartan is a chimera. The Black Watch tartan seems to have been designed specially for the new regiment; presumably, the various setts worn by the independent companies were all rejected to avoid possible local associations causing resentment among those from other districts or clans.

The pipers of the Black Watch do not wear the regimental sett and it seems that from the beginning they wore a red tartan. Today they wear the Royal Stewart, but this cannot be the 'Royal' tartan of legend. If such a tartan existed at that time (and it is almost certain it did not), it would hardly have been chosen for a British regiment in the service of a Hanoverian monarch while the Stewart claimant was perched in France waiting to take over.

The best evidence of what tartans were worn before the Forty-five comes from contemporary portraits. It suggests overwhelmingly that choice of tartan was eclectic to say the least. It is not uncommon to see, as in the Grant portraits, two or even three different tartans worn together. A painting in the possession of the MacDonald family dating from this period shows two children wearing four different tartans, none of which resembles a modern MacDonald sett.

Tartan is associated with the Highlands and Sir Walter Scott used to deny that it had anything but the briefest heritage in the Lowlands. It appears that it was widely adopted in the south after the Act of Union with England (1707), which was more strongly resented there than by the Highlanders, who tended to ignore it. A 1720 portrait of Sir Robert Dalrymple, a Lowland laird, in the Scottish National Portrait Gallery shows him wearing tartan. On the other hand, some distinguished Highland chiefs, like the Campbells of Argyll, did not wear Highland dress for their portraits.

The Grant Piper (1714) by the itinerant artist Richard Waitt, with Castle Grant in the background. The tartan, though unlike the modern Grant tartan and different from the tartans of various Grant gentlemen of the period, is similar to that worn by Alastair Grant, the Laird's Champion, in another portrait painted by Waitt at the same time.

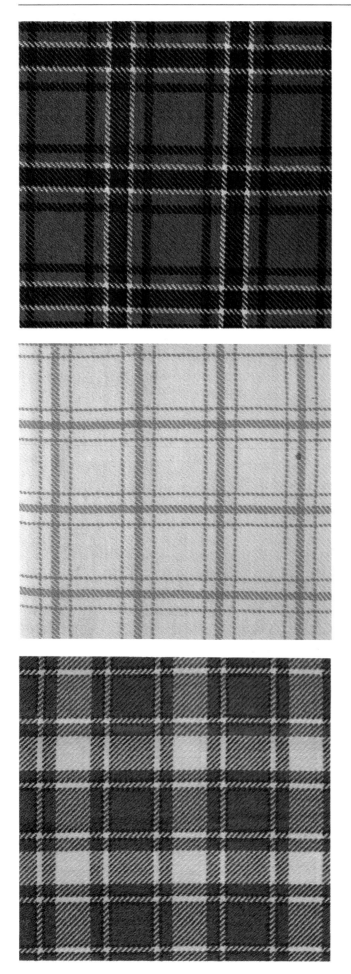

Opposite: Detail of *The MacDonald Children*, attributed to Jeremiah Davison and dating from the period when Highland dress was proscribed. None of the tartans worn by these young sportsmen can be identified with any modern MacDonald sett.

In 1983 hitherto unknown mural paintings of several figures in Highland dress were discovered at Loevestein Castle in the Netherlands. They appear to have been painted by a Scottish officer of the garrison not later than 1753, possibly by William MacKay, a subaltern whose death at Loevestein between 1750 and 1753 might explain why the murals are unfinished. Under the direction of Henk Hovenkamp the tartans worn by a man dancing (*below*) have been meticulously recreated by Dutch weavers (*left*). None of these resembles a modern tartan, nor do others appearing in the paintings with the possible exception of a piper's kilt which resembles, probably coincidentally, the modern MacNab.

There can be little doubt that by the time of the Forty-five certain tartans, besides the 'government' sett (the Black Watch), had acquired something of a clan identity, though whether they possessed the tribal symbolism they acquired later is more doubtful. As so often, much of the available evidence – rather scanty considering how comparatively recent the events are – can be used to argue both sides of the case. For instance, a MacDonald officer at the battle of Culloden complained later that he and his men

found it difficult to distinguish themselves from other Highlanders fighting on the other side, which could mean either that men on both sides wore similar tartans or that tartans had no identifying significance.

A well-known picture of an incident in the battle by a Swiss artist, David Morier, shows seven Highlanders being routed in an improbable manner by well-drilled Hanoverians, and close study reveals that they are wearing twenty-two different tartans, none of which is recognisable as a modern clan tartan. It is usually said that the models were actual Highlanders who had been taken prisoner in the battle, but this has recently been questioned. Even if they were Highlanders, they may not have been wearing their own clothes, although the dress of the English troops is depicted accurately. Practically all the other evidence argues against a clan tartan system, and few if any of the tartans known to have been worn at Culloden, which include a few actual relics, correspond with modern tartans.

Morier's well-known painting of an incident in the battle of
Culloden (*Episode of the Rebellion*). He probably used captured
Highlanders as models, and they possibly wore clothes that did not
belong to them. Morier was an accurate observer, as is proved by

his depiction here of the men of Barrell's Regiment and by his other
paintings of British regiments. This picture does not prove anything
about the tartans worn in 1746, but it certainly suggests that clan
tartans, if they existed at all, were not very common.

There is plenty of room for argument still, but the most likely conclusion is that the clan tartan system very largely post-dates the events which destroyed the clan social system.

One of the acts of repression in the wake of the Jacobite defeat was the so-called Dress Act, which forbade the wearing of Highland dress, including tartan, by anyone other than soldiers of Highland regiments. The act remained in force from 1747 to 1782, though less rigidly enforced in the later years. Very few tartans survived that long eclipse, and this break in tradition is chiefly responsible for our relative ignorance of clan tartans before 1745.

However, as governments never learn, one way to increase the popularity of anything is to make it illegal, and it is not hard to imagine the intense nostalgia that tartan inspired in the defeated Highlanders, nor indeed to conceive how a particular sett, perhaps worn only by a beloved chief long dead, came to be identified with the clan in the minds of his surviving followers.

Moreover, the banning of tartan in the Highlands did not mean that it ceased to be made. On the contrary, the popularity of tartan associated with the 'Celtic revival' in the early 19th century was foreshadowed even in the days of proscription.

The impetus came from two sources: from emigrant Highlanders in the colonies, especially North America, and from the army.

There were only two Highland regiments in 1745, but by the time the restrictions of the Dress Act were lifted there were ten, and a number of others had been raised and disbanded in the interval. At first they wore a variety of tartans, but in the interests of uniformity all eventually adopted the Black Watch or

'government' sett. To the casual observer this is far from obvious: the Gordons or the Seaforth Highlanders appear to wear a different tartan, but it is only the colours of the stripes that change; the pattern is the same.

There was one exception: Cameron of Erracht was allowed to devise his own tartan for the Cameron Highlanders, designed by his mother, it is said. This is perhaps surprising, but he was a determined man and raised the regiment at his own expense, without the usual government bounty. Their colonel, who would not enlist non-Gaelic speakers, was also able to resist successfully an attempt to draft his men into other regiments in 1795 and to retain the kilt when other Highland regiments were converted to 'trews' in 1804.

Tartan was not confined to Highland regiments: many Lowland regiments wore tartan trews, and the blue and yellow Johore tartan was devised for an Indian regiment.

After the restrictions on Highland dress were removed in 1782 tartan became swiftly both respectable and desirable. The new textile mills could turn it out at a great rate. However, the situation in the Highlands had now changed entirely. Tartan had formerly been the normal, everyday wear, but the ban had made it into a symbol – a symbol of nationhood, or pride, perhaps in some cases of defiance. Now when a man put on a kilt it was not at all like putting on his trousers. To a certain extent he was consciously dressing up.

The outsider's, particularly the Englishman's, conception of the Highlands had also changed. It was no longer a barren land of treacherous savages. It was a country of infinite romance, as portrayed in the novels of Sir Walter Scott. The Jacobite rebellion was far enough away to suggest no threat of danger but near enough for vivid, though often unreliable, memories. The Scot who had replied to an inquiry as to whether his family had a tartan with the words, 'Thank God, no, my people could always afford trousers,' would now be eager to reply affirmatively, if he could. And if he didn't have a tartan, he could very easily get one. He went along to a suitable supplier who on the most flimsy evidence would assure him that he belonged to a sept of this or that famous clan and was entitled to wear that tartan. Sometimes, no doubt, it was simpler than that. 'Why, sir, to be sure, the MacNothings have a tartan, and I happen to have a bolt or two to hand.' The customer went away satisfied and the merchant congratulated himself on unloading an unsuccessful line.

A vast number of purely ornamental patterns were produced, some named after districts, others after persons or even events. They included a 'Wellington'

and a 'Waterloo'. There is now a 'Wilson' tartan which was designed by a prominent tartan supplier as a wedding present for his wife, and at least one example of a tartan named after a fictitious character, Scott's Meg Merrilees.

The climax of the tartan revival was the visit to Scotland in 1822 of George IV, the first king to do so for nearly 200 years. Like many episodes in the life of that under-rated sovereign, this constantly teetered on the brink of farce, but in the end was a resounding success and a credit to all concerned, not least Sir Walter Scott and General Stewart of Garth, joint comperes of the show. The king himself, a plump but still impressive figure, proposed a toast to 'the Chieftains and the Clans' and appeared resplendent in Highland dress. He wore the Royal Stewart tartan.

The Fording of the Poll Tarf by Carl Haag, 1865. A critic wrote that 'the equanimity which the whole group maintains under circumstances not a little agitating is subject to admiration'. Queen Victoria's forays into the Highlands were extremely energetic by modern standards; remarkable distances were covered, and the queen's enthusiasm never dimmed. 'I can only say that the scenery is lovely, grand, romantic, & a great peace and wildness pervades all, which is sublime.'

The origins of this famous tartan are shrouded in mystery, but the ancient origin sometimes claimed for it is doubtful and the alleged connection with Prince Charles Edward non-proven at best. It may even have been designed for the occasion, though there are slightly earlier references to it. Stewart of Garth, who should have known better than anyone, had written some years earlier that he did not know of any Stewart tartan.

Tartan became the rage. Highlanders, wrote J. Telfer Dunbar, 'were no longer clansmen, they were the Scottish nation'. But as Sir Thomas Dick Lauder complained in a letter to Scott in 1829, 'the most uncouth coats of many colours are every day invented, manufactured, christened after particular names and worn as genuine'. Royal patronage continued under George IV's niece, Queen Victoria, who developed a passion for Scotland and all things Scottish. Balmoral, her Deeside home, symbolises the peak of the tartan cult. Even the carpets and curtains were tartan. The Balmoral tartan itself was designed by Prince Albert and, unlike the Royal Stewart which rightly or wrongly crops up in all manner of circumstances, the Balmoral tartan is still reserved for the Royal Family. It is not to be found in the most recondite tartan shops.

The amazing proliferation of tartans in the Victorian era was not confined to the invention or discovery of clan and district tartans. People were no longer content with a single tartan, and special editions were devised for special occasions. Even hunting tartans were not worn by the clans, who never showed much interest, whether on the battle- or the hunting field, in the concept of camouflage. The old tartans were made with vegetable dyes and were less brilliant than many modern ones. One observer in the 1730s said plaids were 'composed of such colours as altogether, in the mass, so nearly resemble the heath on which they lie, that it is hardly to be distinguished from it . . .' and in the 17th century tartans were often brown. Mourning setts, made in black and white, seem particularly absurd, and the

'dress' tartan on a white ground, sometimes worn today as evening dress, has been condemned on the grounds that it is traditionally women's wear. The old arisaid – the female equivalent of the belted plaid – is believed to have been predominantly white.

Ever since the time of Queen Victoria, the royal family has generally displayed a properly enthusiastic regard for their northern kingdom and a willingness to don Highland dress when appropriate. Nowadays, the Balmoral tartan, worn here by the Prince of Wales, is the generally preferred Highland dress of the royal family.

TARTAN TODAY

The commercialisation of tartan has led to its appearance in a variety of unsuitable contexts, a development which is best seen as an indication of its popular appeal and durability. Strictly a tartan should be worn only by members of families which have a historical claim to it. The Lord Lyon King of Arms, the Chief Herald of Scotland, has laid down that the right to wear a tartan belongs to those with the appropriate surname. But a tartan is not like a coat of arms and few are likely to object to slight infringements of the rule. The fact (if indeed it *is* a fact – there appears to be some doubt about the current position) that the Royal Stewart is properly reserved for the Royal Family does not inhibit the sellers of scarves in Knightsbridge or Princes Street. It can even be argued that an eclectic attitude to tartan is historically authentic, since the relatively rigid clan tartan system which grew up in the 19th century was alien to the ancient clans. Informal research conducted at the seat of a great clan chief a few years ago revealed that of the kilted young men acting as guides and attendants (university students mainly), only one was wearing the tartan of the clan concerned and none wore the tartan which his surname would have led one to expect.

New tartans are constantly being devised, not only in Scotland but in many other countries. Among the growing number of district tartans may be counted the Welsh, Manx and Cornish tartans. Many Canadian groups of one kind or another have adopted a tartan. There is even one for the pipe band of the New York City Fire Department. If no more specific tartan can reasonably be claimed, there are general tartans like the Caledonian or the Jacobite which can be worn by anyone.

The rule, such as it is, has been condemned as particularly unjust to those whose claim to a tartan depends on descent through the female line, but even in cases which seem clear enough on the surface, the truth may be other than it seems. There are probably people named MacDonald today who are not as they may suppose members of Clan Donald, but are descended from someone named (for example) Donald Campbell. In Sir Walter Scott's time, and perhaps later, one could encounter a gillie named Gordon who

admitted that he had formerly been known as MacPherson, 'but that was when I lived on the other side of the hill'. Another example from the same period was that of two Irishmen who came over to build drains for Colonel Andrew McDouall of Logan ('a horrid man for improvements'). One was named O'Toole, the other O'Dowd. They married and settled down, and their sons became Mr Doyle and Mr Doud, their grandsons McDouall and Dodds.

Few people nowadays wear a kilt other than on special occasions. The late bursar of a public school in the south of England, whose name is not to be found in Black's *Surnames of Scotland* and whose ancestors, so far as was known, included not a single Scot, was nevertheless such an admirer of that nation that he regularly wore a kilt (the tartan is not recorded). To deprive him of this affectation would certainly have been unkind, though it is perhaps desirable that such eccentricities do not become too common.

As even the possession of an established clan name does not prove a blood relationship – does not, in fact, make one particularly likely – it follows that the question of eligibility becomes more difficult as the relationship becomes more distant. Confusion over names is aggravated by variant spellings, by the difficulty of transliterating Gaelic into English, which leads to some curious adaptations, by simple translation (e.g. Goba = Gow = Smith), by the names of septs (often connected with more than one clan) and more distantly connected groups, and by the results of proscribed clans adopting other names. In this case the MacGregors are the obvious example: proscribed during much of the 17th and 18th centuries, they adopted a large variety of names – nearly a hundred have been traced – including such genealogically problematic ones as Smith and Brown. If your surname is Smith, the chances of your being descended from the MacGregors are slight to say the least.

The wearing of Highland dress is governed by good taste and common sense rather than strict rules. Take the question of the correct length of the kilt, which should reach to the top of the knee and not, despite frequent assertions, to the middle of the kneecap, an uncomfortable length, particularly if out walking in the wet. The backs of the knees soon become raw. It is

Highland dress has continued to evolve, and while traditions should be preserved allowance should also be made for the inevitability of change. There were, after all, no strict sartorial rules in the Highlands in the days when the clan system flourished. Nowadays, it is a question of striking an appropriate balance between

preserving tradition without becoming encumbered with finicky
rules of an almost military nature. Strictly speaking the kilt is a male
garment and should be worn only by men. Women should wear
tartan skirts or the Aboyne dress for dancing.

"FULL DRESS" HIGHLAND COSTUME.

(BLACK CLOTH, SILK VELVET, VELVETEEN, OR CELTIC-GREEN, DOUBLET AND VEST).

Left: Full Highland dress, from Forsyth's catalogue in the early years of this century. Nowadays the military influence is more restrained.

Below: Highland targe (shield) and a pair of broadswords. The targe was made of wood covered with leather and studded in metal – often ornamental. It was carried on the left forearm, leaving the left hand free to wield a dirk, and was sometimes fitted with a central spike. The basket-hilted broadsword was the main weapon in the dreaded Highland charge and 'would split heads straight down to the brogues'. Most of the blades were apparently made in Germany or Spain, and such a sword was sometimes called a *Ferrara*, after the famous Venetian swordsmiths one of whom allegedly (but improbably) settled in Scotland in the reign of King James V. The broadsword replaced the two-handed claymore of earlier centuries.

Overleaf: Loch Etive, looking north towards the ridges of Buchaille Etive Mor and Buchaille Etive Beg.

said that an order to make military kilts out of carded rather than combed yarn, which is harder, resulted from Queen Victoria noticing the scratched and cut knees of her bodyguard after a march in the rain.

Nowadays the upper garment is usually a tweed jacket, preferably of plainish weave. An ordinary sports jacket looks peculiar: the jacket should be cut with a kilt in mind. Kilt jackets often have double cuffs, shoulder straps and buttons of horn or leather. Being more briefly skirted and cut away at the front, they do not interfere with the sporran, which is simply a purse (kilts having no pockets) slung around the waist by a strap or chain – the former if you want your kilt to last. There is a temptation to go overboard in the matter of the sporran. Those lengthy horsehair models are all very well for the military, but leather is preferable. The tassels, which are now purely ornamental, represent the strings which in former times closed individual pockets in the purse.

Except for evening wear, the diced or tartan hose seen in old portraits are not worn today, plain stockings being preferred. Nor is it necessary to carry the massive armoury of the Highlander in the bad old days. An exception is made for the *sgian dubh* (black knife) which is tucked into the top of the stocking. It is not a weapon within the meaning of the act, as it was used for skinning and was adopted by the Highlanders when they were deprived of their weapons (including the dirk) after the Forty-five.

Highland dress is not fancy dress, and the numerous possible accoutrements are not perhaps desirable today. If a hat is worn it should be a Highland bonnet of the Balmoral or Glengarry type (not a tam-o'-shanter), on which the clan badge is worn. Chiefs are entitled to three eagle's feathers.

Women do not wear kilts but pleated tartan skirts, or maybe only a tartan scarf, sash or shawl. Official bodies such as the Committee of the Aboyne Gathering have prescribed dress for Highland dancing which is broadly traditional, or looks it, and is certainly preferable to what James Scarlett calls 'the appalling spectacle of small girls capering through the Highland Fling decked out in the full panoply of a Victorian Highland chief'.

Evening dress involves more ceremonial and stricter rules. Women wear a normal evening dress with a tartan sash, the arrangement of which denotes social status according to rules laid down by the Lord Lyon. Highland evening dress for men offers much greater variety, and it would be pointless to list the possibilities here. Most of them seem to derive from Victorian and military traditions. The lace jabot with a tunic that buttons up to the neck is perhaps less often seen today, which is a pity.

Highland dress can be extremely elegant, and it is more colourful and more varied than Sassenach city clothes. As it is also practical, it is not surprising that it continues to be worn.

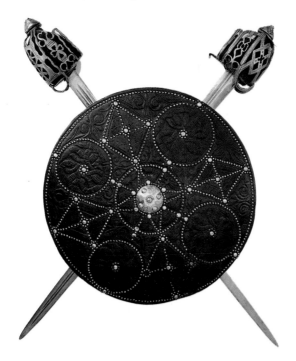

CLANS

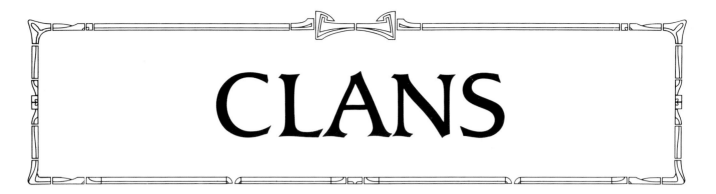

The following list of clans and families is arranged in alphabetical order, but where there are several clans of the same name, they will be found grouped together in order of seniority or chronological importance. This applies even in cases of different spelling, like MacDonald and MacDonell.

Traditionally, in names beginning 'Mac', meaning 'son of', the prefix is followed by a capital letter. Exceptions, such as Mackenzie or Mackay, occur when the first letter is an intruder not to be found in the Gaelic original. (However, people may spell their names as they like.)

Abercromby

No one would claim that Fife is the most beautiful part of Scotland, yet the old fishing ports along the north shore of the Firth of Forth have a powerful charm and, since the construction of the Forth Road Bridge, have become rather too popular with rich folk from Edinburgh. Abercrombie lies less than ten miles south of St Andrews. It was a barony in the Middle Ages and in 1296 was held by William de Abercrombie. His name appears in a list of inquest jurors in the same year as William de Haberchrumbi, and the many 16th-century variants of the name include Abarcrumby, Abbyrcrummy and Eabercombie. William is the earliest of the Abercrombys of that ilk so far discovered. The line died out in the 17th century, but another branch, the Abercrombys of Birkenbog, Banffshire, baronets since 1636, is current.

The Abercrombys remained Roman Catholics at the Reformation. One of them, John Abercromby, who was a Benedictine monk, was executed for attacking the doctrines of Knox, and another, Robert Abercromby, was a Jesuit priest who was imprisoned but escaped and, despite the offer of a huge reward for his capture, succeeded in getting out of the country. He died in exile in 1613.

Although Sir Alexander of Birkenbog was a Covenanter, suffering as a result of having Montrose's troops quartered on his estate during the civil war, the faith was maintained in the next generation. Patrick Abercromby (died c. 1716), who was briefly physician to King James VII/II in 1685, was a Catholic. So was his brother Francis, created Lord Glasford by James VII, and another contemporary, David Abercromby, was a Douai-educated Jesuit. He returned to Scotland as a missionary only to be converted to Protestantism himself in 1682, a sensation at the time. The circumstances suggest it was a genuine spiritual conversion rather than a political one.

There is a story that Patrick Abercromby, who was born in Forfar, wrote a book about the family, but it was apparently never published and the manuscript has not been found. However, to judge by the same

Crail, one of the picturesque old fishing ports on the coast of Fife, a few miles north-east of Abercrombie (St Monance).

Abercromby

author's weighty *Martial Achievements of the Scots Nation* (1711-16), it might not have been reliable historically.

In modern times Abercrombys have served with distinction in the army and in politics. The most outstanding was Sir Ralph Abercromby (1734-1801), a fine professional soldier of strikingly liberal opinions and courage in stating them. His avowed sympathy for the American colonists accounts for his retirement in 1783, but when the French wars began again ten years later he returned to the colours. After a string of successes he was given command of the forces in Ireland, at that time guilty of numerous outrages against the civilian population. The army in Ireland, said Abercromby, was in a state of 'licentiousness which rendered it formidable to everyone but the enemy'. The quotation has a Wellingtonian flavour, and indeed Wellington learned much from Abercromby. He would hardly have achieved his own famous victories without the army reforms which Abercromby played a large part in effecting. Abercromby's opinions, however, resulted in his being forced to resign his Irish command. He was mortally wounded at Alexandria in 1801 during a victorious operation against the French in Egypt.

One of his sons also became a general; the eldest, George, became Lord Abercromby of Tullibody and a third, James, was Speaker of the House of Commons and later Lord Dunfermline.

Anderson

Anderson is a common name, especially in the Lowlands. The name fiz Andreu is recorded in Peebles and Dumfries in the 13th century; the usual Highland form is MacAndrew. The Gaelic form, often rendered Gillanders, means St Andrew's gillie (servant), and it is sometimes said that this applies to all Andersons and MacAndrews, though their origins are probably more diverse.

In the 17th century Donald MacGillandrish was said to be the progenitor of Clan Andrish, from Ross-shire, and the MacAndrews are described as a sept of Clan Chattan.

In the 16th century arms were granted to an 'Anderson of that ilk', but neither the family nor the place (implied by the word ilk) has ever been discovered. However, it was possible for such a grant to be made by the Lord Lyon King of Arms on the grounds that an Anderson chieftain 'represented' the clan or 'community' of Andersons. The most notable branches of the clan in modern times have been the Andersons of Dowhill, traced to the early 16th century, the Andersons of Wester Ardbreck in Banffshire and the Andersons of Candacraig in Strathdon.

One early hero of the MacAndrews was *Iain Beag MacAindrea* (Little John MacAndrew), famous for his bowmanship. In 1670 a party of twelve cattle lifters from Lochaber, having carried out a successful raid, were pursued by the deprived tenants led by William Mackintosh of Kellachie and his attendant

Anderson

Iain Beag. Surprised in the bothy where they had taken shelter, every one of the robbers was killed, *Iain Beag* accounting for their leader, MacDonell of Achluachrach, and, some said, most of the others too. Thereafter *Iain Beag* led a harassed existence avoiding the vengeance of the dead men's kin, but he eventually died peacefully in his bed. Despite this feud, there is a tradition of association between the MacAndrews and the MacDonells.

A number of Andersons have been noted for their intellectual and technological accomplishments, a recent example being the statesman John Anderson, Lord Waverley (1882-1958), who commissioned the household bomb shelter named after him and was a member of the Churchill cabinet during the Second World War. 'Davie-do-a'-things', David Anderson of Finshaugh, was famous for his versatile talents in the early 17th century, his most notable exploit being the removal of an obtrusive rock from the harbour at Aberdeen. His cousin Alexander, also resident in Aberdeen, excelled in theory, publishing volumes of geometry and algebra 'conspicuous for their ingenuity' in Paris during the second decade of the 17th century.

James Anderson (1662-1728) was a noted Scottish historian of his day and author, during the controversy preceding the Act of Union, of *An Historical Essay showing that the Crown and Kingdom of Scotland is Imperial and Independent* (1705). Another James Anderson, from Mid Lothian, not known to be related, was a contributor to the first edition of the *Encyclopaedia Britannica* (1773), writing an article on 'Monsoon' which predicted discoveries made by Captain Cook on his voyage to observe the transit of Venus. A prolific author, he published a periodical called *The Bee* in Edinburgh, the eighteen volumes of which are said to have been written largely by himself.

There are many Andersons in the United States and one, Adam Anderson, was one of the original trustees of the colony of Georgia, whose fort, St Andrews, and the famous civil war prison of Andersonville, serve as reminders of the large Scottish contribution to the early history of that state.

Armstrong

The Armstrongs were one of those families who kept the Borders in constant turmoil up to the 17th century. According to legend the Armstrongs derive from a man named Fairbairn who was the king's armour-bearer. The king's horse was killed in battle and Fairbairn hoisted the monarch on to his own horse out of danger. This fortuitous act gained him the name Arm-Strong and estates in the Borders.

However, the Armstrongs were probably of English origin, as there were Armstrongs in Cumbria

Armstrong

and other parts of the north of England well before they are first heard of on the other side of the border. Gilbert Armstrong was steward of the household to King David II in the 1360s, but the first reference to them in Liddesdale, their chief centre, occurs as late as 1376. The residence of their chief was at Mangerton: an Alexander Armgstrand was Laird of Mangerton in 1378. A lesser chieftain was established at Whitehaugh in the early 16th century.

At that time the Armstrongs were so numerous they extended into beautiful Eskdale and even Annandale. A contemporary report says they could put 3,000 mounted men into the field which, even if somewhat exaggerated, explains why they were practically invincible in the Borders. They were eventually overcome, as so often happened, by a piece of skulduggery as bad as any of their own.

Their leader at this time was the brother of the Laird of Mangerton, Johnnie Armstrong, known as Gilnockie. He built the Hollows Tower in Eskdale, still standing today, which in 1528 was sacked by Lord Dacre, the English warden of the borders. The Armstrongs' prompt response was to burn Netherby in Cumbria. They were also involved in a fierce blood feud with the Johnstons, and in 1530 King James V, on a progress through the Borders, decided to put an end to the anarchy of Liddesdale. Johnnie Armstrong of Gilnockie was persuaded (or chose) to meet the king and arrived accompanied by a 'tail' of forty-odd men –

unarmed, as protocol demanded. 'What wants yon knave that a king should have?' growled the king, observing the company, and he gave orders for them to be seized and hanged. Gilnockie's attempts to arrange a compromise having been rejected, he remarked, 'I am but a fool to seek grace at a graceless face, but had I known you would have taken me this day I would have lived in the Borders despite King Harry and you both', a fair enough supposition.

The death of Gilnockie is commemorated in a well-known ballad of the Borders, though the view of him as a patriot who would have kept the English at bay must be taken with a pinch of salt. Another Armstrong hero commemorated in ballad is Kinmont Willie, ambushed by the English in Liddesdale during a truce, who escaped from prison in Carlisle with the aid of the Scotts.

The Armstrongs were largely dispersed early in the 17th century. Archibald Armstrong of Mangerton was executed in 1610 and the Armstrong lands passed into the possession of the Scotts, another powerful Borders family, one-time allies and occasional enemies. The famous court jester of King James VI was called Archie Armstrong. Gilnockie would surely not have approved of his role.

Baird

Baird

A Richard Baird obtained a charter in Lanarkshire in the 13th century; he belonged to a family who usually appear as de Bard or de Barde, landholders in Lanarkshire, a generation or two earlier and took their name from their estate. An old and doubtful legend ascribes the good fortune of the Bairds to an incident in which their progenitor saved the life of King William the Lion by killing a wild boar, but similar legends are rather common.

Robert Baird was given the barony of Cambusnethan by King Robert I, and the family later spread to Banffshire and Auchmeddan in Aberdeenshire. 'There shall be an eagle in the craig while there is a Baird in Auchmeddan', goes the old saying. Their stature was enhanced by marriage into the great Keith family. The Bairds provided a long line of sheriffs in Aberdeenshire (a hereditary office).

A branch of this family, the Bairds of Newbyth, produced several distinguished men, including a 17th-century judge. His grandson Sir David Baird (1757-1829) was a professional soldier who succeeded to Sir John Moore's command after the latter's death

at Corunna, where Baird himself lost an arm. Other branches of the family were established at Saughtonhall and Balmaduthy.

More recent bearers of the name include John Baird of Kirkintilloch, who built elevated railways in New York City in the 19th century; John Logie Baird (1888-1946), the son of a minister in Dumbartonshire the pioneer of television; and John Lawrence Baird, Lord Stonehaven (1874-1941), a governor-general of Australia in the 1920s.

Barclay

The name Barclay is of Anglo-Norman origin and probably comes from Berkeley in Gloucestershire, the scene of the murder of the English king, Edward II, although some claim Berkeley in Somerset. It occurs in Scotland in the 12th century when a Walter de Berchelai of Gartly was chamberlain of Scotland. He is regarded as the first chief of the Barclays.

The name seems to have been fairly common in Fife and Aberdeenshire in the Middle Ages, and Barclays were hereditary sheriffs of Banffshire for several generations.

The Barclays of Mathers can also be traced to an immigrant Englishman in the 12th century, whose descendant Alexander acquired the estate when he married a Keith in 1351. The modern spelling of the name was adopted by about 1400.

In 1456 the chiefship passed to the Barclays of Towie, where it has remained, though the line is not direct and in recent times has migrated to California

Barclay

and back to England: the present chief lives in Essex.

Colonel David Barclay of the Mathers branch, having lost the family estates through sale in the previous generation, became a leader of the notable band of Highland mercenaries who fought for Gustavus Adolphus in the Thirty Years' War. He subsequently bought Urie in Kincardineshire and, during a brief imprisonment after the Restoration of 1660, was converted to the beliefs of the Society of Friends – the Quakers. His son Robert (1648-90), despite being educated at the Catholic Scots College in Paris where his uncle, another Robert Barclay, was rector, also adopted the Quaker faith and became, along with William Penn, a highly efficient propagandist for the Quakers. His *Apology for the True Christian Divinity* (1676) has been called one of the most impressive theological writings of the 17th century – when there was plenty of competition. From him are descended the Barclays of Buryhill. Other notable families were the Barclays of Collairnie in Fife, the Barclays of Pierston and the Barclays of Ardrossan.

In the 16th century a member of the Barclays of Towie settled in Russia and founded the most eminent of all the Barclay houses, the Barclays de Tolly. Michael Andreas, Prince Barclay de Tolly (1761-1818), a distinguished soldier, was given command of the Russian army against Napoleon in 1812. Fierce opposition to the appointment of a 'foreigner' plus his defeat at Smolensk forced his resignation, but he was later reinstated and commanded the Russians at Dresden, Leipzig and during the final invasion of France.

Among other notable Barclays were Alexander Barclay (1476-1552), poet, monk and author of the English translation of the German satirical classic *The Ship of Fools*, and Captain Robert Barclay-Allardyce of Urie (1779-1854), a notable Regency sportsman who once walked 1,000 miles in 1,000 hours for a wager – a feat which is said to have encouraged popular interest in professional athletics.

Beaton (MacBeth)

Beaton is an anglicised form of the Gaelic *mac beatha* (son of life), which also occurs as Bethune or Mac-Beth. The name MacBeth was fairly common in Scotland in the Middle Ages; it is a personal name, not a patronymic like most 'Mac--s', and its most famous holder was the king of Scots who reigned from 1040 to 1057, eponymous hero of Shakespeare's tragedy (and, according to the historians, much maligned by the dramatist).

The Beatons were distinguished as the hereditary physicians of the lords of the Isles and other West Highland chiefs. According to tradition they came over from Ireland in the 13th century, following the Irish princess who married Angus, Lord of the Isles, and they held land in Islay, the seat of the old lordship, in the 14th century.

After the fall of the lordship of the Isles they became hereditary physicians to the MacLeans of Duart in Mull and to the Frasers, as well as to the Munros of Foulis and the earls of Sutherland. One branch in Skye was supported by both the MacLeods of MacLeod and the MacDonalds of Sleat, despite the fierce feud between those clans.

The success of Presbyterianism was one of the causes of their decline in the 17th century, together with the deliberate oppression of Gaelic culture

MacBeth

which resulted in the near-extinction of Gaelic as a written language by 1700. When Lord Lovat became ill in 1662 he was attended by a doctor from Perth; there is no record of the Beaton family physician attending him at that date, though whether this had any connection with the fact that Lord Lovat's malady proved fatal would be unwarranted supposition.

A tombstone in Iona commemorates a Dr Beaton who died in 1658, having been family doctor of the MacLeans. John Beaton, a clergyman, retired from Mull to Ireland, where he died some time before 1715, but the contents of his remarkable manuscript library were recorded by the keeper of the Ashmolean Museum in Oxford. Some manuscripts written in Irish script and dating from the 14th to the 16th centuries have survived. Some of them are now in the British Museum, and they bear eloquent testimony to the highly advanced Gaelic culture which was lost with the suppression of the lordship of the Isles. One medical treatise has corrections made as late as 1671, and there were reports of people called Beaton with an extensive knowledge of wild plants living in the Outer Hebrides in the 19th century.

Like John Beaton, 18th-century members of the family seem to have often entered the Church, and it is with that profession that the name Beaton is also notably connected.

It has been claimed that the Beatons of Skye were descended from a family in Fife, from where also came the famous family of Reformation ecclesiastics. The egregious Cardinal David Beaton (1494-1546) owed his rapid ascent in the hierarchy to his uncle James Beaton (died 1539), who preceded him as Archbishop of St Andrews and Primate of Scotland. Cardinal Beaton was responsible for the burning of the reformer George Wishart, an act which, added to his general unpopularity, led to his own murder – in particularly unpleasant circumstances – in 1546 at St Andrews. Another James Beaton (1517-1603), a nephew of the cardinal, was the last Roman Catholic Bishop of Glasgow, driven out in 1560 and thereafter resident in France.

The Sound of Mull. A prominent branch of the Beatons, or MacBeths, practised in Mull, holding Pennycross of MacLean of Duart, to whom they were hereditary physicians. One of them is said to have been sitting on the deck of the Armada ship which blew up in Tobermory Bay in 1588, but survived the experience.

Pipers of the Black Watch traditionally wear the Royal Stewart tartan rather than the Black Watch, but there is some controversy concerning the origin of the tradition. Probably they wore a red tartan from the beginning, but it would hardly have been the Royal Stewart.

Black Watch

After the Jacobite rising of 1715, when the amiable General Wade was commander-in-chief in Scotland, it was decided to create a local militia, or watch, in six independent companies of 114 men each under reliable local commanders. In 1739 four additional companies were raised to form a new regiment, the 43rd (from 1749 the 42nd). It took the name which had been applied originally to the independent companies, the Black Watch, to distinguish them from the red-coated regulars, and wore the famous tartan it still wears today.

The origin of the Black Watch tartan has already been mentioned in the chapter on tartan. The sett (though not the colours) is the same as the modern Campbell tartan, and since three of the original six commanders were Campbells (the others were a Grant, a Munro and, rather surprisingly, a Fraser – Lord Lovat), it is tempting to suppose that the Black Watch adopted the Campbell sett. However, there is no evidence for the existence of the modern Campbell tartan before 1739 (the old Campbell tartan, or one of them, appears to have been red). A number of other tartans, such as the Grant hunting tartan, are also apparently derived from the Black Watch. The MacNab tartan too, for example, has the sett of the Black Watch although the change of blues and blacks to reds and greens makes it look altogether different.

Many of the rank and file of the newly created Black Watch were men of some social standing. A well-known story relates how two of them were sent to St James's Palace in London for inspection by George II, who had expressed interest. He approved their tartan, admired their sword dancing, and gave them each a guinea. On their way out, they tossed the coins to a porter.

Their original dress was the belted plaid. The 'little' kilt was worn off duty and was not in Black Watch tartan. The government provided musket and bayonet and basket-hilted broadsword (sometimes wrongly called a claymore), but the men could also carry their own pistols, dirk and even target (round shield).

Their first 'engagement' was – paradoxically in view of their future staunchness – a mutiny. It resulted from a rumour that despite the government's promise that they should serve at home, they were to be sent to the West Indies. Although the trouble was

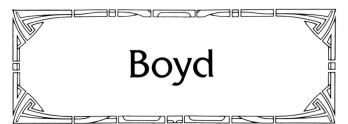

42nd Regiment, the Black Watch

soon over, three men were shot as traitors in the Tower, 'all sons of gentlemen and members of Clan Chattan'. They were regarded in the Highlands as heroes, especially as the rumours proved true: 200 men were drafted to the American or Mediterranean garrisons. The rest of the regiment was sent to Flanders in 1744, fighting with great distinction and amazing the Flemings by their dress.

During the Forty-five the regiment was stationed in Kent. It is a moot point what effect its presence in Scotland might have had on the fortunes of the Jacobites. Today, the official name of the regiment is the 1st Battalion Royal Highlanders, the Black Watch, and their headquarters are in Perth.

Boyd

The name Boyd is thought to derive from the Gaelic for Bute, and the original family to take their name from that island probably arrived in Scotland as vassals of the De Morevilles, a powerful Anglo-Norman family with vast estates in the Lowlands. The earliest record of them is in the burgh of Irvine in 1205, and the name soon became fairly common, especially in Ayrshire. Duncan Boyd was executed in 1306 as a partisan of Robert Bruce, and Boyds were to be found at court under the early Stewarts. In the 15th century they came very near the throne.

Robert Boyle, created Lord Boyle in 1454, became regent for the infant King James III after an accident with a siege gun had carried off James II in 1460. He arranged the marriage of the king to a Norwegian princess. This liaison resulted in the return of the Orkneys and Shetlands to the Scottish Crown, but Boyle's ambitions were viewed with suspicion and when he grew old enough James III, with the enthusiastic backing of Boyd's many enemies, got rid of him. He was forced to flee to England; his brother, less quick off the mark, was executed for treason.

His son Thomas, who in better times had married the king's sister Mary and acquired the titles Earl of Arran and Lord Kilmarnock, also fled abroad. A contemporary reported that he was 'the most courteous, gentlest, wisest, kindest, most bounteous knight,' and certainly his widow was not pleased at being compelled to marry the elderly Lord Hamilton, whose family then supplanted the Boyds in nearness to the throne. The Hamiltons gained not only a royal wife from the Boyds but also the earldom of Arran.

The line continued through the second son of Lord Boyd the Regent, and the Boyds remained supporters of the Stewarts. The tenth Lord Boyd was made Earl of Kilmarnock in 1661 by Charles II, but his great-grandson lost the title – and his life – for his part in the Forty-five when he commanded a troop of cavalry.

One of the fourth earl's sons became, through inheritance in the female line, Earl of Erroll, and he adopted the name of Hay, the former holders of that title. In 1941, on the death of the twenty-second Earl of Erroll without a male heir, his daughter became Countess of Erroll and Chief of Clan Hay, while his brother changed his own name back to Boyd and became known as Lord Kilmarnock and Chief of Clan Boyd.

Boyd

Glen Sannox, a notable beauty spot on the Isle of Arran, where the Boyds were briefly dominant until displaced by the Hamiltons. In 1306 Sir Robert Boyle with other supporters of Bruce took Brodick Castle (see page 130), from whose battlements, according to Scott, Bruce watched for the signal inviting his prompt descent on the Ayrshire coast.

Brodie

The Brodies are one of the few clans whose origins can be ascribed without serious doubts to Pictish times. They come from Moray, and their castle near Forres still stands, along with the ditch or *broth* which, some believe, gave them their name.

The burning of Brodie Castle in 1645 by Lord Lewis Gordon destroyed the family archives, although in 1972 a pontifical (book of offices for a bishop) turned up which has been dated to about 1000 (it is now in the British Museum). We know from a charter of King Robert I in 1311 that Michael de Brodie inherited Brodie from his father, and the family was certainly established much earlier. It has been said that they may have been descended from the Pictish kings called Brude, although the scarcity of early evidence, partly accounted for no doubt by the disaster of 1645, may also suggest that they were not of any great importance. There appears to have been a thane of Brodie in the mid-13th century – the first chief – and it is said that Brodie was confirmed in his possessions in Moray by King Malcolm IV a century earlier.

A number of the Brodies of Brodie featured in both local and national affairs in the late Middle Ages, but the first to achieve eminence was Alexander Brodie, the eleventh Chief of Brodie. He was one of the commissioners sent from Scotland to the Hague in 1649 to negotiate terms for the return of Charles II (the terms included signing the National Covenant, a disagreeable prospect to the king who later looked with disfavour on those who had forced him into it). Another Alexander, the fifteenth chief, as Lord Lyon King of Arms in the 18th century, had the dubious duty of attending the Duke of Cumberland during the campaign which ended at Culloden in 1746.

In general the family never aspired to the public station for which their heritage and status, not to mention their connections with many of the greatest Scottish families, were appropriate. Perhaps that is why there is still a Brodie of Brodie in Brodie Castle who still retains the ancient lands of his ancestors.

Cadet branches of the clan include Brodie of Lethen and Brodie of Idvies. Other Brodies may be descended from O'Brolochains, who often anglicised their name as Brodie.

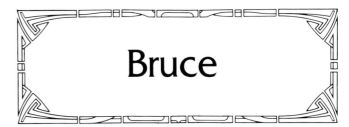

Bruce

The first Robert de Brus, or Bruis, came to England with William the Conqueror. The 11th-century seat of his family, the Château d'Adam, survives in Normandy, not far from Cherbourg. His son, known as Robert le Meschin (the cadet), was associated with King David I at the English court and received from him the grant of Annandale (the charter, undated but probably granted about 1125, still exists). There is a story that at the battle of the Standard (1138), this Robert Bruce fought on the English side while his son fought with the Scots, and was taken prisoner by his own father.

The fifth Lord of Annandale married a descendant of King David I and his son became regent and

Brodie

Bruce

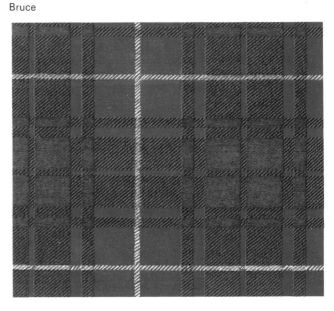

guardian of King Alexander II in 1255. On the death of the Maid of Norway he had a claim to the crown, but his overlord the English King Edward I, to whom all sides appealed, gave his judgement in favour of John Balliol. He had been advised that Balliol, Toom Tabard (Empty Coat) as the Scots called him, would prove more pliable than Bruce. Balliol had the better claim under the laws of succession. The decision was accepted by Bruce, essentially still a great Anglo-Norman noble rather than a Scot. He and his son, who outlived him by only a few years, remained reasonably loyal vassals of Edward I during the growing imposition of English control in Scotland and the guerilla war of William Wallace.

The eight Robert Bruce, Lord of Annandale, is popularly known as 'the Bruce' and his story belongs of course to all Scotland. Crowned at Scone, he cemented his kingship and assured Scottish independence in the splendid victory of Bannockburn (1314), dying, the greatest of Scotland's national heroes, at Cardross, Dumbartonshire, in 1329 at the age of 55.

Bruce's less inspiring son, King David II, died childless. In 1359 he granted the barony of Clackmannan to another Robert Bruce, whose exact relationship is not known. In the late 18th century the Earl of Elgin, who was also descended from the Bruces of Clackmannan, became head of the family, as is the present earl. Clackmannan Castle's remains still overlook the Forth, though Lord Elgin's seat is at Broomhall in Fife.

The Bruces were also established on the south side of the river in the 15th century, and the Bruces of Kinnaird, Stirlingshire, produced the most famous holder of the name since King Robert, the 18th-century explorer James Bruce (1730-94), whose entertaining account of his travels in Ethiopia is 'a blend of romance, grandeur, bestiality and violence, devious intrigues and bold ploys – a weird combination of Machiavelli and Tolkien'. Bruce used to carry a folding blunderbuss (now in Lord Elgin's possession) which he was able to conceal under his robe, producing it at moments of crisis.

The fine equestrian statue of Bruce by C. d'O. Pilkington Jackson erected in 1964, the 650th anniversary of Bruce's most famous victory, as part of the 60-acre memorial centred on the Bore Stone, where Bruce's standard allegedly stood during the battle of Bannockburn.

Buchan

Those who took their name from the district of Buchan in Aberdeenshire were not connected with the various families, including the Comyns, Stewarts and Erskines, who at one time or another held the ancient Scottish earldom of Buchan. Ricardus de Buchan was a clerk in the diocese of Aberdeen in the early years of the 13th century and others of the name are found in Aberdeen, Edinburgh and elsewhere in the late medieval period. Walter de Bochane or Buchan was Archdeacon of Shetland in 1391. The clerical connection often reappears: another Buchan was Bishop of Caithness earlier in the same century.

The most prominent of the Buchans in Aberdeenshire were the Buchans of Auchmacoy, who are first heard of in the early 15th century. Thomas Buchan of Auchmacoy was a Jacobite general in the 17th century, succeeding Graham of Claverhouse (Bonnie Dundee) after the latter's death at Killiecrankie. He did not last long and in 1692 fled to the exiled court of James VII/II in France. He insisted that his family were descended from the earls of Buchan.

The Buchanites were a small (46 members at full strength) and fanatical religious group in Scotland in the 1780s, named after their founder, Elspeth Buchan, who claimed to be the woman mentioned in Chapter 12 of the Book of Revelations: 'a woman clothed with the sun, and the moon under her feet, and upon her head a crown of twelve stars . . . [She]

Buchan

brought forth a man child, who was to rule all nations with a rod of iron . . .' Buchan was her married name however, her father being an innkeeper from Banffshire named Simpson.

The most distinguished individuals among the Buchans were Alexander Buchan (1829-1907), a meteorologist who inaugurated an observatory on the summit of Ben Nevis, and John Buchan, Lord Tweedsmuir (1875-1940) who besides being the author of *The Thirty-nine Steps, Greenmantle*, many other adventure stories and a notable biography of Montrose, was governor-general of Canada from 1935 to 1940.

Buchanan

In Gaelic *both-chanain* means the seat of the canon, suggesting an ecclesiastical origin. A Buchanan was called *Mac-a'-Chanonaich*, son of the descendant of the canon. However, the name really comes from the district bordering Loch Lomond. There the Earl of Lennox bestowed lands on his seneschal in the 13th century, a grant which was later confirmed by royal charter. Sir Thomas Innes of Learney suggested that part of the land may have been held through old Celtic hereditary clerical tenures. The ninth Laird of Buchanan, Sir Maurice, was the first to assume the surname, but it is said there were Buchanans in the French forces at Agincourt.

The war cry of the Buchanans is *Clar Innis*, the name of an island in Loch Lomond opposite Balmaha, where the clan once gathered. Now a bird sanctuary,

Buchanan

it was bequeathed to the Buchanan Society (said to be the oldest clan society in Scotland) in 1939.

The various branches of Clan Buchanan include Leny, Carbell, Drumakill, Auchmar, Auchintorlie and Spittal. This last family, founded in the 16th century, acquired the chiefship in 1762 when the senior line became extinct on the death of the twenty-second laird, John Buchanan of that ilk. By that time the Buchanan lands had already been sold – in 1682 to the Marquess of Montrose whose heirs have retained them ever since. The last chief of the house of Spittal died in 1919.

William Buchanan of Auchmar, who died in 1747, was a noted Scottish genealogist, author of a work on Scottish surnames and a genealogical essay on the Buchanans themselves. He recalled a time when the laird of Buchanan could entertain fifty men, all living within easy walking distance, who bore his own name or that of the Buchanan septs of MacAuslan, MacMillan, MacColman and Spittal. From this time, however, the Buchanans were gradually scattered. Some settled in Ulster, among them the ancestors of James Buchanan (1791-1868), fifteenth president of the United States.

The Buchanans have produced a more than average number of scholars and poets, of whom the best known was George Buchanan (1506-82) of Killearn. A humanist who later turned strict Calvinist and became Moderator of the General Assembly, he was universally acknowledged as a great scholar and was tutor to two generations of royalty. The last of them was King James VI, who had the elderly Buchanan (he was 64 when appointed James's tutor) to thank, very largely, both for his own erudition and for the miseries of his childhood, the tutor's methods being harsh even by the rugged standard of those times. Buchanan is also blamed for poisoning his charge's mind against his mother, Mary Queen of Scots, whom he assisted to the block by testifying to her authorship of the Casket Letters and publishing an indictment of her that contained deliberate falsehoods. Whatever the felicities of his Latin style, George Buchanan was surely not a very pleasant man.

Dugald Buchanan (1716-68) helps correct the moral balance. He has been called the Milton and Bunyon of Gaelic Scotland and the most inspired religious poet that Scotland ever produced. Kinloch Rannoch, where he was a teacher, became in his later years a place of pilgrimage. There is a memorial to him at Strathyre.

A burn making its way down to the loch near Rowardennan on the eastern side of Loch Lomond, now part of Queen Elizabeth Forest Park, formerly Buchanan territory, with MacGregors close by.

Cameron

The Camerons are one of the greatest of the Highland clans and one of the most ancient, for ever associated with the wild and beautiful country of Lochaber. For many generations they held on to their land, commanding the Road to the Isles, without legal title and with continual harassment by the sword, earning in the process a reputation for bravery and ferocity which they later displayed with equal effect in the British army.

An old and picturesque tradition ascribes the name Cameron to the Gaelic *cam shron* (crooked nose) and traces them to the late Middle Ages, when they were established in Lochaber as subjects, allies, sometimes opponents, of the lord of the Isles. More recently, however, the late Sir Iain Moncreiffe of that ilk, Highland genealogist and historian and one-time Lord Lyon King of Arms, has suggested an earlier origin and a different derivation of the name.

Early versions of Cameron include Cambrun, Cambroun, Caumberen and several others sharing that intrusive B. The inference is that the Camerons take their name not from some broken-nosed ancestor but from *cam brun* (crooked hill), the name of a place in the old kingdom of Fife, which has long been regarded as the principal place of origin of Lowland Camerons. It seems to have been the original home of the Highland Camerons too. There is a striking similarity in the coat of arms of the MacDuff earls of Fife and the Cameron chiefs, and there is other evidence which strongly suggests a connection between the famous old Clan MacDuff and the Camerons.

There were Cameron chiefs in Lochaber by about 1400. The oldest branch is believed to be the MacGillonies, allegedly descended from a 7th-century king of Lorne, and their sept, the MacMartins of Letterfinlay on Loch Lochy. However, the chiefship passed to another branch, one of whom, Donald *Dubh*, married a MacMartin heiress. He is reckoned as the eleventh chief, but is the first of whom there is a documentary record. He is said to have led the clan in support of the lord of the Isles at the bloody battle of Harlaw in 1411, where the Islemen's march on Aberdeen was halted and the great MacLean chief, Red Hector of the Battles, met his end.

Donald *Dubh* left two sons, Allan, who succeeded him as twelfth chief, and Ewen, founder of the Camerons of Strone.

In 1528, during the time of the thirteenth chief (also called Ewen), the lands he held were erected into the barony of Lochiel, and he was the first to call himself Cameron of Lochiel. The Cameron chiefs have borne this name ever since.

Above: **Cameron** *Below:* **Hunting Cameron**

Cameron of Lochiel

The disappearance of the lord of the Isles created a power vacuum in the west, and for centuries the Camerons held the lands from Loch Oich to Glen Loy by force against incursions by the Mackintoshes in particular, and the efforts of the earls of Huntly to gain control of the western clans (in 1547 Ewen

Cameron of Lochiel was beheaded by Huntly).

Throughout the successive crises of the 17th and 18th centuries the Camerons, under a line of remarkable chiefs, were loyal supporters of the Stewart dynasty. Sir Ewen Cameron of Lochiel, 'the Ulysses of the Highlands', was the last Highland chief to hold out against Cromwell in the 1650s. He had been brought up under Campbell tutelage. The Campbells had sometimes been a useful counterweight to the power of Clan Chattan and the Mackintoshes, as well as the MacDonalds, though in this case the reason for the future Lochiel's residence at Kilchurn and Inveraray was as hostage for the good behaviour of the Camerons. He was apparently not influenced by the Covenanting sympathies of Argyll, nor by his wavering political loyalties, and in 1647, at the age of 18, he took up his duties as chief.

After the execution of Charles I and the flight of Charles II Lochiel supported the rising led by the Earl of Glencairn, and when this failed he continued to

Detail of a posthumous portrait of the 'Gentle Lochiel', by George Chalmers. He died in exile in France. Of his brothers, one, a doctor (Archibald) was executed and another (Alexander) died in captivity.

Cameron of Lochiel

harass General Monk, the Commonwealth's commander in Scotland, by guerilla warfare. In the end it was Monk, of course, who changed sides, and Lochiel accompanied him on his memorable march to London which led to the Restoration of Charles II (1660). After James VII/II lost his throne in 1688, Lochiel again rose to assist the king's futile campaign in Ireland, and the Camerons were among the force commanded by Bonnie Dundee at Killiecrankie.

In this shortlived campaign a regiment called the Cameronians featured. They distinguished themselves on the government side in a fierce skirmish at Dunkeld. This regiment was originally composed of followers of a Richard Cameron, son of a shopkeeper in Fife, who had been a Calvinist exile in Holland and had no connection, nor sympathy, with the pro-

Stewart, Catholic Camerons of Lochaber.

After this last act of defiance 'the Great Lochiel' finally took the oath of allegiance to William and Mary, thus avoiding the fate planned by the Master of Stair which overtook the MacDonalds of Glencoe.

Lochiel lived to see the failure of the Jacobite rising of 1715, dying at peace in 1719, one of the most renowned warriors in Highland history. It is said of him that he once bit out the throat of a Cromwellian officer in combat by Loch Arkaig. He was certainly a giant: someone who had shaken hands with him complained that Lochiel's grip had made his fingertips bleed. Lochiel was perhaps growing absentminded – he was 87 years old at the time.

His son John, the eighteenth Lochiel, fought in the Fifteen, for which he was attainted and went into exile. His grandson was Donald, 'gentle Lochiel', the man who in 1745 had to make a fateful decision.

The nineteenth Lochiel has been called 'perhaps the finest Highland chief there will ever have been' – a tragic hero if ever there was one. Like practically all the Jacobite chiefs (except MacDonald of Clan Ranald) he was appalled by the landing of Prince Charles, unsupported, in the Hebrides. He urged him to think again, or at least wait until promised French armaments arrived. The prince said to Lochiel's emissary (his brother, Dr Archibald Cameron, who

was to be executed in the customary barbaric manner eight years later), 'Lochiel, whom my father esteemed the best friend of our family, may stay at home, and learn his Prince's fate from the newspapers'. Lochiel's famous reply was, 'I'll share the fate of my Prince, and so shall every man over whom nature or fortune hath given me any power.'

One can only admire and deplore this Athenian heroism. Since the other chiefs were waiting for Lochiel's response, it was decisive; had he held aloof,

the prince would have got nowhere. As Sir Iain Moncreiffe wrote, 'the hush of relief when the Cameron pipes were heard approaching the Prince's gathering-place at Glenfinnan was one of the dramatic moments of history'. It was also, in retrospect, a

Early morning at Loch Arkaig, Cameron country. Bonnie Prince Charlie spent a night soon after Culloden at the home of Donald Cameron of nearby Glenpean on the loch, and later in a hut on Tor-a-muilt nearby, where an old and rusty sword was found many years later and was said to belong to the prince's party.

very bad moment indeed, for it led directly to the destruction of the clans.

At Culloden, where the Camerons were described by the future General Wolfe as the bravest of the Highlanders, Lochiel had both ankles broken by grapeshot, but he was carried from the field by four of his men. He hid in the hills and eventually rejoined the prince. They sailed on the same ship to France, where Lochiel died less than two years later.

During the Jacobite retreat towards Glasgow in 1746 Lochiel had exercised all his prestige to prevent the city being ravaged. That is why, whenever his descendant enters the city today, the bells of Glasgow ring out in his honour.

The lands of Lochiel were instead ravaged by Cumberland's men. His seat, Achnacarry castle, where he had been planting an avenue of beech trees when the news of the prince's landing was brought to him, was burnt down with most of its beautiful furniture still inside. The usual acts of savagery took place.

The lands of the Camerons suffered again during the Clearances, when the evictions and consequent sales of land are said to have produced the money for rebuilding Achnacarry on a grandiose scale. The present Lochiel lives there now.

Cameron of Erracht

After the horrors of Culloden and its aftermath, the martial pride of the Camerons was salvaged by the creation of the regiment best known as the Queen's Own Cameron Highlanders (now merged with the Seaforths as the Queen's Own Highlanders), raised by Alan Cameron of Erracht in 1793.

In the 16th century Ewen, the thirteenth chief, who first took the name 'of Lochiel', married as his second wife Marjory, a Mackintosh, and their sons Ewen and John both founded branches of the clan, of which the more notable is Cameron of Erracht. Relations between the Camerons of Lochiel and of Erracht were variable. There was a good deal of intermarriage but also, when no other enemies threatened, a good deal of fratricidal violence.

Donald, the seventh Cameron of Erracht, was about 30 at the time of the Forty-five and was second in command to Lochiel when Prince Charles raised his standard at Glenfinnan and set off on his victorious march to Edinburgh. After Culloden Erracht went into hiding for three years. His eldest son was Sir Alan

Cameron of Erracht who as a young man had killed an enemy in a duel and fled to Mull. He was for a time a clerk in the Customs at Greenock. He then emigrated to America, where he joined the army and was unfortunately captured during the American War of Independence, spending two years as a prisoner in Philadelphia before returning to Lochaber. For a brief period Alan Cameron successfully claimed the chiefship of the Camerons, but the Lyon court eventually

restored the chiefship to Cameron of Lochiel.

The circumstances in which Cameron of Erracht raised the 79th regiment, the Cameronian Volunteers (later the Cameronian Highlanders) have been related in an earlier chapter. The Cameron of Erracht tartan which the regiment wore was designed, tradition says, by the Colonel's mother, a MacLean whose father died at Culloden. It is supposedly based on an old Lochaber sett and has a close

The Cameron Highlanders, in fatigue dress, embarking at Gibraltar, from a painting by R. R. McIan, about 1870. An old tradition maintains that the regimental tartan originated as an amalgamation of a MacDonald sett with yellow lines as suggested by Cameron of Erracht's mother, but more recent research also suggests a more general sett and a MacLean influence as well. Red tartans were considered unsuitable in the army because they clashed with the red tunics.

Cameron of Erracht

affinity with MacDonald. The yellow line, however, is distinctive.

The regiment was broken up in 1797 but the following year Sir Alan Cameron and his officers raised a second 79th regiment, with a second battalion following in 1804. Cameron of Erracht remained colonel of the regiment until his death at 78 in 1828. The male line died out on the death of his grandson, William Cameron of Erracht, in 1903.

Campbell

When the clan system came to an end in the 18th century the Campbells were easily the most powerful clan in the Highlands. The Campbell heritage is as old as any clan's and the Campbells had played an important part in both local and national affairs since the Middle Ages.

Success does not make for popularity and animosity to the Campbells was strong enough to survive to the present. The stories one hears of inn-keepers in the West Highlands who will spit on the floor at the mention of the name Campbell may owe more to attempts to impress visitors than to genuine antipathy. Nevertheless, an instinctive, hostile reaction undoubtedly remains, encouraged but not entirely explained by the romanticism that has infected views of Scotland's past since the 19th century. Alasdair Alpin MacGregor, writing less than fifty years ago, recalled the 'hatred of anything connected with Clan Campbell' in his childhood home.

There are certainly acts of treachery and atrocity in the history of the Campbells, but so there are in other clans. That the Campbells were devious and cunning is perhaps a biased way of saying that they were clever and politic. Generally, the success of the Campbells was based on their support of the right, i.e.

Loch Long, a branch of the Firth of Clyde between Argyll and Dumbartonshire, roughly marked the south-eastern limit of the territory of the later earls of Argyll.

winning, side, which almost invariably meant the government's. They were adherents of the Bruce and later of the Stewart dynasty. They lost their way somewhat in the difficult conditions of the 17th century, but after the Revolution of 1688 they were firm supporters of the Whig, later Hanoverian, party,

Campbell, Old Colours

being the chief anti-Jacobite power in the Highlands – indeed, in the whole country. From the 18th century and often earlier, their outlook, or that of their leaders, was more British than Scottish. In the words of one of their historians, Colin M. MacDonald, 'the prominence of the nine Campbell earls of Argyll in Scottish history and of the subsequent eleven dukes in the history of Great Britain is unsurpassed by any other single noble British family'.

The Campbells expanded steadily over the centuries by taking advantage of the failure and feuds of their neighbours, playing one clan off against another and, as agents of the government in the Western Highlands, moving in on the lands of defeated rebels. They always secured legal title to those lands, sometimes obtaining charters from the Crown, but they also used force when necessary – for instance in carrying off a useful heiress.

A recent member of the Argyll family, in a moment of dynastic fervour, is said to have traced his ancestors back to ancient Egypt. That does seem excessive, but long-accepted legend does take us back deep into the Celtic mists.

The armorial device of the Campbells is a boar's head. This commemorates the animal allegedly slain by the Ossianic hero, founder of Clan Diarmaid (to which all Campbells belong), in Kintyre. While measuring the slain beast, Diarmaid's bare foot was pierced by a deadly bristle and he died.

The conjectural genealogy given by Sir Iain Moncreiffe of that ilk follows the Campbells back through the MacDougall lords of Lorne to the famous Somerled, regulus (sub-king) of Argyll, who was killed in 1164, and through him to the ancient Norse and Irish kings. Another old Gaelic tradition gives the Campbells an unspecified descent from the legendary Romano-British hero Arthur via the

ancient British house of Strathclyde. A Campbell ancestor probably married an *Ó Duibhne* (O'Duin) heiress and through her inherited an estate in Lochow (i.e. Loch Awe). The 13th-century descendant of this line was *Cailein* (Colin), from whom the chief of the Campbells of Argyll takes his Gaelic name, *Mac Cailein Mór*.

The name Campbell, generally spelt Cambel until the 16th century, is thought to derive from the Gaelic *cam beul* (crooked mouth) presumably a deformity of some Campbell ancestor. It is at least equally likely, however, that it comes from a placename.

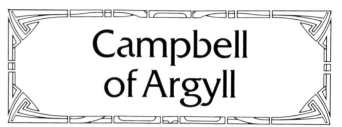

Campbell of Argyll

In the days when *Cailein* lived in Lochow the chief powers in the region were the MacDougall lords of Lorne and the MacDonald lords of the Isles. Sir Colin, who was knighted by King Alexander III in 1280, supported Bruce against the MacDougall lieutenants of Balliol, but the resulting feud ended with the defeat of the Campbells and the death of Sir Colin in 1294 in battle in the String of Lorne.

When Bruce fled to the Western Highlands after his defeat at Methven he found staunch support in Sir Neil, the first *Mac Cailein Mór*. Bruce's eventual victory caused the decline of the MacDougalls and the rise of the Campbells. Sir Neil, who fought at Bannockburn with three of his brothers, married Bruce's sister. His son Colin captured Dunoon Castle in 1344, and the Campbells have remained keeper of that castle (and several others) since those days, paying 'rent' of one red rose a year.

The Campbell estates in Argyll continued to expand, especially under the third Sir Colin (d. 1413), known as *Iongantach* (marvellous). His son Sir Duncan spent some time in England as a hostage for the annual ransom payments for King James I. His grandson and successor was Colin, the first Earl of Argyll, created in 1457, whose marriage to a Stewart of Lorne brought him most of the lands of the lord of Lorne together with other land in Knapdale and elsewhere. He also moved his seat from Loch Awe to Inveraray on Loch Fyne, thus opening up access to the coasts and islands and posing a clear threat to the

A castle at Inveraray on Loch Fyne (River Aray in the foreground) has been the seat of the earls and dukes of Argyll since the 15th century. The original plans of this early (1744-61) example of the Gothic Revival were by Roger Morris, and they were put into effect by William Adam (father of Robert), among others.

already stumbling authority of the lord of the Isles. The earl preferred peaceful acquisition to conquest and following the collapse of the lord of the Isles he acquired, by very devious means, a substantial part of the MacDonald lands, including Kintyre. He also played a skilful part in national affairs as chancellor and as a conspirator against King James III. He doubled the Campbell lands in his lifetime and more than doubled the power of his house. Expansion continued under his son (killed at Flodden) and later earls, who benefited considerably from the dying spasms of the MacDonald lordship of the Isles.

It was said of one of the chiefs of the Campbells of Argyll that 'he served his country well, his county better and his clan and family best of all'. These were the general priorities. The series of constitutional disturbances that began with the Reformation and ended two centuries later with the final defeat of the Jacobites offered unrivalled opportunities for advancement but also heavy odds against always being on the right side at the right time – not that the earls of Argyll were ruled entirely by cynical motives. There is for example no reason to doubt the sincerity of the religious conversion which resulted in Argyll's signature appearing at the top of the list on the National Covenant (1557).

Archibald, the fifth Earl of Argyll, nevertheless commanded Mary Queen of Scots' forces at Langside (1568) but unfortunately had a seizure as the battle was about to begin, which 'contributed not a little to the defeat of Mary's forces'. He soon made his peace with the Protestant lords, though his brother and successor became embroiled in the quarrels over the regency of King James VI. On his death there were similar divisions among the Campbells over the chiefship, a rare dispute by comparison with other clans. The tentacles of this complicated plot, involving

Campbell of Argyll

the murder of Campbell chieftains at the instigation of other Campbells, stretched everywhere and provoked warfare between the Campbells of Argyll and the Gordons, in a sense their counterparts in the east. It was ended after the king enforced a reconciliation.

The most famous of the long line of Campbell chiefs of Argyll was of course the Marquess of Argyll (1607-61), the squint-eyed adversary of Montrose during the civil war. He was not a particularly attractive character, but he has suffered unduly by comparison with his highly romanticised opponent, the dashing Montrose.

Many of the accusations against him – lecherous designs on Lady Ogilvie, cowardice in the face of the enemy – are mere propaganda, perpetrated by Argyll's enemies and embraced by later writers. His

Carrick Castle, an ancient Lamont stronghold on the west side of Loch Goil, which became a Stewart hunting lodge with the Campbells as hereditary keepers.

execution after the Restoration was exceedingly unjust.

The marquess's eldest son, as Lord Lorne, had joined the revolt in favour of Charles II in 1653, but was unable to save his father from execution. He was a wild fellow for a Campbell chief, perhaps the result of an accidental bullet wound in the head. He repaired the devastation caused by Montrose in Argyll, but he was always held in some suspicion by the government. He undoubtedly had Covenanting sympathies, though he avoided making them dangerously obvious, and he was eventually convicted of treason on a charge connected with the Test Act which prompted Lord Halifax to remark that in England 'we should not hang a dog on the grounds on which my Lord Argyll has been sentenced'.

He escaped from Edinburgh Castle disguised as his step-daughter's page and fled to Holland. He now become a rebel in earnest, invaded the Western Highlands in support of Monmouth's futile rebellion (1685), failed even to take Inveraray, and was caught and executed under the old sentence. On the day of his execution he took his midday nap, as usual.

With the accession of William and Mary the Argylls' political difficulties were over, and the tenth earl was advanced to a dukedom in 1701. The second duke, who as a small child fell from a third-floor

window without harm on the day his grandfather was executed for treason, became a distinguished soldier, serving under Marlborough (very restlessly it may be said). His support of the Act of Union did not make him popular in Scotland, nor did his command of government forces during the Fifteen.

Later dukes have been men of many distinctions in Argyll, in Scotland and in a wider arena. Many of them were also considerable historians and Gaelic scholars. The most famous is the eighth duke, whose long political career almost spanned the reign of Queen Victoria. He would probably have been prime minister had it not been for Gladstone. His son, the ninth duke, married a daughter of Queen Victoria.

The present *Mac Cailein Mór* is the twelfth Duke of Argyll, hereditary Lord Justice and Admiral of the Western Coasts. He lives in the charming blue-stone castle (the fairy turrets are Victorian) of Inveraray.

Campbell of Breadalbane

Sir Duncan, known as Lord Campbell, fifth *Mac Cailein Mór*, who died in 1453, is the ancestor of the Campbells of Glenorchy, whose chieftains became earls and marquesses of Breadalbane. Though a cadet branch, the Campbells of Breadalbane became a mighty clan in their own right and at the beginning of this century it was said that the Marquess of Breadalbane could ride for a hundred miles in a straight line without leaving his own estates.

Glen Orchy, a valley to the east of Loch Awe, came into Campbell possession with a MacGregor heiress in the early 14th century. Sir Duncan left it to his second son, Black Colin of Glenorchy, who augmented his inheritance by marrying an heiress of the Stewart lords of Lorne. He also built Kilchurn Castle, now a picturesque ruin at the head of Loch Awe.

The Campbells of Glenorchy continued to expand, mainly at the expense of the MacGregors, and the downfall of their rivals was completed by the proscription of Clan MacGregor in 1603, in which the current Colin of Glenorchy had a hand. He renovated Balloch, later called Taymouth Castle, near Aberfeldy. Black Duncan, the seventh of Glenorchy,

The ruined Kilchurn Castle on Loch Awe, below Ben Cruachan. It was built by Colin Campbell of Glenorchy about 1440, and provided a springboard for Campbell expansion eastward.

Campbell of Breadalbane

was also a keen builder, constructing or acquiring
seven forts at various points in his ever-expanding but
frequently threatened estates. He was created a
baronet in 1625.

The most famous leader of the Campbells of
Glenorchy was Sir John, *Iain Glas*, eleventh in line
from Black Colin, who was born in 1635 and created
Earl of Breadalbane in 1681. He is remembered in
particular for his machinations in connection with the
earldom of Caithness. He obtained from the ruined
Earl of Caithness his lands and jurisdictions in 1672,
on payment of 4,000 pounds a year. He did not have to
pay this long because when the earl died a few years
later he married his widow. He then invaded
Caithness with a small army and dispossessed the
earl's heir, though he was finally thwarted in his
ambition by the courts. The episode was unusual in
that it opposed Campbells and Gordons, who usually
kept to their own spheres of influence.

The first Lord Breadalbane was described by a
biased observer as 'cunning as a Fox, wise as a
Serpent, and supple as an Eel'. He was for a time the
most powerful man in Scotland after the senior
Campbell chief, Argyll. During the plots, counter-
plots, revolts and recriminations caused by the collapse of the Stewart dynasty, he kept his head, turned
a pretty penny or two, and occasionally played a
double game. It is unfair to convict him of
responsibility for the massacre of Glencoe. Although
the Campbells of Glenlyon, who carried out that
fearful act, were a sept of the Glenorchies and
Breadalbane was certainly hostile to the MacDonalds, he had no knowledge of the planned attack and
subsequently condemned it in private correspon-
dence.

He was succeeded in 1717 by his son, known as 'Old
Rag', but the line died out with his grandson the third
earl, a diplomat of some standing and a supporter of

Loch Tulla, north of Glen Orchy. Campbell expansion in this region was largely at the expense of the MacGregors and the Fletchers.

Walpole in Parliament, in 1782. The title then passed to a cousin, who was created Marquess of Breadalbane in the British peerage in 1831. Another cousin succeeded in 1862. The marquessate ended in 1922 with the end of another line, but the Scottish title continues. The family still holds Glenorchy and estates in other parts, though Taymouth Castle, built in the 19th century on the site of Balloch, is currently vacant.

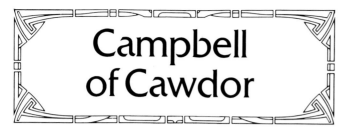

Campbell of Cawdor

In Cawdor Castle, said to be the last privately inhabited castle (complete with drawbridge) in Scotland, there is a monumental fireplace, built by Sir Hugh Campbell, Thane of Cawdor, in the late 17th century to commemorate the marriage in 1510 from which his line sprang.

The death of John, Thane of Calder (Cawdor) in 1494 was shortly followed by the birth of an heiress, Muriel. The baby's maternal grandfather, Rose of Kilravock, who intended the heiress as a future wife for his grandson (her cousin), was at that time under arrest after some Highland affray. The Justice-General was Archibald Campbell, second Earl of Argyll, and presumably the two came to a mutually advantageous agreement, which eased Argyll's task in obtaining wardship of the Cawdor heiress from King James IV. Argyll wanted her and her dowry for his younger son, John. To make sure of the plan, he sent a party sixty strong under Campbell of Inverliver to seize the child. An extremely grisly legend relates that to thwart a possible substitution the child's mother branded her with a red-hot key, and/or the

Campbell of Cawdor

child's nurse bit off the top joint of one of her fingers.

The abductors were pursued by the Calders and while some made off secretly with the child the others fought to the death in defence of a hastily contrived dummy. Someone later remarked to Inverliver that it would be a pity if after all the Campbell losses in this fight the child were to die. He replied, 'Muriel can never die as long as there is a red-haired lass on the shores of Loch Fyne'. Presumably, however, the 15-year-old who became the mother of the Campbells of Cawdor was the real Muriel.

In the vault of Cawdor Castle, amid the fertile country south of the Moray Firth, there is an ancient hawthorn tree, lovingly protected now by a wire cage. In 1454 the Thane of Cawdor resolved to build a new

castle, and he dreamt that he should place a chest of gold on a donkey and set it to wander. Where it stopped would be the place to build. It stopped at the hawthorn tree, and the castle was built around it.

In the early 17th century some of the Cawdor lands were sold to facilitate the wresting of Islay from the MacDonalds. Islay, though far removed, remained the property of the thanes of Cawdor until it was sold to another Campbell family, Campbell of Shawfield, in 1726. The thane's title was elevated to an earldom in 1796, and the earls of Cawdor still live in Cawdor Castle.

The military record of the Campbells generally has often been remarked, and of the Campbells of Cawdor in particular. Sir Iain Moncreiffe calculated that the fifty-odd male descendants of the Thane of Cawdor in the past hundred years who were of an age for military service in wartime won 22 British awards for bravery between them, including three Victoria Crosses.

Carnegie

The Carnegies of Southesk are descended from John de Balinhard, whose forebears held lands of that name in Angus at the beginning of the 13th century. In the 14th century the Balinhard lands were sold to pay for the lands of Carrynegy (Carnegie) in the parish of Carmyllie, Angus, and the family thus acquired their modern name.

The line of descent from John de Balinhard died out in the 16th century, and the Carnegie chiefs of the house of Southesk derived from his younger son Duthac. His son, the second Duthac, gained Kinnaird through marriage but was killed soon afterwards at the battle of Harlow (1411).

A later Carnegie, John of Kinnaird, died at Flodden. His son Robert was a judge and ambassador who fought at Pinkie Cleugh and died in 1565. His nephew David (1575-1658), eighth Carnegie of Kinnaird, was created Earl of Southesk in 1633.

The Carnegies were generally loyal adherents of the Stewart dynasty. The second Earl of Southesk, who was known as the Black Earl because of his alleged familiarity with the black arts, was imprisoned during the Commonwealth, and the fifth earl, James, came out for King James in Angus during the Jacobite rising of 1715. He is commemorated in song in 'The Piper o' Dundee'. After the defeat of the Jacobites he lost his earldom.

The Carnegie tartan appears to be based on that of MacDonell of Glengarry, and it is said that his association dates from the Fifteen, when Lords

Carnegie

Southesk and Glengarry acted in close co-operation.

The fifth earl had no children and the succession passed to a cousin, Sir James Carnegie of Pitarro, who was descended from a younger son of the first earl and was able to buy back the Southesk estates. Sir Alexander Carnegie of Pitarro, a scholar and Knight of the Thistle, succeeded in having the attainder reversed in 1853 and accordingly became ninth Earl of Southesk. The present earl and Carnegie chief still lives in Kinnaird Castle, Angus.

Another branch of the family, descended from Lord Lour, a younger brother of the first Earl of Southesk, became earls of Ethie, later changed to Northesk, in the 17th century. The family produced two British admirals, most notably William, Earl of Northesk (1758-1831), who was third in command at the battle of Trafalgar (1804) and later commander-in-chief at Portsmouth. A cadet branch of this house is Carnegie of Lour. The Carnegies of Balnamoon are connected with the Southesk house.

The most famous bearer of the name was of humbler birth. Andrew Carnegie (1835-1919) was the son of a weaver in Dunfermline who emigrated to Pennsylvania in the 1840s. Starting work in a cotton mill at the age of 13, Andrew Carnegie rose to become a leading railway magnate and the greatest steelmaster in the United States. He was an exceedingly generous philanthropist and his native country benefited greatly from his fortune. Having himself profited as a boy from reading in a free library in Pittsburgh, he founded the Carnegie free libraries in Scotland as well as other educational projects. He rebuilt Skibo Castle in Sutherland as a home for himself.

Chisholm

There are only three people, it is said, entitled to a definite article: the King, the Pope and the Chisholm (alternately, the Queen, the Devil and the Chisholm). This isn't true of course, even among Highland chiefs several of whom are known as 'the --'. The chief of the clan has, however, been known as the Chisholm (*An Siosalach*) since the 17th century, though the chiefship has since migrated and the title sounds a little odd when applied to a Suffolk farmer.

The Chisholms are first found in the Borders, taking their name from a barony in Roberton, near Hawick in Roxburghshire. The Border family continued into modern times, the last Chisholm of that ilk

The Chisholm, painted by Kenneth MacLeay in 1869.

Chisholm of Strathglass

perishing in the Boer War. The name, however, is of Anglo-Norman origin, the early spelling being 'de Cheseholm'.

The move into the Highlands occurred in the 14th century, when Robert Chisholm of that ilk became Constable of Urquart Castle, near Inverness, as a result of inheritance through his mother. This key position, commanding the northern end of the Great Glen, made him a powerful force in the region, especially as he also inherited lands in Moray through another grandparent. His younger son remained Chief of the Border Chisholms, and *his* son become the founder of the Chisholms of Cromlix, Perthshire.

Sir Robert Chisholm's eldest son Alexander married Mary, Lady of Erchless and Comar and thus acquired the picturesque fortified house of Erchless in Strathglass, which was the seat of the Chisholm until the 1930s. Erchless became a barony in the 16th century.

The Chisholms remained Catholics at the Reformation, and the Perthshire Chisholms produced three 16th-century bishops of Dunblane. However, by the time of the Jacobite risings of the 18th century the Chisholm had changed his allegiance. Despite this, the Chisholms, never a numerous clan, were 'out' in the Fifteen, fighting under the Earl of Mar at Sheriffmuir, and though the Chisholm himself did not take part, he forfeited his lands for a period. During the second great Jacobite rising thirty Chisholms were killed at Culloden, including their leader Roderick, a younger son of the chief. Two of his brothers

Autumn in Glen Affric, Chisholm country. Once famous for timber, much of the original forest was swept away for sheep pastures in the late 18th and early 19th centuries.

fought on the other side and the chief himself was too old or too careful to appear. He seems to have been sympathetic to the Jacobite cause as Prince Charles briefly found shelter in Strathglass during his wanderings after the fatal battle. Three Chisholm brothers were among the famed Seven (actually eight) Men of Glenmoriston who sheltered and protected the prince in their cave for a week, raiding an army baggage train to get him new clothes.

The Chisholms were fortunate to avoid the worst immediate repercussions of the Forty-five, but the clan was steadily reduced by voluntary emigration and finally decimated by the Clearances. Alexander Chisholm was tempted to sell out in the 1780s but, urged by his admirable daughter Mary, eventually issued new 18-year leases to his tenants. By the time the leases expired, however, he had been succeeded by his half-brother William, who had no reservations. Despite the objections of Mary and her mother, the Chisholms were evicted, and a Lowland grazier moved in with his sheep. 'The abode of warriors has withered away,' mourned the bard, 'the son of the Lowlander is in your place.'

Clark/Blue Clergy

A clerk originally meant a man in Holy Orders, from the Latin which also gives us the word clergyman. Early references to a Clerk or Clark generally refer to a man's occupation. Later it might mean a learned man, a scholar, not necessarily a clergyman, and the word continued to be used in both senses long after it

had also become a family surname. It is a common name in medieval Scottish documents, but it cannot be shown to be, without any doubt, a name rather than a description until the 15th century at the earliest. The Gaelic form is *Mac a' Chléirich*.

One district where the name seems to have been especially common is the old bishopric of Caithness, where there is still a place called Clerkhill. There is an interesting letter written by John Eldar, Clerk, who describes himself as a 'Redshanks' (i.e. a bare-legged Highlander) to Henry VIII of England in 1543, in which he stoutly defends his fellow Highlanders against the oppressive actions of royal government. Somewhat later two Scots called Clerk reached high rank in the Swedish navy, and the American explorer George Rogers Clark (1752-1818) was of Scottish descent.

Although there was never a Highland clan of this name, it is found among the clansmen of Clan Chattan, the confederation of clans in the central Highlands mainly under Mackintosh leadership. The Clarks appear to have been a sept of the MacPhersons (another name of ecclesiastical origin), and Clarks or Clarksons were also associated with the Camerons.

It seems quite reasonable to have a Clark tartan, therefore. It is a variation on the 'Blue Clergy' tartan worn by the clergy who, as John Prebble remarked, 'undoubtedly belonged to the Church Militant in the Highlands'. During the religious troubles of the 17th century there was one instance at least of a minister, 'dressed in the kilt and armed with a sword in one hand and a cocked pistol in the other', with his back to the church wall, defying an anti-Presbyterian congregation. The old Celtic Church had been organised very like a clan; their hereditary bishops aroused the ire of St Bernard, though the practice continued centuries later.

Clark

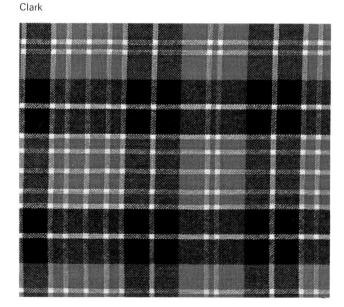

Blue Clergy

The Clark tartan appears to date from the post-1822 revival, although it may have existed earlier, and it is similar to an old version of the MacPherson tartan, in black and white.

Cochrane

Although other sources have been suggested, the name Cochrane clearly derives from a place near Paisley, Renfrewshire. A certain Waldeve de Coueran, or Coughran, was established there in the 13th century. A royal charter of King James II confirming the family possessions was obtained by Allan Cochrane of Cochrane, son of Robert, son of John. Cochrane Castle (now no more), or its tower, was built by William Cochrane in the late 16th century.

The last Cochrane of that ilk left only a daughter, Elizabeth. Her husband, originally Alexander Blair, therefore took his wife's name along with the estates, and their son was created Earl of Dundonald in 1669. The first earl's second son was a Calvinist who went to Holland and returned with William of Orange in 1688. He was also the ancestor of later earls, after the death of the seventh earl in the senior line without issue.

The most famous member of the Cochrane chiefs in modern times was Thomas, tenth Earl of Dundonald, generally known as Lord Cochrane (1775-1860). He inherited a streak of creative oddity apparent in some earlier members of his house. Having held commissions in both army and navy as a child, he first went to sea at 18 in a ship commanded by his uncle, Alexander Cochrane, and made his name when, in command of the sloop *Speedy* in 1800, he captured a Spanish frigate whose crew outnumbered his own by about six to one. This was followed by other exploits equally remarkable, which provided the material for *Peter Simple*, by Captain Marryat, who served under Cochrane. He represented Westminster in parliament, where as an outspoken radical he had a stormy career, antagonising not only the Admiralty but many others, and in 1814 he was deprived of his seat and his profession after his alleged involvement in a stock market fraud (it has been suggested that he was framed).

The republicans in Chile invited him in 1817 to command their fleet in the war of independence against Spain, which he did with dramatic success. He then performed a similar role for Brazil and for

Cochrane

Greece against the Turks, as usual showing great ability and panache and an unrivalled capacity for irritating his superiors. He was equally radical on the technical side, advocating steam-driven warships and inventing several useful devices. His plans for laying smokescreens in battle, drawn up in 1812, remained classified for over a century.

He was reinstated as an admiral in the Royal Navy in 1832, and was extremely upset to be refused a battle command on the outbreak of the Crimean War – he was only 80!

Among others Nelly Bly, born Elizabeth Cochrane at Cochran's Mill, Pennsylvania, the American journalist remembered for her round-the-world journey to beat Phineas Fogg's 80 days, is said to have been of Scottish descent.

The Cochrane tartan was officially approved by the present Earl of Dundonald and Chief of Cochrane, removing earlier doubts as to the appropriate sett.

Colquhoun

During the reign of King Malcolm II Humphrey de Kilpatrick received a grant of the lands of Colquhoun in Dumbartonshire from the Earl of Lennox. His son

Colquhoun

Ingram was the first to take the name Colquhoun. In the 14th century a descendant married 'the Fair Maid of Luss' (was there ever a Scots heiress who was not a 'Fair Maid'?), heiress of the house of Luss and related to the Earl of Lennox. He and his successors added the name Luss to their own.

The family profited by the downfall of their former patron Lennox, and Iain Colquhoun of Luss became a key figure in Dumbartonshire under the early Stewarts. The eleventh Colquhoun of Luss built the castle of Rossdhu, whose ruins now augment the natural beauties of Loch Lomond, and became chamberlain of Scotland.

The Colquhouns suffered at the hands of the invading Islesmen in 1439, when Iain of Luss was killed with many of his men, and there were other feuds with the Buchanans, the MacFarlanes and others. In 1592 Sir Humphrey Colquhoun of Luss had an affair with the wife of a MacFarlane chief which led to grisly retribution. Sir Humphrey was killed, though apparently by his ambitious younger brother rather than the MacFarlanes, but the latter raped Sir Humphrey's daughter and cut off his genitals, which they served up for supper to the adulterous MacFarlane lady.

Nevertheless, the worst of the Colquhouns' enemies were the MacGregors. Early in the 17th century the Colquhoun women enacted a remarkable kind of protest demonstration when they brought the bloodstained shirts of their menfolk killed by the MacGregors to the king at Stirling Castle (it was said, rightly or wrongly, that some of the shirts had been stained with sheep's blood). As a result the chief was given a commission of fire and sword against the MacGregors, but the immediate result was the worst disaster yet.

In 1603 Alexander Colquhoun of Luss assembled all his men, said to have numbered 800, with the fiery cross, only to be ambushed by the MacGregors in Glenfruin, not very far from Dumbarton itself. They were utterly defeated, 200 of them killed, their cattle

driven off and their goods stolen. It was this episode which led to the proscription of Clan Gregor.

The Colquhoun lands were attractive. They also bridged one of the main routes between the Highlands and the Lowlands, and even after the disaster of Glenfruin they continued to suffer depredation and violence. Indeed, the Colquhouns were no longer much of a force, and though they received cash compensation and a Nova Scotia baronetcy, they were permanently reduced. Although expected to provide 100 men in the event of invasion, they could not be taken seriously by the government in military

The Colquhouns have succeeded in holding parts of the desirable country to the west of Loch Lomond for many centuries. They were in possession at the time of the earliest surviving records and they are still there today.

terms. During the Jacobite rising of 1715 their assignment was to deprive the MacGregors of boats in Loch Lomond.

In the 18th century the Colquhouns became mixed up with the Grants in a complicated way. Sir Humphrey Colquhoun, seventeenth of Luss, who died in 1715, had only one child, a daughter. She married

James Grant of Pluscardine, second son of Grant of that ilk. In order to retain the autonomy of his own clan, Sir Humphrey made arrangements to prevent the estate passing to the Grants. On his death accordingly, James Grant changed his name and became Sir James Colquhoun of Luss. However, the death of his elder brother without children in 1719 meant that he then succeeded to the estates of Grant, whereupon he swapped identities again and was succeeded as Colquhoun chief by his own second son, Sir Ludovick. The same thing happened in the next generation. Sir Ludovick's elder brother died unmarried and he became Laird of Grant. His younger brother, another James, was recognised as Chief of Colquhoun in 1781, and from him the present chief is indirectly descended.

That the attractive Colquhoun estates have not been much developed or despoiled is largely due to the determined and unselfish efforts of Sir Iain Colquhoun of Luss (died 1948), who besides being a near-legendary hero of the First World War was chairman of the National Trust for Scotland. His successor lives today in the neo-classical mansion at Rossdhu on the famous bonny, bonny banks of Loch Lomond.

Crawford

Crawford

The ancestors of the Crawfords (or Crawfurds) can be traced back to the 12th century in the old barony of Crawford in Lanarkshire. Sir Reginald of Crawford was Sheriff of Ayr in the reign of King William the Lion. Sir John of Crawford, who died in 1248, had a daughter who married a Lindsay ancestor of the earls of Crawford. Another Crawford daughter, Margaret, married Sir Malcolm Wallace of Ellerslie and became the mother of the great resistance leader Sir William Wallace.

Her brother received a grant of Auchinames from King Robert Bruce in 1320, and the house of Auchinames continued into the present century, when the property was sold and the last representative died in Canada. Another branch, the Crawfords of Crawfordland, trace their ancestors back to Sir Reginald of Crawford in the late 12th century, and a third, the Crawfords of Kilburnie, go back to the 13th-century Sir John Crawford whose daughter married a Lindsay.

The Crawfords of Kilburnie, baronets since 1781,

have a distinguished record in the British armed services in modern times.

Thomas Crawford (died 1603) was a younger son of Lawrence Crawford of Kilburnie. He was taken prisoner at the Battle of Pinkie (1547) but ransomed by his family and later went to France where he became a soldier in French service and a courtier attendant on Mary Queen of Scots. He returned to Scotland with the queen in 1561 and after her marriage to Lord Darnley became a member of the latter's household. In 1569 he denounced certain lords as the murderers of Darnley, although by that time there was little point in such a highly dangerous accusation, whether true or not. In 1571 Crawford captured Dumbarton Castle from Mary's supporters on behalf of the government with a force of only 150 men, who scaled the natural defences with ropes and ladders. He also participated in the capture of Edinburgh Castle from 'the Queen's Lords' two years later.

Lawrence Crawford (1611-45) was a fierce Presbyterian with military experience under Gustavus Adolphus in the Thirty Years' War who fought in the English Parliamentary forces against Charles I. He came into sharp conflict with Cromwell, no lover of Presbyterians, whom he accused of cowardice during the battle of Marston Moor, but the dispute was resolved by Crawford's death in a skirmish some months later.

Cumming (Comyn)

The origin of this name is a matter of dispute. It may be territorial: the town of Commines, near Lisle, is a candidate. More widely accepted is the suggestion that it derives from the herb cummin which, along with Comyn, was a common early spelling of the name.

The family was of Anglo-Norman descent, and the first to settle in Scotland was William Comyn, an associate of King David I who, on his return to his kingdom, made Comyn Chancellor of Scotland. He established his nephew Richard at Allerton, and it is from him that the clan is descended. He married a granddaughter of Donald *Bàn* (Donaldbane), King of Scots 1093-97, and their son married the heiress of Buchan, the first of several Comyn alliances with Celtic dynastic houses which eventually resulted in Comyns holding three of the thirteen Scottish earldoms in the 13th century. From 1270 they also held the military office of constable, the guardian of the king.

Thus on the constitutional crisis caused by the death of King Alexander III in 1286 the Comyns were the most powerful family in Scotland. With the death of Alexander's little granddaughter 'the Maid of Norway' the Comyn chief, known as the Black Comyn, was one of the claimants to the throne, as descendant of Donald *Bàn*. The other two chief claimants, John Balliol and the elder Robert Bruce, were, however, descended from Donald *Bàn*'s elder brother, Malcolm *Ceann Mór* (reigned 1057-93) and thus had better claims according to strict laws of succession. The Black Comyn, like Bruce, eventually acknowledged John Balliol as king, and he married Balliol's sister Marjory. This obviously strengthened the future royal claims of their son John, the Red Comyn. The results, however, were not a crown for the Red Comyn but the ruin of the clan.

When John Balliol was pressed into defiance of his overlord Edward I, provoking the English invasion of Scotland, Bruce was among the Scottish nobles who as vassals of Edward did homage to him when he crossed the border. Balliol indignantly seized Bruce's lands and gave them to his nephew, the Red Comyn.

Edward proceeded to conquer Scotland, as it seemed, removing the Stone of Scone to Westminster Abbey. Balliol departed, leaving the Red Comyn as his successor, but national resistance broke out soon

Cumming (Comyn)

after under the inspiring leadership of Wallace.

The great nobles did not on the whole give much aid to Wallace, but after his defeat and death both Comyn and Bruce were ready to move. A meeting was arranged between them at Greyfriars Kirk, Dumfries, early in 1306. There were plenty of reasons for mutual hostility and the selection of a church as a meeting place suggests precautionary measures against violence. They were ineffective, however: Bruce stabbed the Red Comyn and killed him in the church.

Dearly as one would like to know the details, this incident is likely to remain somewhat mysterious. For one Scottish noble to murder another was not unusual, but it was a most dangerous act and therefore cannot have been planned. Bruce himself was greatly worried by his sacrilege but, being the kind of man he was, he grasped the thistle and proceeded at once to have himself crowned at Scone.

Besides the English, he also had to contend with the Church, since he had incurred automatic excommunication, and the mighty power of the Comyns and their supporters. He was of course successful, and the Comyns were gradually but ruthlessly destroyed. The Red Comyn's only son died at Bannockburn fighting for the English. The hereditary office of constable was given to the Hays of Erroll (who had some Comyn blood), where it has since remained.

One branch of the Cummings remained, relatively

The ruins of the powerful castle of Inverlochy, near Fort William, a place rich in legend and in history (site of a famous victory by Montrose over Argyll in 1645). Inverlochy Castle was held by the Cummings (Comyns) when they were at the height of their power, later by the Gordons.

unharassed, to the north of Badenoch. There, the Cummings of Altyre were descended from a brother of the Black Comyn, who died with his nephew in the church at Dumfries. In time they prospered, though not mightily, and became a power in Moray by the end of the century, conducting blistering feuds with Clan Chattan. It is said that they once dammed Loch Moy to raise the level and flood the castle of the Mackintoshes on an island. Sir Iain Moncreiffe of that ilk speculated that they were the clan which fought the famous mass duel with the Mackintoshes or MacPhersons (?Camerons) in the Battle of the Clans (1396) on the North Inch at Perth. The Cummings were certainly a warlike clan, and their enemies had a saying, 'So long as there is a stick in the wood there will be treachery in a Cumming'.

Robert, thirteenth Chief of Altyre, married a daughter of Sir Ludovic Gordon of Gordonstoun, which was inherited by his grandson. He was the first to adopt the name Gordon-Cumming, which is that of the present chief.

Cunningham

Cunningham

Cunningham is a district in Ayrshire where in the 12th century the land of Kilmaurs (later a Cunningham barony, sold in the 18th century) was granted by Hugh de Moreville, then Constable of Scotland, to a vassal named Wernebald.

His presumed descendant Harvey de Cunningham is said to have fought against the Norwegian king at the Battle of Largs in 1263. The lands were further expanded by a grant of Robert Bruce in gratitude for Cunningham support, and through the marriage of Sir William Cunningham to the heiress of Danielston of that ilk, which resulted in the acquisition of Glencairn.

Sir William's grandson was created Earl of Glencairn by King James III in 1488 but did not live to enjoy the honour long, dying in the same year in the battle of Sauchieburn, which also put an end to James III. His son and heir lost the earldom, but it was restored to his brother Cuthbert. The third Earl of Glencairn (sometimes listed as the fourth) was captured at Solway Moss but released in exchange for his support for the marriage of the English King Edward VI to Mary Queen of Scots, a project which foundered when he was defeated by Hamilton, Earl of Arran.

Alexander, fourth (fifth) Earl of Glencairn, was a stern Calvinist and a friend of John Knox. He is said to have been responsible for vandalising the chapel at Holyrood after the battle of Langside, where Mary Queen of Scots was defeated in 1568.

A feud between the Cunninghams of Glencairn and the Montgomery earls of Eglinton was exacerbated at this time by the Catholic Eglinton's support for Mary. The fourth Earl of Eglinton was murdered by the Cunninghams in 1586.

The eighth Earl of Glencairn, though hesitant at first, became one of the most loyal Stewart supporters, leading the rising of 1653 which is named after him. With Charles II in exile abroad and Cromwell's generals in command in Scotland it had little chance of success. Glencairn was betrayed and captured but managed to keep his head on his shoulders until the Restoration (1660) when he was rewarded with the post of Lord Chancellor. His successor supported the overthrow of James VII/II.

The fourteenth earl, John, is best remembered as the friend and patron of Burns, who on the earl's death in 1791 wrote a *Lament* for him:

The mother may forget the child
That smiles sae sweetly on her knee;
But I'll remember thee, Glencairn,
And a' that thou hast done for me.

As he had no children the earldom became dormant, though it would seem that the claim of the present Cunningham chief, who is descended from Cunningham of Corsehill, second son of the third Earl of Glencairn, could hardly be disputed. The Cunninghams of Craigends and Robertlane (baronets since 1630) and Auchinarvie are descended from a younger son of the first earl; the Cunninghams of Caprington (a barony created by Mary Queen of Scots) from a cousin of the first earl.

Cunningham prowess on the battlefield was exemplified by an odd coincidence during the Second World War, when the three British commanders of army, navy and air force in the Middle East were all named Cunningham or Coningham.

Davidson

The Davidsons are believed to have been a branch of the Comyns. After the destruction of the Comyns by Robert Bruce they were led by David *Dubh* of Invernahaven into the 'security' of Clan Chattan. He was closely related by marriage to the sixth Mackintosh Chief of Clan Chattan and his people were welcomed by William, seventh of Mackintosh. The

Davidson

favour shown to the Davidsons appears to have been partly responsible for the disastrous feuds in which they became involved. In particular the MacPhersons, another sept of Clan Chattan, were inveterate enemies.

According to one tradition the Camerons occupied Mackintosh lands in Lochaber for which they were decidedly dilatory in the matter of rent. The Mackintoshes were accustomed to make good this failure by plundering the Camerons' cattle, and in 1370 the infuriated Camerons marched into Clan Chattan territory. The Chief of Mackintosh sent out the fiery cross and the MacPhersons and the Davidsons were among those who at once responded. An argument then broke out between Davidson of Invernahaven and Cluny MacPherson over who should have the honour of leading the right wing. As the Camerons were advancing, this dispute had to be cut short and Mackintosh precipitately opted for Davidson. As a result the MacPhersons withdrew, and in the ensuing battle the Davidsons were badly mauled. In the end the MacPhersons were provoked into joining in (some say by a trick) and they defeated the Camerons, though too late to save the Davidsons.

A generation later the famous conflict known as the battle of the Clans was staged in Perth, watched by King Robert III (royal policy was to let the Highlanders, whom the king was unable to control, kill as many of each other as possible). It is usually assumed that the combatants were the MacPhersons and the Davidsons. Sir Iain Moncreiffe said the Cummings were the more likely opponents, but in view of the Davidsons' former associations, this may come to the same thing. In any case, others no doubt took part, especially as the Davidsons must presumably have still been sadly depleted as a result of the battle with the Camerons. It is said that only one of the thirty Davidsons who took part survived the combat. He escaped by jumping into the River Tay.

Later the chiefship was held for many years by the Davidsons of Tulloch. At the beginning of the 18th century Alexander Davidson of Davidson married a Miss Bayne of Tulloch, near Dingwall in Easter Ross, and bought the estates from his wife's father.

Douglas

The succession of mighty families who bore this name derived it from the dale south of Lanark where William of Douglas held land in the late 12th century. In Gaelic Douglas means black water. William of Douglas was the grandfather of the founder of the Mortons and the great-grandfather of the man who created the Douglas fortunes in the 14th century.

This was 'the Good Sir James' (1286-1330), who stands with Wallace and Bruce among the heroes of the Scottish wars of independence. He was said to have preferred the lark's song to the mouse's squeak, yet he was a bold and cunning warrior, who captured Roxburgh by disguising his men as oxen, and he certainly showed no revulsion to squeaks when recapturing Castle Douglas (Scott's *Castle Dangerous*) from the English. At Bannockburn he commanded the left wing and thereafter led many raids into England, on one occasion almost capturing Edward I. He was the first to be called – by the English – the Black Douglas. He died fighting in Spain on his way to the Holy Land where he was taking the Bruce's heart in fulfilment of a deathbed promise.

Sir James's son and his brother Sir Archibald (regent for the young King David II) died fighting the English at Halidon Hill in 1333. Sir Archibald's son inherited the estates and was created Earl of Douglas in 1358. By marriage to the Earl of Mar's sister he eventually gained the earldom of Mar, and by the Countess of Angus he had a son, George, who became first Earl of Angus. The second Earl of Douglas and Mar married a daughter of King Robert II and was killed fighting the Percys at Otterburn in 1388, a battle fought by moonlight and celebrated in both Scottish and English ballad ('Chevy Chase'). He left no legitimate heir, but his natural sons William and Archibald became the ancestors of the families of Douglas of Drumlanrigg and Douglas of Craven.

The earldom of Douglas reverted to Archibald the Grim, a bastard son of 'the Good Sir James'. He married the heiress of Bothwell, thus expanding his estates, and in the intervals between fighting the English managed to impose a degree of stability and justice in the Borders, governing from his castle of Threaves in Galloway. The Black Douglas's power was considerably greater at this time than the Crown's under the ineffective King Robert III, and Douglas was able to marry his daughter to the heir to the throne.

His son, the fourth Earl of Douglas, has gone down in history with the nickname of the Tyneman (the loser). As a warrior he was sometimes victorious – his campaigns in France against the English earned him the duchy of Touraine – but in 1402 he was captured by the Percys and, in the following year, fighting with the rebellious Percys at Shrewsbury, he was captured by Henry IV. Not long after gaining his French duchy he was killed in battle at Verneuil (1424).

The enemies of the Douglases were gathering strength. Soon after the death of the fifth earl in 1439 his two sons, both under seventeen, were judicially murdered in Edinburgh.

The power of the Black Douglases was diminished but not annihilated. The Douglas estates passed to the seventh earl, a younger son of the third earl who was also Earl of Avondale, and under his son and successor the family's standing was largely restored. William,

Douglas

Grey Douglas

the eighth earl, regained Galloway by marrying his cousin, 'the Fair Maid of Galloway', and gained favour with King James II (which enabled him to exact revenge on the chief murderer of his young kinsmen in 1440). However, this happy relationship did not last long. The king desired Douglas to withdraw from an alliance with certain other nobles that he had recently joined – such alliances were the bane of royal government – and invited him to discuss the matter, under a safe conduct, at Stirling in 1452. When Douglas refused to withdraw, the king himself stabbed him, his courtiers finished him off, and his body was flung from the battlements.

There was little choice for the ninth earl, the last of the Black Douglases, except rebellion. After a splendid gesture of protest – he rode through Stirling with the king's safe conduct dragging in the dirt behind his horse – he was eventually forced to fly to England in 1453. The Douglas estates were forfeit and the earldom extinguished.

An extraordinary transformation then took place. The brothers of the last Black Douglas were defeated in a battle in Eskdale by the fourth Earl of Angus, George Douglas. He was the leader of the Red Douglases, as they were known in distinction (allegedly due to hair colour) from their distant kinsmen, the Black Douglases. He was a great-grandson of the first Earl of Douglas and in the division of the Black Douglas's estates gained the lordship of Douglas.

To a considerable extent the Red Douglases came to occupy the space left by the extinction of the Black Douglases. The fifth Earl of Angus (died c. 1514) plotted against King James III and later became guardian of the young King James IV and Lord Chancellor of Scotland. He was known as 'Bell-the-cat', from his alleged remark when a group of nobles, dissatisfied with James III, plotted to get rid of the king's favourites. Someone mentioned the mice which hung a bell around the cat's neck as a warning. 'I will bell the cat', said Angus, and took the lead in hanging several of the king's favourites from the bridge at Lauder. He later survived Flodden Field, where two of his sons died. A third son was Gavain Douglas (died 1522), bishop and poet, the first man to translate a great classical poem (the *Aeneid*) into English, and the author of poetic allegories. He too was involved in the feuds of the time and died of the plague while an exile in London.

The sixth Earl of Angus married the king's widow, Queen Margaret Tudor, but had no male heir. He held supreme power in Scotland for a time in the 1520s, but was eventually forced to flee to England. His sister was burned at the stake under King James V. His daughter by Margaret Tudor married Matthew Stewart, fourth Earl of Lennox, becoming the mother

of Lord Darnley and thus grandmother of James VI/I.

The earldom passed to another branch and in 1633 the Douglas title was revived when William, eleventh Earl of Angus, was created Marquess of Douglas. The third marquess was made a duke in 1703 but he died childless and his titles, including the earldom of Angus, passed to the Duke of Hamilton, while the lordship of Douglas, including the chiefship, went, after a famous lawsuit, to Lord Douglas of Douglas in the late 18th century. His 19th-century inheritors were the earls of Home.

Another branch of the Douglas family, probably

Threave (Thrieve) Castle, a Douglas stronghold on an island in the River Dee, a mile or two west of Castle Douglas. After the fall of the Black Douglases it became a royal castle and the hereditary keepership was bestowed on the Maxwells of Nithsdale.

descended from William of Douglas in the late 12th century, gained a small estate in East Calder in the early 14th century. As supporters of Bruce and his successors they advanced rapidly. Sir William Douglas gained the earldom of Atholl in 1341 but later exchanged it for Liddesdale. Known as 'the Flower of Chivalry' and the Knight of Liddesdale, he was killed by his distant kinsman, the first Earl of Douglas, in 1353.

His nephew, Sir James Douglas of Dalkeith, married a daughter of King James I and became Earl of Morton in 1458. The fourth Earl of Morton (died 1581) is the best known of this long line. He was implicated in the murders of both Rizzio and Darnley and was an unpopular regent during the minority of James VI, who had him executed at the first opportunity. Several later earls played prominent and less sinister parts in Scottish history.

Douglas of Drumlanrig

The ramifications of the Douglas family, even if confined to major branches, are enormous. For centuries history seems to have conspired to ensure there was always a Douglas near the centre of events. After the Black Douglases came the Red Douglases of Angus, after them the earls of Morton and finally the Douglases of Drumlanrig.

The second Earl of Douglas (died 1388) had an illegitimate son William, to whom he gave the barony of Drumlanrig. As active supporters of the Stewart dynasty the family reaped rewards in the reign of Charles II, who made Sir William Douglas of Drumlanrig a viscount and then, in 1633, Earl of Queensberry. His grandson, also William (1637-95), held high posts in Scotland and his earldom was raised to a marquessate and then to a dukedom.

His son James, the second Duke of Queensberry, followed in his father's footsteps but, by error rather than design, became implicated in the plotting of the devious Simon Fraser, Lord Lovat. He extricated himself successfully from this embarrassment and was largely responsible, as commissioner to the Scottish parliament, for securing passage of the Act of Union (1707), by a judicious combination of diplomacy, bullying and bribes.

The third duke married the witty and fashionable Catherine Hyde but had no direct heirs and was succeeded by his cousin, the fourth Duke of Queensberry ('Old Q', 1724-1810), a well-known character and patron of horse racing, who was mocked by Burns among others. On his death the title passed to the Duke of Buccleuch. The marquessate passed to Sir Charles Douglas of Kelhead, whose descendants included the egregious eighth marquess, regulator of boxing and father of Oscar Wilde's lover Lord Alfred Douglas. From Archibald the Grim and the Knight of Liddesdale it seems a long, long way to Lord Alfred Douglas.

Drumlanrig Castle, Nithsdale; built in the late 17th century for the first Duke of Queensberry who, it is said, spent only one night there because the cost of its construction turned him against the place.

Drummond

It is said that a major contribution to Bruce's victory at Bannockburn was an anti-cavalry device known as caltrops, four-angled prongs which were always alight with one point sticking up. This was the work of Sir Malcolm de Drymen, or Drummond, who took his name from Drymen in Stirlingshire and, after the victory of Bruce, was granted lands in Perthshire. The ancestry of the Drummonds can be traced, speculatively, much farther back to the ancient Celtic earls of Menteith and Lennox in the early 13th century.

Having prospered in Bruce's train, Sir John Drummond, *An Drumanach Mór* (the Great Man of Drymen) as the chiefs of Drummond are called, married in 1345 the heiress of Stobhall, where the present chief, Lord Perth, still lives. Both his sister and his daughter were married to kings of Scots, the latter becoming mother of James I.

The Drummonds have a talent for producing beautiful women; at least, several of them have attracted a royal eye, but not always with happy results. A century after this Margaret Drummond, 'the diamond of delight', daughter of the first Lord Drummond (created 1488), was adored by the susceptible young James IV. James, however, was destined to make a dynastically more useful match to Margaret Tudor and Margaret Drummond (who may have been privately married to James) disappeared from the scene. Her two sisters also died mysteriously; natural causes were not suspected.

The fourth Lord Drummond was made Earl of Perth by James VI in 1605, soon after he had succeeded to the throne he owed to his grandfather's politic marriage.

The Drummonds had a talent, admittedly not rare among the clans, for a prickly temper, commemorated in the prayer of their neighbours, 'From the ire of the Drummonds, Good Lord deliver us.' The first Lord Drummond was imprisoned at the age of 76 for

The beautiful Italian gardens at Drummond castle. The original castle was built in 1491 by John, Lord Drummond.

Drummond of Perth

Dunbar

The ruins of the old castle of Dunbar still remain above the harbour, but Dunbars were also to be found in many other parts of Scotland, in particular in Moray.

In the 11th century Cospatrick, the Celtic Earl of Northumberland, was deprived of his earldom by William the Conqueror and fled to Scotland, where he was granted lands in East Lothian, including Dunbar, by Malcolm *Ceann Mór*. The king of Scots

striking the Scottish herald, and one of his sons was executed for burning a number of Murrays, currently feuding with the Drummonds, in a church.

By the 17th century the Drummonds had expanded considerably, establishing the cadet branches of Carnock, Meidhope and Hawthornden, whose laird William Drummond of Hawthornden (1585-1649) was the famous poet, man of letters and sage. The first Earl of Perth was head of a considerable host which contributed powerfully to the Stewart cause in the troubles of the 17th and 18th centuries.

, In 1688 the fourth Earl of Perth and his brothers the Earl of Melfort, with whom he had 'ruled Scotland' under James VII, and Lord Strathallan followed their king into exile. Perth and Melfort each received dukedoms as reward for their loyalty. In the Jacobite rising of 1715 the second duke (fifth earl) commanded the Jacobite cavalry at Sheriffmuir, and 30 years later the Drummonds were out again. At Culloden the third Duke of Perth, not a strong man since a childhood accident, commanded the left wing of the Jacobite army, made up mainly of exhausted and hungry MacDonalds embittered because their normal, honoured position was on the right. 'If you fight with your usual bravery,' the duke declared, 'you will make the left wing a right wing!' He also promised that if they fought well he would himself assume the honourable name of MacDonald. Afterwards the duke escaped to France. His brother Strathallan, mortally wounded in the battle, took communion in whisky as no wine was to be had.

The Drummond estates were forfeit but were regained in the General Act of Restoration of 1784. The old Drummond lands passed through an heiress to the earls of Ancaster. Medieval Stobhall has been restored by the seventeenth Earl of Perth, who is descended from the Strathallan killed at Culloden.

was his first cousin, Cospatrick being the son of King Duncan I's daughter.

His descendants acquired land elsewhere, in England as well as Scotland, but the seat of the earls of Dunbar remained at Dunbar Castle. The eighth earl, Patrick, was one of the numerous claimants to the Scottish crown in the 1290s, though not perhaps a very serious one. His son, the ninth earl, was for a time hostile to Bruce, and after Bannockburn he received Edward II at Dunbar and assisted his withdrawal to England. However, he came around later: he was one of the signatories of the Declaration of Arbroath

The harbour and castle of Dunbar, where Black Agnes held out against the English in 1337. The Dunbars spread all over Scotland. One branch acquired the former Keith stronghold of Ackergill Tower, Wick.

Dunbar

(1320), the famous address to the Pope in support of Bruce and Scottish independence, and he married a daughter of Bruce's friend Thomas Randolph, Earl of Moray.

This lady was the famous 'Black Agnes' of Dunbar – 'that brawling boisterous Scottish wench' as the English balladeer called her – who in the earl's absence held the castle for several months against a besieging English army in 1337. 'Black Agnes' also became Countess of Moray in her own right, but she outlived her children and the estates of Dunbar and Moray both went ultimately to the children of her sister Isobel, who had also married a Dunbar. This marks the beginning of the Dunbars as a Highland clan.

The earldom of Dunbar was lost in 1435 when James I, regarding it as undesirably powerful, annexed it, but in Moray the Dunbars prospered, in spite of an unremitting feud with their neighbours the Inneses. The boundary between their territories was set at the cairn of Kilbuick, between Forres and Elgin: no Innes was supposed to be seen west of that point, no Dunbar east of it. The Dunbars of Westfield held the hereditary office of sheriff of Moray until it was sold to the Stewart Earl of Moray in the 19th century.

Many other cadet branches were founded, as distantly spread as Hempriggs in Caithness and Mochrum in Galloway. The latter family included Gavin Dunbar, who was Archbishop of Glasgow and Lord Chancellor of Scotland in the reign of James V. Another Gavin Dunbar, Bishop of Aberdeen in the 16th century, was a member of the Westfield family and uncle of his namesake, tutor to the young James V.

The most famous bearer of the name Dunbar, William Dunbar the poet (died c. 1515), was of obscure origin, though probably born in or near Dunbar itself.

A Franciscan friar, he travelled widely in Britain and France and was a member of the embassy which negotiated the marriage of King James IV to Margaret Tudor in 1501. His first major poem, *The Thrissil and the Rois*, is an allegory on the theme of that marriage. His literary reputation today stands very high, and many would say he comes close to Burns as Scotland's greatest poet.

Duncan

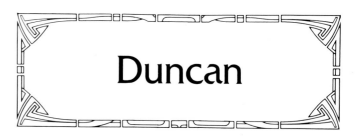

Duncan is the old Gaelic name *Donnchadh*, and *Clann-Donnchaidh* is the name of the Robertsons, who claim descent from royal 'kindred of St Columba' and take their name from a chief named Duncan who led them into battle on behalf of the Bruce at Bannockburn.

At the time of the Norse invasions some of the relics of St Columba were taken from Iona for safety to Dunkeld, and the hereditary abbot of Dunkeld came from the same royal line as St Columba himself. There was an Abbot Duncan of Dunkeld in the 10th century, who was killed in battle in 965 (Celtic clergy were less retiring in military activities than stricter Romans). He was probably the great-grandfather of King Duncan I, who reigned from 1034 until his death (probably killed by MacBeth) in 1040. From a younger son of King Duncan I descended great landholders in Atholl, the country of *Clann Donnchaidh* (the children of Duncan).

Eventually the chief and most of the clan adopted the name Robertson, but some were called Duncan-

Duncan

son, Duncan, MacConachie or Donachie.

By the time surnames were becoming common in Scotland Duncans and Duncansons cropped up in many places, especially in the south-east.

The Duncans of Lundie held land in Forfar and Perthshire. Sir William Duncan was an 18th-century physician who was created a baronet in 1764 for services to George III, but died without an heir ten years later. The Duncans of Lundie had been Jacobite sympathisers in the Forty-five, but Adam Duncan (1731-1804), a younger son of Sir Alexander Duncan of Lundie, entered the Royal Navy in 1746 and rose to become one of the most distinguished British admirals in an age when they were remarkably plentiful. A very big man, immensely strong (as well as handsome), his sheer personality was effective in preventing worse trouble when his ships were involved in the naval mutinies of 1797. (He held one mutineer, with one arm, over the side of the ship, saying, 'Look, lads, this fellow would deprive me of my command.') For his overwhelming victory over the Dutch fleet at Camperdown he was created Viscount Duncan of Camperdown in 1800.

Elliot

It is said that some Elliots took their name from Eliot in Forfarshire, though the common early form of the name was the old English Elwold. Modern branches of the family spell the name in several different ways, those of Stobs, the leading house, preferring Eliott initially and Eliot today. An old rhyme commemo-rates these differences:

> The double L and single T
>> Descend from Minto and Wolflee,
> The double T and single L
>> Mark the old race in Stobs that dwell,
>> The single L and single T
>> The Eliots of St Germains be,
> But double T and double L,
>> Who they are nobody can tell.

A list of variants of the name current in the 17th century numbers about seventy, from Allat to Hellewald.

The Elliots were a famous, indeed notorious, Border clan, like the Armstrongs. Their territory was around Upper Liddesdale, where they conducted their more or less profitable banditry for many centuries. The principal family in the early days was the Elliots of Redheugh, who often held the captaincy of Hermitage Castle – still to be seen, squat and impregnable, on the moors south of Hawick. One of the Elliots of Redheugh, forefather of the Elliots of Arkleton, fell at Flodden (the beautiful lament for that disaster, *The Flowers of the Forest*, was written

Hermitage Castle in Liddesdale, built in the 13th century as a stronghold for the De Soulis family and one of the most famous of Border fortresses. After 1341 it was held by the Douglases, its walls have sheltered the holders of many famous names, including Lord Bothwell, visited here by his future wife, Mary Queen of Scots.

Elliot

Erskine

by Jane Elliot, sister of Sir Gilbert Elliot, first Baronet of Minto, in the 18th century).

The Elliots of Stobs go back to Gawain Elliot of Stobs in the late 16th century, who was descended from the Elliots of Redheugh. Since the 17th century, when Border plundering was finally suppressed, they have been the principal among the many cadet houses. Gawain was succeeded as Laird of Stobs by Gilbert, known as 'Gibbie wi' the gowden gartens', and from one of his sons the baronets and earls of Minto are descended.

Of this line, several of whom were distinguished as judges and empire builders, the most famous were George Elliot, vegetarian and teetotaller who as governor of Gibraltar in 1779 conducted the heroic and successful defence of the Rock when it was besieged by Franco-Spanish forces, and Gilbert Elliot, first Earl of Minto, a notable governor-general of India in the early 19th century.

His great grandson Gilbert, fourth Earl of Minto (1845-1914), is remembered in the sporting world for having broken his neck riding in the Grand National. The mishap had no permanent effects and he was Governor-general of Canada before succeeding Lord Curzon as Viceroy of India in 1905. He was the chief architect of the Morley-Minto Reforms, regarded as dangerously radical in some circles at the time though, as it turned out, insufficient to stem the tide of Indian unrest.

The seat of the present Earl of Minto is Minto House, in Hawick, and of the present Eliot of Stobs, chief of the clan, at Redheugh.

The Erskines were perhaps more of a dynasty than a clan, and their name is bound up with the long and complicated history of the earldom of Mar.

The name is derived from the barony of Erskine in Renfrewshire, where Henry de Erskine held land in the reign of King Alexander II. Sir Robert Erskine of that ilk (died 1385) profited from the success of Bruce and was for some time Chamberlain of Scotland. He gained the lands of Alloa, north of the Forth, and two of his sons were dynastic progenitors. From Thomas, the elder, who married Lady Elyne of Mar, came the Erskines of Dun (through a younger son), and from Malcolm came the Erskines of Kinnoul.

Robert, son of Thomas, the first Lord Erskine, claimed the earldom of Mar, which derived from an ancient Pictish title and had never been conferred by a king of Scots, but the confiscation of the Alloa estates forced him to withdraw. The title was not confirmed to the Erskines until the reign of Mary, who not only restored it but also created a new earldom of Mar, so that the beneficiary, the sixth Lord Erskine, became eighteenth and first Earl of Mar. The reason for this curious contrivance was presumably to secure the earldom against a possible future cancellation of Mary's restoration. Today the two earldoms of Mar are separately held.

It shows in what affection the Erskines were held by the Stewart dynasty. This affection dated from the appointment of the fifth Lord Erskine as guardian to James V after his father (and Lord Erskine's father, incidentally) had been killed at Flodden. A position of responsibility in relation to a royal infant can lead to future benefit or to future disaster, but in this case Erskine performed so well that James V later put him in charge of the future Mary Queen of Scots when she was sent to France to escape the unwanted attentions of the English. The association continued into the next generation when Mary's infant son, the future James VI, was given into the care of Lord Erskine's son the Earl of Mar, who carried the baby at the coronation in 1567. He later became regent and, after his death in 1572, his wife remained in charge of the young king. She later received James's son into her care – the fourth successive generation of Scottish royal heirs under Erskine guardianship.

The Regent Mar's grandson, Lord Treasurer of Scotland under James VI, was the builder of Braemar

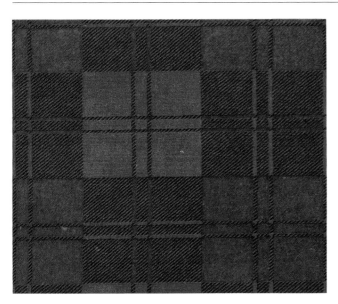

Erskine

Castle on Deeside and from his sons are descended other important Erskine families who became in course of time earls of Rosslyn and earls of Buchan.

The sixth earl (1675-1732), maintaining the close alliance of his family with the Stewart dynasty, was the Jacobite commander-in-chief during the rising of 1715, although he had previously been an advocate of the Union (1707) and a Scottish Secretary of State under Queen Anne. Having been deprived of office under George I he returned secretly to Scotland, where he told the Highland chiefs the Union had been a mistake, that he now favoured Scottish independence, and raised the banner of the Jacobites at Braemar. But Lord Mar, 'Bobbing John' as he was called, was no great general and lingered at Perth while his opponents, at first outnumbered, gathered strength. His only serious sortie resulted in the battle of Sheriffmuir which, if not an actual defeat, was certainly no glorious victory. Eventually, Mar withdrew to France along with 'Old Mr Melancholy', James Edward Stewart. Later he changed sides again, accepting a pension from George I and abandoning the Jacobite court.

He was made a duke in the Jacobite peerage but naturally forfeited his earldom, and his attainder was not reversed for over a hundred years. His brother James Erskine, Lord Grange (1679-1754), a judge and MP, is remembered for a famous scandal involving his wife, 'a woman of disorderly intellect' whom he had abducted in 1732 and kept secretly in the Hebrides while her 'funeral' was staged in Edinburgh.

Braemar Castle, on Royal Deeside, was built by the second Earl of Mar during the reign of Charles I. It was sacked by the Jacobites in 1689 and partly rebuilt in the 18th century.

Farquharson

The Farquharsons, 'the dear ones', were members of the Clan Chattan confederation, although latterly they were an independent clan. In origin they were apparently descended from Farquhar, son of Shaw of Rothiemurchus, and were thus a branch of the Shaws. The Gaelic name of the Farquharson chief is *Mac Fhionnlaigh*, after Finlay, royal standard-bearer at the battle of Pinkie – where he was killed – in 1547. A harp now in the Edinburgh National Museum of Antiquities is said to have been given to Finlay *Mór*'s widow by Mary Queen of Scots – it is a rare survival of the old Celtic harps which predominated before the rising of the pipes.

The Farquharsons acquired Invercauld on upper Deeside by the marriage of Donald, father of Finlay, to the heiress Isobel Stewart. They produced a number of cadet branches – Monaltrie, Inverey, Whitehouse, Finzean, etc. – several descended from Donald Farquharson, grandson of Finlay. The Farquharson lands were held from the Earl of Mar, though during the 17th century they obtained royal charters for some of them. In that troubled period Sir Robert Farquharson of Invercauld, an Aberdeen merchant, greatly improved the family fortunes by his commercial and political activities, and later the Farquharsons acquired the former seat of the earls of Mar, Braemar Castle, which they still hold today.

The Farquharsons of Inverey fought under Montrose and at the battle of Worcester in 1651. Bonnie

Dundee had Farquharsons among his forces in 1689, including John Farquharson of Inverey, 'the Black Colonel' celebrated in ballad. In the 1715 Jacobite rising John Farquharson of Invercauld, with 140 men, fought in the Clan Chattan regiment. He was taken prisoner at Preston, but was able to convince the government that he had become involved in the rebellion unwillingly as vassal of the Earl of Mar.

His daughter 'Colonel Anne' married the Mackintosh and, though only 20, played a leading part in raising Clan Chattan for Prince Charles in 1745 in the absence of her husband, who commanded a company of Hanoverian militia and was taken prisoner. There was a legend current in the Hanoverian army that she had led her husband's men in person at the battle of Culloden. There were also 300 Farquharsons fighting for the Jacobite cause at Culloden, led by Francis Farquharson of Monaltrie, 'Baron Ban', but James Farquharson of Invercauld fought on the government side. Farquharson of Balmoral was among the Jacobites and although Monaltrie was later returned to its former owner, Balmoral was forfeited permanently, returning to the Gordons who were later to sell it to Queen Victoria.

Fergusson

It is doubtful whether all 'sons of Fergus' are in fact descended from a single ancestor, and although there was a clannish sympathy between families of that name, the Fergussons were not a clan in the full sense of the word. The name occurs in widely scattered

Farquharson

Fergusson

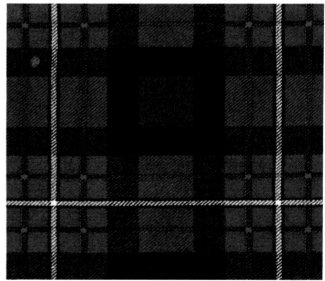

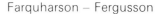

'Queen Mary's Harp', probably made in the 15th century and at one time in Farquharson possession. The harp and the clarsach were to some extent replaced by the bagpipes in the Highlands during the 16th century perhaps because 'the clans . . . required a more resonant martial instrument than the harp . . .' (I. F. Grant).

locations in Scotland at an early date.

The best-known family is that of Fergusson of Kilkerran, descendants of Fergus, son of Fergus, who was granted lands in Ayrshire by King Robert Bruce in the early 14th century. In later times a number of families in that area regarded Fergusson of Kilkerran as their chief, and the later Sir James Fergusson, Keeper of the Records of Scotland and a famous scholar and historian, was so regarded by Fergussons everywhere. Sir Bernard Fergusson, the great guerilla leader of the Chindits in Burma during the Second World War, was his brother. The baronetcy of Kilkerran dates from 1703.

Other families included the Fergussons of Dunfallandy in Atholl, who acquired that estate by the old Highland device of killing the current Baron of Dunfallandy and forcibly marrying his heiress to their own heir; the Fergussons of Baldemund in Perthshire; the Kinmundy, Baddifurrow and Pitfour Fergussons of Aberdeenshire; and the Fergussons of Craigdarroch in Dumfriesshire, one of whom married the Annie Laurie of the well-known song. Fergussons said to have been connected with the Fergussons of Kilkerran held lands on Loch Fyne until the 19th century.

There were Fergussons of Dunfallandy, who claimed descent from the princes of Galloway, among the men of Atholl in Montrose's force during the civil war, and under the banner of Prince Charles during the Forty-five. A Captain Fergusson of HMS *Furnace* earned an evil reputation ferrying the oddly named Captain Caroline Scott around the Western Isles after Culloden in a search for the prince. He was described by a contemporary historian of the campaign as 'a fellow of very low extract, born in Aberdeenshire', and appears to have been related to the Fergussons of Pitfour. Otherwise, Fergussons have been more notable for learning and scholarship than savagery, and the name often appears among the lists of the judiciary.

Robert Fergusson (1750-74), the Scots poet, who was born in Edinburgh, was one of the leaders of the 18th-century revival of writing in the Scots vernacular and an important influence on Burns whom, had he lived longer, he might have rivalled. He died insane after an accidental head injury and Burns himself was responsible for erecting a monument on his grave. His contemporary Adam Ferguson (1732-1816) was Presbyterian chaplain to the Black Watch and took part, sword in hand, in their charge at the battle of Fontenoy. He lived to become professor of philosophy at Edinburgh University and a commissioner appointed to negotiate with the American colonists in 1778. His epitaph was written by his friend Sir Walter Scott.

Fletcher

Fletcher is a trade name, like Smith or Gow, and derives from an Old French word for feathers. A 'fletcher' was one who fitted the feathered flights to arrows, later simply an arrow-maker. In the days when bows and arrows were common weapons all the clans therefore had their Fletchers, and at the time when surnames were becoming common in Scotland Fletchers are found in many places. By the 17th century bows were becoming obsolete, although Scots who fought with Gustavus Adolphus in the Thirty Years' War carried them and they were occasionally used during Montrose's famous campaign.

In that era of idiosyncratic spelling in the 17th century, the name became understandably confused with 'Flesher', another trade name, meaning a butcher. A Fletcher today, therefore, may well be descended from a butcher rather than an arrow-maker.

Around the end of the 15th century the Fletchers are to be found seeking support from the Stewarts of

Fletcher of Dunans

Appin against the MacDonalds. There were also Fletchers in Glenorchy: they claimed to be the original inhabitants, predating the Campbells, a claim expressed in the old saying, 'Clan Fletcher raised the first smoke to boil water in Orchy.'

The Fletchers of Glenlyon were associated with the MacGregors, and one of them is said to have saved the life of Rob Roy when he was wounded in a skirmish with government forces. The most notable representative of this family, however, was Archibald Fletcher, a lawyer – 'one of the most upright men that ever adorned the profession' – and friend of Charles James Fox.

In the 17th and 18th centuries the Fletchers of Innerpeffer in Angus and of Saltoun (Salton) near

Haddington in Lothian produced a number of notable men, of whom the most famous is the Scottish patriot Andrew Fletcher of Saltoun (1655-1716). In his youth the future bishop and historian Gilbert Burnet was Minister of Saltoun and played some part in his education. He had a high opinion of Fletcher's mental capacities but remarked less favourably on his political opinions and his somewhat volcanic temperament – which led him to shoot a brother officer dead, admittedly after severe provocation, during Monmouth's rebellion (which he supported). He was later associated with William Paterson in the unfortunate Darien Scheme (1690) and became one of the most powerful opponents of the Union of Scotland and England. His oratory in 1703-04 almost turned the

Glenorchy, whose water, according to the old saying, was first boiled by resident Fletchers. MacLeister and other forms such as McClester are of the same origin. Many Argyll MacLeisters are said to have changed their name to Fletcher.

tide in the Scottish parliament. His writings, praised by the philosopher David Hume, contain the famous remark about a wise man who 'believed if a man were permitted to make all the ballads, he need not care who should make the laws of a nation'.

His namesake and descendant, as Lord Milton, was a judge at the time of the Forty-five. He advocated colonising the Highlands with sober Protestant southern gentry and consigning able-bodied beggars to permanent servitude.

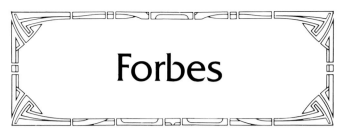

Forbes

The name Forbes was originally pronounced as two syllables (when the new pronunciation became general someone remarked that it would 'throw Lady Fettes into Fits').

Aberdeenshire is peppered with the houses and castles which belonged, or belong, to various branches of the clan. According to tradition the clan took possession of the Braes of Forbes after killing a ferocious bear which, having killed nine maidens at the well that commemorates them, had kept previous settlers at bay. The present Lord Forbes, the premier baron in the Scottish peerage, still retains part of the ancestral lands on Donside.

Clan Forbes is traditionally connected with the Urquharts, though no one now knows how. The name comes from the Gaelic *forba*, meaning a field or district, and Duncan Forbes held a charter for his lands from King Alexander III in the 13th century. Sir Alexander Forbes, who married a granddaughter of King Robert III, was raised to the peerage in 1445. In the same year, however, the Gordons acquired the earldom of Huntly, a less welcome elevation for Clan Forbes. For some 300 years the Gordons were extremely hostile and dangerous neighbours.

Broadly speaking the Gordons adhered to the 'Right' – they were Catholics, pro-Stewart and pro-Jacobite – while the Forbeses embraced the 'Left' – becoming Protestants, Covenanters and Whigs. There were exceptions however, and the eighth Lord Forbes married a daughter of the Earl of Huntly. Their sons, Catholics naturally, became friars, and the ninth Lord Forbes (died 1581) was their Protestant half-brother.

By the 17th century some decline was apparent at the centre: the tenth Lord Forbes was described as 'a naked life-renter of a small part and portion of his old estates'. But there were other prominent families, notably Forbes of Pitsligo, of Tolquhon and of Brux, with their numerous cadets, who descended from younger brothers of the first Lord Forbes. At the end of the 16th century Lord Forbes had been able to

Forbes

Craigievar Castle, one of the most elegant – and authentic – Scottish tower houses of the 17th century. It was built by William Forbes, a merchant and brother of a bishop who traded with Baltic ports and was known as Danziq Willie. It is now the property of the National Trust for Scotland.

provide a thousand men for the king's service, and he could raise nearly as many in 1628 for service in the Thirty Years' War.

Clan Forbes played a notable part in the Jacobite risings, with representatives on both sides. Alexander Forbes, fourth of Pitsligo (1678-1762) was 'out' in the Fifteen, and it says much for clan loyalty that he was able to hide out in the Forbes country for years after the Forty-five, despite the contrary loyalties of most of his fellow-clansmen.

The Rev. Robert Forbes of Leith made an invaluable collection of stories of the Forty-five, published as *The Lyon in Mourning*. But the greatest figure, a man in some ways the very symbol of that disastrous conflict, was Duncan Forbes of Culloden (a branch of Forbes of Tolquhon), Lord President of the Court of Session and virtually the sole representative of the government in the north. He was a man of honour, good sense and sympathy, whose brave efforts to influence the government after the battle of Culloden to adopt more humane and productive policies were almost totally ignored. The loutish Duke of Cumberland referred to him as 'that old woman'.

Fraser

The flowers of strawberries (French *fraises*) appear on the Fraser coat of arms, but this is probably just a heraldic pun. The origin of the name is certainly French – early forms include de Fresel and de Frisselle – and possibly derives from Freselière in Anjou. The first known Simon Fraser, who held lands in Keith, East Lothian, in 1160, was probably a descendant of the Frezels of Anjou.

The Frasers are genealogically somewhat complicated. By no means all Scots of that name belonged to the Highland clan, and the lands and families of the Frasers were spread over a wide area. The original estates soon passed to another family, which took the name Keith, while the Frasers acquired Tweeddale and Oliver Castle through marriage.

A famous member of this family was the Scottish patriot, Sir Simon Fraser, who fought with Wallace and Bruce. He is justly celebrated for defeating the English in three separate engagements on one day at Rosslyn in 1302, but he was eventually captured and suffered the barbaric type of execution which the English had also inflicted on Wallace. His more

the Highland clan, Fraser of Lovat, who bear the Gaelic name *Mac Shimi* (son of Simon).

This original Simon Fraser is assumed to have been the patriot who fought with Wallace. The first known chief was Hugh Fraser, Lord of Lovat near Beauly in the Aird in 1367, and it is certain that he was a kinsman of Fraser of Philorth. The Frasers subsequently acquired, mainly through marriage, considerable territories in Inverness and Aberdeenshire, but their heartland remained the districts on either side of Loch Ness.

The Frasers took a fearful battering in the great clan battle against the MacDonalds in 1544, *Blar-na-Léine*, the battle of the Shirts. Only five Frasers and eight MacDonalds are said to have survived this bloody engagement, yet within a hundred years the

Fraser

Hunting Fraser

fortunate contemporary Sir Alexander Fraser fought at Bannockburn, married Bruce's sister and became Chamberlain of Scotland. His grandson, also Alexander, married a daughter of the Earl of Ross and so acquired the lands of Philorth in Buchan, plus the castle of Cairnburgh, which remains the seat of the Fraser chiefs to this day. Fraserburgh was founded by his descendants as a rival port to Aberdeen, and the ninth Fraser of Philorth married the heiress of Lord Saltoun, a title since borne by the Fraser chiefs.

For a time the chiefship was in dispute between the Frasers of Philorth and another branch, which also sprang from Tweeddale, the Frasers of Muchal-in-Mar. Their seat, Castle Fraser, was built in the early 17th century by Andrew Fraser, who was created Lord Fraser in the reign of Charles II. The peerage expired with the fourth Lord Fraser, who died in 1716 while on the run as a result of his participation in the Fifteen.

Probably the best known Frasers are the chiefs of

Frasers were stronger than ever before. (See Mac-Donald of Clan Ranald.)

Undoubtedly the most famous – or notorious – of the Frasers of Lovat was Simon, eleventh Lord Lovat (1667–1747) who, despite being the second son of a third son, assumed the title in 1699 after a scandalous episode in which he forcibly married the widow of the tenth Lord Lovat and fled to France from a charge of rape (the lady, though forced into bed at the point of a dirk, her protests drowned by the playing of bagpipes, is said to have grown fond of him later).

The usual verdict on this remarkable man is that he was 'a born traitor and deceiver'. He certainly earned such a reputation, and the double game he constantly played is not easy to follow nearly 300 years later (and possibly harder at the time), but there was perhaps more to him that his popular image suggests. Had the Jacobites been capable of carrying out his suggested strategy for a rising in the Highlands, they might have fared much better.

Detail of a portrait of Major James Fraser of Castle Leathers, by an unknown artist, dated 1723. The Major is wearing, incidentally, a very early example of a tartan jacket but surely not, as some books say, a 'tartan sporran'.

His manifold duplicities eventually brought him to a grisly end. Though old and sick at the time of the Forty-five, he contrived as usual to play both sides, but the government classed him, with undeniable accuracy, as a traitor and he was hunted down, conveyed to London on a litter and after a trial lasting a week in which he conducted his own defence, beheaded – the last peer to suffer this type of execution – in front of a huge and fascinated crowd.

His last words were an apposite quotation from Horace. Though undoubtedly a tremendous rogue, he remains one of the most fascinating characters in the history of the Highlands.

His son, having fought on the Jacobite side at his father's insistence (old Simon told Forbes of Culloden a different story), was pardoned, and later raised the Fraser Highlanders in the service of George II. Their service in North America in the Seven Years' War partly explains the frequency of the name in Canada (Simon Fraser University in British Columbia is named after one of them).

The line became extinct in 1803 and the chiefship eventually passed to the Frasers of Strichen, a family which has produced many distinguished men, including the sixteenth Lord Lovat, who raised the Lovat Scouts in the Boer War, Brigadier Lord Lovat, twenty-second *Mac Shimi*, the dashing commando leader who is said to have landed in France on D-Day wearing a white polo-neck sweater and preceded by his piper, and his brother, Hugh Fraser, the politician and businessman.

Galbraith

The name comes from Gaelic words meaning 'Foreigner-Briton', and the Galbraiths were originally Britons from the kingdom of Strathclyde, which did not become part of Scotland until 1124. Inchgalbraith (Island of the Foreigner-Briton) in Loch Lomond was once their stronghold.

The first recorded Galbraith chief appears in the 12th century (i.e. very soon after the incorporation of Strathclyde in the Scottish kingdom), and it is clear that his house was of noble status (Sir Iain Moncreiffe suggested a possible connection with the old royal house of Strathclyde), for this chief married a daughter of the Earl of Lennox. The fortunes of these two houses were long to remain intimately connected.

The fourth chief, Sir William Galbraith, married a daughter of the Black Comyn, though he was also involved in the coup d'état which removed the young King Alexander III from Comyn control. He was powerful enough to make himself one of the co-regents of the kingdom in 1255. His son Sir Arthur (a favourite name among the Galbraiths, reflecting, no doubt, their British origin), married a daughter of 'the Good Sir James' Douglas and fought for Bruce. He was possibly the originator of the Galbraiths of Culcreuch in Strathendrick, a cadet branch to which the chiefship had passed by the end of the 14th century.

When King James I set about diminishing overmighty subjects, including his own kinsmen, the Galbraiths supported the Earl of Lennox. They were reported to have been involved in the sack of

Galbraith

Huntly, Old Colours

Dumbarton in 1425, following which they fled westward, to Kintyre. The twelfth chief, Thomas Galbraith of Culcreuch, was, with Lennox, opposed to the conspirators of 1488 but, after the death of James III, was captured and hanged. Similarly the fourteenth chief, Sir Andrew, was involved with Lennox in the attempt to rescue the young King James V from the Douglases in 1526.

The Galbraiths were in the thick of things throughout the 16th century, and many of their activities were far divorced from moral or legal principle (though they were not alone in that). However, the sixteenth chief, Sir James, administered the Lennox estates in a capable and responsible manner during the absence of the duke, Esme Stewart. His successor Sir Robert, seventeenth chief, was, however, a thorough bandit whose misdeeds included the ambush and attempted murder of his brother-in-law, to whom he owed money. The attempt failed, he was forced to surrender Culcreuch Castle and, declared a rebel, he fled to Ireland, where he died. The Galbraiths thereafter faded from the scene.

Gordon of Huntly

Speculation on the origins of the Gordons run rife. One of the wilder suggestions is that the name derives from Gordium, from where it was brought back by one of the Crusaders! There seems little reason to doubt that it really derives from the district in Berwickshire where the family held land in the 12th century. However, at some early time the Gordons were genealogically linked with the Swintons, neighbours and rivals in the Middle Ages, who had exactly the same coat of arms, and there is evidence of a link with a prominent 13th-century English family named Gurdon (the Swintons also held land in England), giving the Gordons an Anglo-Norman provenance.

Sir Adam, Lord of Gordon during the wars of independence, originally supported the Red Comyn, who was killed by Bruce, and thereafter he was inclined to support the English. However, after the death of Edward I of England less sensible commanders allowed their men to harry the Gordon lands in the Borders and thus effectively alienated a useful ally. From 1313 Gordon became a loyal supporter of Bruce, and he was one of those who carried the Declaration of Arbroath to the Pope in 1320.

His services to Bruce brought the Gordons to the north, to Strathbogie in Aberdeenshire. Their fortunes expanded rapidly. On the extinction of the senior male line in 1402 the heiress Elizabeth Gordon married Alexander Seton of that ilk and their son became the first Earl of Huntly. The earldom passed to the first earl's second son, who took the name of Gordon.

In their efforts to bring the Highlands under control the early Stewart kings of Scots were compelled to employ local agents or to set clan against clan. Their agents in the west were the Campbell earls of Argyll, and in the east the Gordon earls of Huntly. They, like the Campbells, were able to exploit their vice-regal authority to further their private interests and to create – as long as the authority of the Crown remained weak – their own 'empire' in the north-east.

Their greatest success was acquiring the earldom of Sutherland in 1514 following the destruction of so many of Scotland's leaders at Flodden. Their attempt to wrest Findlater away from the Ogilvies by a plot of truly baroque proportions was ultimately unsuccessful, and they were defeated in battle at Corrichie in 1562, the fourth Earl of Huntly, the most powerful nobleman in Scotland but fat and asthmatic, suffering a fatal stroke in the field.

Under King James VI the power of the Gordons threatened to spread still further, as the Earl of Huntly, elevated in 1599 to a marquessate, was granted a royal commission to extend his operations into the Western Isles, with the object of extirpating 'the hole Clan Donald in the North'. However, there were problems over the terms on which the expedition should be undertaken, and the king, no doubt realising the stupidity of the plan, changed his mind, while the Catholic Huntly's personal authority was jeopardised by his excommunication by the Kirk.

The first marquess had a colourful existence: not many men have been elevated in noble rank within a few years of fleeing abroad to escape a charge of treason. His private wars against Grants, Mackintoshes, Stewarts and others included the murder of the Bonnie Earl of Moray, commemorated in ballad.

The Gordons gained overlordship of the Mackay territory of Strathnaver, from which they prepared an (unsuccessful) assault on the earldom of Caithness, but in the 17th century the power of Huntly, 'the Cock of the North', was in decline. The second marquess, though brought up in England as a Protestant, met the humiliating fate of execution at the hands of the Covenanters in 1649.

A Gordon Highlander in the 19th century. The first Gordon regiment was the 89th Highland Regiment, raised during the Seven Years' War and afterwards disbanded. The Gordon Highlanders (92nd Regiment) were raised in 1794, recruits being encouraged by a promised kiss from the glamorous Duchess of Gordon.

Gordon

It has often been said that the Gordons were never a clan, since the relationship between lord and men was strictly a feudal one. Nevertheless, the Gordons for a long period dominated much of the north-east. There were a number of families in that region called Gordon who did not belong to what became the house of Huntly, though most could probably claim Sir Adam of Gordon as an ancestor (genealogists have recorded over 150 main branches of the Gordons).

The estate of Haddo was acquired by the Gordons of Methlic in 1533. Although comparatively junior in genealogical terms, this family was to prove perhaps the most eminent. The Gordons of Haddo were also remarkable for longevity. One of them obtained royal charters for his lands from Kings James III, IV and V, whose reigns covered a period of over 80 years. The

fifth Gordon of Haddo fought for King Charles I, was captured in 1643, imprisoned in 'Haddo's Hole' in St Giles's Cathedral in Edinburgh, and later executed.

The family's properties were restored in 1660 and in 1682 Sir George Gordon of Haddo was created Earl of Aberdeen. The beautiful Haddo House of Robert Adam, now National Trust for Scotland property, was built in the 18th century and the estate was greatly embellished by the fourth earl, who was prime minister at the time of the Crimean War. The seventh earl and first marquess was governor-general of Canada in the 1890s.

Many other titles are associated with branches of the Gordons. The first Viscount Kenmure, created 1633, was Sir John Gordon, of the Gordons of Kirkcudbright, who traced their descent from the

Gordon

Detail of Raeburn's portrait of the famous fiddler, Niel Gow. Dance tunes for the fiddle were composed in Strathspey in the 17th century, though the characteristic 'Scotch Snap' – a short note on the beat followed by a longer one until the next beat – came later.

original Berwickshire family. He married a sister of the Marquess of Argyll and was a keen Covenanter, but the sixth viscount adhered to the Jacobite cause: he was captured at Preston and executed in 1716.

The dukedom of Gordon was created for the fourth Marquess of Huntly by Charles II. The title became extinct in 1836 (it was later recreated for the Duke of Richmond when he inherited the Huntly estates), but the Marquessate of Huntly passed to the Earl of Aboyne, a direct descendant of the first marquess. This line has since held the chiefship and Aboyne Castle, though not the large estates that once went with it. Huntly Castle is today a magnificent ruin; Gordon Castle itself, the Bog o' Gight as it was once called, which was the principal seat of the marquesses of Huntly, is also largely ruined, though what remains is well preserved.

Gow

The name Gow is a corruption of the Gaelic *gobha*, meaning a smith, or armourer. The Gaelic name is *Mac a' Ghobhainn*, or MacGowan. Gows and MacGowans were to be found among many clans

therefore, though they are particularly associated with Clan Chattan and the MacPhersons. According to MacPherson historians the ancestor of the Gows was a younger son of a captain of Clan Chattan. The place name Balnagowan, found throughout the Highlands, marks the site of a former smithy, and some Gows and MacGowans who moved south appear to have changed their name to Smith. Another name connected with their trade, incidentally, is MacEachern, smiths to the MacDonalds and others.

An old tale relates how at the famous clan battle on the North Inch at Perth in 1396 one side found itself a man short and therefore hired *an Gobha Crom* (a crooked smith) who swiftly despatched his opponent but then ceased to take any further part in the battle until he was promised additional remuneration. The character, Hal o' the Wynd, was immortalised by Scott in *The Fair Maid of Perth*, but the suggestion that he was the ancestor of the Gows is unfounded.

The most famous bearer of this name in the Highlands was Niel Gow (1727-1807), 'the Prince of Scottish fiddlers'. He was born (and died) at Inver, near Dunkeld, and began to play the violin before he was 10 years old. Someone took him along to Dunkeld

House, the Duke of Atholl became his patron, and he was taken up by the nobility. He wrote many popular reels and strathspeys and was succeeded by his son Nathaniel (1766-1831).

Taught by his father and later, more formally, at Edinburgh, Nathaniel Gow was something of a fashionable band leader when the 'Celtic Revival'

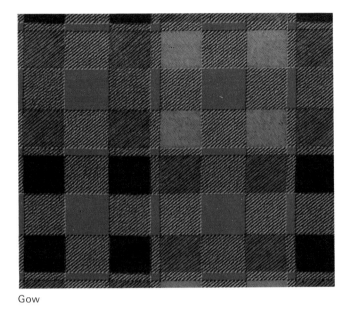

Gow

was in full swing. He played at private parties for the Prince Regent and at the fashionable balls at Almacks, where London society ladies delighted to dance to Scottish country music. His and his father's compositions run to half a dozen published volumes.

Niel Gow's portrait was painted several times by Raeburn (according to Sir Iain Moncreiffe of that ilk, popular engravings of these works 'were hung up in several English country-house lavatories'), and on each occasion the sitter wore tartan breeches of the same pattern. This is now the Gow tartan, and it is therefore one of the oldest tartans with an authentic history – although, of course, there is no evidence that it was worn by other Gows in the 18th century.

Graham

There is a legend of a Graham chieftain in ancient Caledonia repulsing the Roman legions, but historically the first of the Grahams was one of those Anglo-Norman barons who came to Scotland when King David I came to the throne in 1124. He was William de Graham, who took his name from the English manor of Graegham (Grey Home), which is men-

tioned in the Domesday Book. He acquired the lands of Abercorn and Dalkeith.

The Grahams have a noble tradition of patriotism and military leadership, which dates back to the Scottish wars of independence. Sir Patrick, son of Sir David Graham of Dundaff (who is regarded as the real founder of the house of Montrose) was keeper of

Graham of Montrose

Stirling Castle. He died while carrying the royal standard against the English in 1296. His nephew Sir John was called the 'Richt Arm' of Wallace; he fell at the battle of Falkirk in 1298.

Sir Patrick was the first to hold lands in the Highlands as a result of his marriage into the old Celtic house of the earls of Strathearn, and his son was the first to hold lands at Montrose in Angus – as a result of an exchange with the king – in 1325. In 1445 Patrick, the current Graham chief, became Lord Graham, and his grandson, the third Lord Graham, who was to die at Flodden, became Earl of Montrose in 1505.

The most distinguished military leader this house produced was unarguably James, fifth earl, and from 1644 Marquess of Montrose. Although his achievements have been obscured by clouds of romance now very hard to dispel, the bald facts of his campaign in the Highlands remain astonishing – the almost incredible speed of movement, the succession of smashing victories against superior numbers. How much of the credit was due to the Clan MacDonald war leader Alasdair MacColla is irrelevant.

Not the least remarkable fact about Montrose was that he was originally a supporter of the Covenant – his name appears at the head of those signing the National Covenant of 1638 – and a Lowlander. It is doubtful that he spoke much Gaelic.

What caused Montrose to change sides was largely

his concern at the ambition of Argyll. It looked as though King Charles would be replaced by King Campbell. But in the field the squint-eyed Marquess of Argyll was always a step or more behind the dashing Montrose.

Montrose (without MacColla) was eventually defeated by Leslie's army of seasoned regulars. He returned to assist Charles II but was betrayed and executed in 1650 with all the barbarities of the time. After the Restoration the various parts of his body were collected from the places where they had been put on vulgar display and he received a grand funeral. The head of Argyll replaced the head of Montrose on the spikes of the Tolbooth.

The other great military hero of those grim times was Bonnie Dundee, John Graham of Claverhouse, Viscount Dundee, scourge of the Covenanters and know to them as 'Bloody Clavers', who died at Killiecrankie fighting for King James VII/II.

The fourth Marquess of Montrose became a duke in 1707. The third duke should be remembered gratefully as the man who in 1782 secured the annulment of the act which proscribed Highland dress.

Of the many cadets of the Grahams the most notable houses were those of the earls of Menteith and Strathearn. There is a separate tartan for Graham of Menteith, branches of which include Graham of Duchray and Cunningham-Graham of Ardoch. The seat of the Graham dukes of Montrose was the now-ruined Buchanan Castle, built on the site of a former Buchanan stronghold by Loch Lomond and acquired by the Grahams in 1680. The former seat was Mugdock Castle, later renamed more becomingly Montdieu, in Strathblane.

Grant

The name is generally agreed to derive from the French *grand* and thus means the same as the Gaelic *mór*. But assuming the Grant chiefs had an Anglo-Norman ancestor, that does not explain the origin of the clansmen who adopted his name. Here legends cluster. There is a strong tradition which holds that

Grant

the Grants belonged to *Sìol Ailpein*, the stock of
Kenneth MacAlpin, first monarch of all Scotland.
According to this belief the Grants are kin to the
MacGregors, Gregor *Mór* MacGregor being their
12th-century ancestor. Significantly the Grants were
good friends to the MacGregors at the time when that
clan was proscribed.

Again, tradition alone supports Sir Laurence le
Grant, Sheriff of Inverness in the 1260s, being the son
of Gregor and ancestor of Grant chiefs. His son John,
who was captured by the English in 1296, held land in
Strathspey (later lost but repurchased), but there is a
gap before Sir Ian, the first chief from whom an
uninterrupted line can be traced, appears as Sheriff of
Inverness in 1434.

At that time there were other Grant families
around. Grants were already established in
Glenmoriston and Glenurquhart, and Sir Ian's marriage secured them their lands in Strathspey, later
increased by purchases. His son Sir Duncan was the
first Grant of Freuchie (later Castle Grant), as the
chiefs were known until the late 16th century.
Freuchie became a barony in the time of his grandson
John, in 1494.

Loch Morlich, near Aviemore, at the head of Strathspey, not far
from Craigellachie, the Grants' gathering place from whose
'swelling base, and rifted precipicies, the birch trees wave in
graceful cluster'.

Clan Grant's history is less sensational than many other clans', but is comparatively well documented. In the troubles of the 17th and 18th centuries the Grants were generally Whiggish, though the Grants of Glenmoriston, who secured relative independence from the laird of Grant, remained loyal to the Stewart dynasty. One of the Seven Men of Glenmoriston who succoured Prince Charles was named Patrick Grant.

Until the 17th century the chief power in the north-east was the 'Cock of the North', the earl of Huntly, with whom the lairds of Grant usually remained on good terms. Numerous bonds of manrent between the two families survive. This did not save the Grants from the raids of Camerons or MacDonalds, and by the end of the 16th century relations between Grants and Huntlys were cooling: the Grants fought for Argyll against the Gordons in the battle of Glenlivet (1594). In the 17th century the decline of Huntly power tended to the advantage of the Grants.

The seventh Laird of Grant was a moderate Covenanter in the civil war, which led to Montrose's occupation of Strathspey and, after he had secured the Grants' submission, similar trouble from the army of the Covenanters. At the battle of Worcester in 1651 150 Grants from Strathspey were on the royalist side, but the chief supported William of Orange in 1688 and the Hanoverian succession subsequently. After the 1715 Jacobite rising the Laird of Grant, who had played a part in regaining Inverness from the Jacobites, managed to repurchase Glenmoriston for his kinsman, forfeited because of Glenmoriston's participation on the Jacobite side – an example of clan loyalty despite ideological differences.

Like other loyal Highlanders, the Grants were poorly treated by the government, and Ludovick Grant (the chief's son then living in London), was not very enthusiastic in his support for the Hanoverians in 1745 (there was also a conflict with Forbes of Culloden). The Grants defending Inverness did not put up much of a fight against the besieging Jacobites, and many cadets, including Glenmoriston, fought for the prince. Colquhoun Grant of Burnside, a member of Prince Charles's bodyguard, is the hero of many tales of derring-do. Sir Ludovick was most active after Culloden in hunting down Jacobite fugitives.

In an incident known as the Elgin Raid (a minor political riot in fact), which took place in 1820, the Grants were summoned to the aid of their chief by the fiery cross – the last occasion in which a clan was raised in that fashion.

Grantown-on-Spey was founded by Sir James Grant in 1766 as part of his effort to avoid Clearances and discourage emigration. King James VI/I is said to have offered to make the fifth Lord of Freuchie Earl of Strathspey, an offer declined with the famous words, 'And wha'll be Laird of Grant?', and the Grants of Grant continued to reject ennoblement until 1855, when the chief became Lord Strathspey in the United Kingdom peerage. The Scottish earldom of Seafield was acquired through marriage some years earlier. Today the titles are divided; Sir Patrick Grant of Grant is fifth Baron Strathspey and thirty-second chief, the present Earl of Seafield being his first cousin once removed.

A Grant story concerning *Iain Mór*, founder of the Grants of Glenmoriston (pictured below), relates how he was promised as a reward for his duellistic prowess anything he could carry from Edinburgh Castle. His father and the Laird of Mackintosh being prisoners therein, he carried them both on his back.

Gunn

It is usually said that the Gunns were of Norse origin and that their name derives from the Norse *gunnr*, meaning war – a suitable enough name for a very warlike clan. However, the researches of Sir Iain Moncreiffe of that ilk suggest that the name comes from Gunni, who is known from a Norse saga of the Orkney jarls (earls). He inherited estates in Caithness and Sutherland through his wife about the end of the 12th century, and his descendant Ottar, living on the mainland in 1280, was the assumed progenitor of the chiefs of Gunn.

In the 15th century the Gunns were engaged in a ferocious feud with their neighbours, the Keiths. In one romantic story the Fair Helen, only daughter of Lachlan Gunn, was betrothed to her cousin when carried off by Keith of Ackergill, whose advances she had earlier rejected. She subsequently threw herself from the top of the tower at Ackergill.

Clan Gunn suffered several defeats at the hands of the Keiths and in 1464 their chief, Crouner (Coroner) George Gunn arranged a meeting to discuss peace. Each side was to bring twelve horsemen, but the Keiths interpreted this as twelve horses, and mounted two men on each horse. In the ensuing fight all the Gunns were killed, including the chief and four of his sons, despite taking refuge in the chapel of St Tyr. The dead chief was robbed of his badge of office from which he was known as *Am Bràisdeach Mór*, 'He of the Big Brooch'.

Revenge was later exacted by the grandson of Crouner George, who killed Keith of Ackergill and ten of his men at Drummoy. This grandson was the first to hold the title *Mac Sheumais Chataich*, 'son of James of Caithness' (his father).

Though fierce fighters the Gunns were not a large clan and their history is largely one of retreat and retrenchment. They were harassed by the Mackays to the north-west, and were caught up in the feud between the Gordon earls of Sutherland and the Sinclair earls of Caithness during the 16th and 17th centuries. They inflicted some notable defeats on their enemies at times, particularly in a famous raid on the Sinclairs led by Alasdair Gunn of Killearnan in 1589.

In the end it was the Clearances of the early 19th century that did the most damage to the Gunns. Driven from Kildonan and their homelands in the hills

Gunn

on the Caithness-Sutherland border, some descended to the coast and became fishermen in little ports without harbours, where boats had to be perilously landed on the beach. From this milieu emerged the fine Scottish novelist Neil M. Gunn, whose novels based on his childhood in Dunbeath present a marvellous picture of those communities at the end of the 19th century (and include the finest description of salmon poaching ever written).

Hamilton

Hamilton is an illustrious name in Scottish – and British – history, though it is not the name of a Highland clan except in a very limited sense.

The first known member of the family in Scotland was Sir Walter Fitz Gilbert of Hameldone (probably deriving from a Northumbrian place name), who held land in Renfrewshire in the late 13th century. Although he at first supported the English, after Bannockburn he wisely changed his allegiance and was rewarded by Bruce with confiscated Comyn lands and the barony of Cadzow (later renamed Hamilton), where the remains of the old castle still

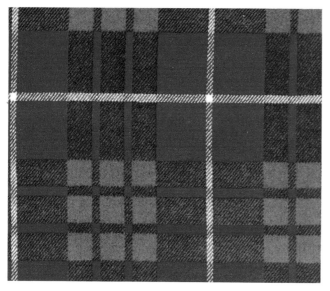

Hamilton

Hamiltons, who thus acquired Highland property. They built Brodick Castle (later, much expanded and now a National Trust for Scotland property) as their Highland home.

As a result of Lord Hamilton's marriage the Hamilton chiefs were closest, as heirs presumptive, to the throne and thus involved in high affairs of state. The frequent minorities of the sovereign made things all the more fraught.

That their political success in this favoured position was not greater has been put down to lack of determination, of which Mary of Guise accused the second Earl of Arran, Regent of Scotland for the infant Mary Queen of Scots. His international machinations, however, did earn him the dukedom of Châtelherault from the king of France.

Disputes over precedence lay behind the vicious feuds of the Hamiltons with the Stewart earls of Lennox and the Douglas earls of Angus in the 16th century. The former ended only when Lennox's son

stand above the Clyde. He is said to have married a sister of the Earl of Moray, Bruce's close associate, and his son David was captured along with King David II by the English at Neville's Cross (1346).

The sixth Lord of Cadzow was raised to the peerage as Lord Hamilton in 1445. He married as his second wife a daughter of King James II, the young widow of the Master of Boyd who had been Earl of Arran. The island and the earldom subsequently passed to the

Brodick Castle (below left) the old home of the dukes of Hamilton in Arran, below Goat Fell and overlooking Brodick Bay, now belongs to the National Trust for Scotland. It contains a remarkable collection of sporting pictures and trophies, as well as silver and porcelain.

Lord Darnley married Mary Queen of Scots; the latter was never completely resolved until this century when the Duke of Hamilton became Earl of Angus.

In a famous incident in the Hamilton-Douglas feud in 1520 their followers clashed by chance in Edinburgh and the Hamiltons were driven out of the city. It is remembered as 'Cleanse the Causeway'.

A memorable character who took part in this bloody episode was Sir James Hamilton of Finnart, a bastard son of the first Earl of Arran. Six years afterwards he was responsible for killing the Earl of Lennox, after Lennox had surrendered his sword to him. He also helped to bring about the burning of his kinsman Patrick Hamilton, the first Protestant martyr in Scotland, in 1528, but was himself executed on a probably unjust charge of treason in 1540.

Yet Finnart was also largely responsible for introducing the ideas of French Renaissance architecture into Scotland. The façade of Falkland Palace is his work.

Another illegitimate son of the first Earl of Arran became Archbishop of St Andrews (succeeding Cardinal Beaton) and was hanged by partisans of Lennox partly in revenge for the murder of the Regent Moray by a Hamilton.

In 1599 the Earl of Arran became Marquess of Hamilton, and in 1643 the marquess became a duke. The first duke was beheaded in the same year as Charles I, and his brother, the second duke, was mortally wounded at Worcester in 1651. His niece and successor married a Douglas, who was created Duke of Hamilton in 1663. The Hamilton earls and dukes of Abercorn were descended from a younger son of the second Earl of Arran who fought for Mary Queen of Scots at Langside in 1568. The earls of Haddington are another ennobled cadet house. Today the chiefship remains with the Duke of Hamilton, the premier peer of Scotland.

Hay

The chief of Clan Hay is Earl (recently Countess) of Erroll and also hereditary lord high constable, who enjoys precedence over all other holders of hereditary titles in Scotland outside the royal family. The family has held that honour since the time of King Robert Bruce.

The chiefs of Hay are of Anglo-Norman descent, and stem from William de la Haye, who received the

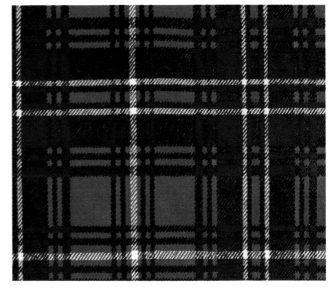

Hay

barony of Erroll in 1178. The name comes from La Haye in Normandy, meaning 'stockade' or 'hedge', and the Gaelic name of the chiefs, *Mac Garaidh Mór*, is, rather unusually, a translation of this term.

According to tradition the Hays played a leading part in a victory against Danish invaders, employing ox yokes for lack of more orthodox weapons, but the battle is not recorded in history. This colourful story, commemorated in Hay heraldic device, relates that as reward for the victory a falcon led the way to Erroll and outlined the boundaries of the barony in flight before alighting on the Falcon Stone (now at Bowness, near Port Erroll). The legend may have come from the family of the wife of the first Lord of Erroll, or that of his son, who married into the old Celtic house of the earls of Strathearn.

The third Hay of Erroll was twice co-regent of Scotland and married a Comyn. The fifth, Sir Gilbert, as a loyal adherent of Bruce was rewarded with the castle and estate of Slains, formerly Comyn property, on the Aberdeenshire coast (his successors live in a modern house built within the ruins) as well as the hereditary office of constable, the king's personal guardian.

Two of his successors fell in battle against the English, at Neville's Cross and Flodden, where 87 gentlemen of the name of Hay, including the ancestor of the earls and marquesses of Tweeddale, are said to have been killed along with Sir Thomas de la Haye, seventh Lord of Erroll and fourth High Constable, whose wife was a daughter of King Robert II. His grand-nephew William, Lord Hay, became Earl of Erroll in 1452.

By this time cadets of the house of Erroll had considerably extended Hay territories. A younger son of Sir Thomas was the ancestor of the Hays of Delgaty, from whom came Montrose's chief of staff

Sir William Hay, who was executed in 1650. Another branch held land in Lochloy.

The earls of Erroll continued to play an important part in national affairs. The ninth earl was an ardent Catholic and leader of that cause after the death of Mary Queen of Scots. With his allies Angus and Huntly he secretly negotiated with Spain to depose Elizabeth of England and unite Britain under a Catholic James VI. The king was privately not unsympathetic to such a project but after Argyll's government forces had been defeated by the Counter-Reformation earls in 1594 (Erroll being wounded leading the charge with his personal war cry, 'The Virgin Mary!') he was compelled to take more authoritative action, which included blowing up Slains Castle (no less effectively, it would appear, than the attempt to demolish its equally robust successor at Bowness early in this century).

As (generally) adherents of the old religious and political regime the Hays were heading for trouble in the events of the next half-century, but in the end they survived more or less unscathed. The thirteenth earl was a powerful opponent of the union with England (1707) and arranged for the Old Chevalier to be guided up the Firth of Forth in the botched Jacobite rising of 1708, undergoing a spell of imprisonment in Edinburgh Castle as a result.

He was succeeded by his sister, the redoubtable Mary, Countess of Erroll in her own right, under whom New Slains became a receiving centre for Jacobites entering the country secretly (as a later visitor, James Boswell, remarked, Erroll's nearest neighbour was the king of Denmark). She raised the clan for Prince Charles in 1745. The prince's secretary at the time of Culloden was a certain John Hay, described by John Prebble in his account of the battle as 'a weak and silly man', in some degree responsible for the logistical failures which sapped the fighting spirit of the Highlanders before the battle.

The earls of Erroll tended to be men of intelligence and fine physical stature. The lord high constable at the coronation of George III, a great nephew of the countess (and as son of the executed Jacobite Lord Kilmarnock, a Boyd by birth) was described by Horace Walpole as 'the noblest figure I ever saw'. The nineteenth earl (died 1891), founder of Port Erroll, was a splendid Victorian patriarch, accustomed to take early-morning baths at Slains in sea water pumped daily up the cliffs by his 'fool'.

Slains Castle, at Bowness above Cruden Bay, was the home of the earls of Erroll from the early 17th century to the 1920s. It was considerably altered in the early 19th century and after it was sold by the twentieth Earl an attempt was made to demolish it. As this photograph shows, it resisted pretty well.

Henderson (Mackendrick)

Traditionally the Hendersons, Clan *Eanruig*, inhabited Glencoe long before the arrival of the MacIain MacDonalds, and their ancestor was *Eanruig Mór Mac Rìgh Neachtain*, 'Great Henry, son of King Nectan', a preposterous claim according to one authority.

The line of chiefs supposedly descended from this legendary ancestor terminated in an heiress, daughter of Dugald MacHendry, who married a brother of the lord of the Isles. Their son Iain was the first MacIain MacDonald of Glencoe.

The assimilation of Hendersons and MacDonalds seems to have proceeded smoothly – not always the case elsewhere. The Hendersons, who had a reputation for physical strength, enjoyed certain honorific duties reflecting their priority, forming the MacIain chief's bodyguard and, on his death, bearing his coffin. Hendersons were also hereditary pipers to the clan.

There were other groups of Hendersons, or Mackendricks (Gaelic *Mac Eanruig*) in other parts, apparently unconnected with the Hendersons of

Henderson

Glencoe. One group, possibly a sept of the Elliots, has been located in Upper Liddesdale in the Borders. The Hendersons of Caithness in the far north were a sept of Clan Gunn, descended from Hendry, a son of Crouner George Gunn, hereditary coroner of Caithness in the 15th century, who is said to have separated himself from his numerous brothers as a result of some family quarrel.

The tartan illustrated is that of Henderson of Fordell, perhaps the most distinguished family. James Henderson (originally Henryson), who moved from Dumfriesshire to Fife in the 15th century and was Lord Advocate in 1494, was the first Henderson of Fordell. From a branch of his family descended Alexander Henderson (1583-1646), who is regarded as the greatest leader of the Reformation in Scotland after Knox.

Henderson was born in Fife and went to St Andrews University, where he became a professor of philosophy in his twenties. When he first went as minister to Leuchars he was received without enthusiasm because of his episcopalian views, but he soon changed them and within a few years was one of the most respected Presbyterian leaders. He was largely responsible for drafting the National Covenant (1638), and he was chosen by acclamation as moderator of the historic assembly at Glasgow which completely reformed the Scottish Kirk on Presbyterian principles. He was also the chief influence in drafting the Solemn League and Covenant (1643) and went to Westminster to see it pass the English parliament. His personal relations with Charles I, despite their vast ideological differences, were good, and Henderson's death in 1646 ('mourned throughout Scotland' says a biographer, but one can think of places where this was unlikely) was reported to have resulted from a broken heart.

Home

The name Home is pronounced, and often spelt, Hume. Apparently the Polwarth branch of the family generally adopted the U spelling while the earls of Home preferred the O. The great philosopher David Hume is said to have spelt his name thus because he was so irritated by Englishmen pronouncing it to rhyme with comb.

The name comes from the barony of Home in Berwickshire, and the holders of that barony, later earls of Home, may be descended from the Northumbrian earls of Dunbar. Aldan de Home was a probable 12th-century ancestor. His presumed 14th-century descendant Sir Thomas Home of that ilk gained the barony of Dunglas in East Lothian through marriage. His son Sir Alexander died with Douglas fighting in France against the English at the battle of Verneuil in 1424. His grandson (died 1491) became Lord Home, and the first Lord Home's son and heir, in alliance with Archibald Douglas and supported by the Campbell Earl of Argyll, was leader of the conspiracy which sought to replace King James III with his young son and led to the king's death after the battle of Sauchieburn in 1488. The third lord, called Alexander like most of his predecessors and successors, survived the slaughter of Flodden, where many of his name died, but was executed by the Regent Albany, against whom he had been plotting with the English, in 1516.

The second lord was Warden of the March, an office frequently held by the Homes, who were at least partly responsible for the greater order (or lesser disorder) in the Borders on the east than the west.

The religious divisions of the Reformation also split the Homes. The fifth Lord Home became a Protestant but was a supporter of Mary Queen of Scots for a time. His estates were forfeit but they were returned to the sixth lord, a close adviser to King James VI/I who was created Earl of Home in 1605. The second earl died childless and the title passed to a distant relative who was descended from John Home of Whiterigs and Easton, younger son of the first Lord

Home. The fourteenth earl renounced his title to become prime minister (1963-64) as Sir Alec Douglas Home and was later created Lord Home of the Hirsel, the family seat in Berwickshire.

The Homes proliferated fairly rapidly in the early years and a number of other important cadets should be mentioned. Sir David Home of Wedderburn near Duns, ancestor of the Homes of Polwarth and earls of Marchmont, was a younger son of Sir Thomas in the 14th century. His descendant Sir Patrick Home, an adherent of William of Orange whose court in the Hague he attended, became Lord Polwarth and later Earl of Marchmont. Sir David's Wedderburn descendants included 'The Seven Spears of Wedderburn', sons of the third Home of Wedderburn, who in turn became ancestors of the Homes of Blackadder, Broomhouse and other families.

David Hume (1711-76), perhaps the greatest British thinker of the 18th century, was son of Joseph Home of Chirnside, Berwickshire, and the Homes include an unusual number of writers. Among them are the playwrights John Home (a Lowlander who fought for the Jacobites in 1745), the author of *Douglas*, a melodrama which prompted patriotic if critically inept Scots to crow, 'Where's your Willie Shakespeare now?', and William Douglas Home, brother of the prime minister. The famous spiritualist medium of the 19th century, Daniel Dunglas Home, was alleged to have been the son of a natural son of the tenth Earl of Home.

Home

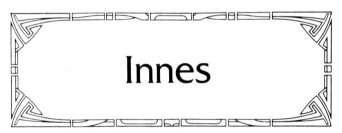

Innes

When the twenty-fifth Chief of Innes succeeded to the duchy of Roxeburgh in the early 19th century he had a history of Clan Innes published to prove to those dazzled by ducality that 'he was of as good blood on his father's side as on his great-grandmother's' (through whom he inherited the Kerr dukedom). An early account of the family had ascribed their good fortunes to three facts: the heirs of Innes had always been male, none had ever married a bad wife, and they had never been in debt.

The barony of Innes – the name means 'greens' – lies on the Moray Firth between the Spey and the Lossie, and by a charter of King Malcolm IV in 1160 it was granted to Berowald, a Fleming, whose grandson was apparently the first to use the name in the early 13th century.

Innes

The chiefs of Innes built up very large family estates, thanks partly to the ninth chief's marriage to the thane of Aberchirder's heiress, and spawned many cadets. Perfect amity did not always reign among them, however, nor were all the chiefs men of admirable character. The eleventh Laird of Innes, who took part in the battle of Brechin in 1452, was a man of bad reputation, known as 'Ill Sir Robert' in contrast to his grandfather 'Good Sir Robert' (died 1381). The eighteenth chief was murdered by the head of another branch, Innes of Invermarkie, in a quarrel over the succession in the 16th century. Sir Robert Innes of Balveny, Constable of Redcastle on the Beauly Firth, who was descended from a younger son of the 'Ill Sir Robert', was a supporter of Mary Queen of Scots and was killed after being betrayed by his son and successor.

Sir Robert, twentieth chief, was a Covenanter, but supported Charles II, whom he welcomed on his arrival in Scotland in 1650. He was the builder of Innes house (his father, nineteenth chief, had been responsible for founding Garmouth, east of Elgin, in 1587). Balveny Castle on Speyside was built by Sir Robert Innes of Invermarkie, grandson of the murdered constable, whose family's support for Charles I was disastrous for their fortunes.

Croxton Tower was built in the 16th century by a branch of this family. The Ineses of Croxton, like most of their name, were loyal Jacobites. Sir Alexander Innes of Croxton fought with Dundee at

Killiecrankie and was prominent in the failed rising of 1708. His son was fatally wounded at Sheriffmuir.

Johnston

The name Johnston is of territorial origin, but there are many 'John's towns' or 'John's tuns' (farms or agrarian settlements) in Scotland and there is little doubt that the Johnstons were not all descended from a common ancestor.

The Devil's Beef Tub, a 500-foot-deep hollow amid green hills near Moffat where there is now a Covenanters' Memorial, was a handy place to conceal stolen cattle in the bad old days on the Borders. Nowadays one is more likely to encounter young tourists with backpacks than the booty of the Johnston's raids.

Johnston

The name was in use as a surname in the late 12th century. The presumed progenitor of the famous Border clan of Johnston received a charter for lands in Annandale, the home of the clan thereafter. The well-known beauty spot near Moffat where the River Annan rises is now called the Devil's Beef Tub, but its proprietor was formerly said to be not the devil but the Johnstons, which some of their neighbours would have regarded as much the same thing.

For the Johnstons were a characteristically tough and violent clan for whom raiding was a way of life. They were also prolific, and besides Annandale itself they were eventually to be found in the nearby valleys of Moffat Water and other tributaries. Their stronghold was at Lochwood.

Sir Gilbert de Johnstoun, son of John, is the first to appear in historical records, at the end of the 12th century. Sir John, of the fifth generation after Sir Gilbert, had one son, Adam, who was the ancestor of several branches of the clan, including (by different wives) the Johnstons of Westerhall and of Elphinstone. Sir James Johnston became Lord Johnston in 1633 and Earl of Hartfell ten years later. His son was also made Earl of Annandale, and in the next generation the earl became a marquess. In the 18th century this line became extinct and the Johnstons of Westerhall in Dumfriesshire became the leading family of the Border clan.

The Johnstons generally supported the monarchy, and a Johnston of that ilk often held the office of warden of the Western Marches (he sometimes interpreted his duties rather loosely). They were great rivals of the Maxwells of Nithsdale, earlier holders of the office, which gave rise to one of the last great Border feuds, in which both Johnston and Maxwell chiefs fell about the end of the 16th century. King James VI/I was responsible for reconciling the two clans in 1623.

There were also Johnstons in Strathspey, unconnected with the Johnstons of Annandale. They originated from the marriage of Stephen the clerk to the heiress of Sir Andrew Garioch in the 14th century, which brought them the land of Johnston. In the 18th century they fought on the Jacobite side in the major risings and are at present represented by an American family.

Archibald Johnston, who came from Annandale and is known as Johnston of Warriston (the title he held as a judge), was with Alexander Henderson author of the National Covenant in 1638. He was a stern, unbending Covenanter and though he supported Charles II after he had accepted the Covenant his lectures aroused the king's bitter dislike. Moreover, he made the mistake of accepting judicial office under Cromwell in 1657. At the Restoration in 1660 he was excluded from the general pardon and was hanged in Edinburgh in 1663.

Keith

The Keiths were an ancient Celtic family of great distinction, hereditary holders of the office of marischal (since 1458 earl marischal) of Scotland. The earliest known holder of the office was Harvey Keith in the reign of King Malcolm IV. He held lands in Buchan, although his name probably derived from estates in East Lothian. It was not until the time of Bruce that the Keiths became really powerful, and by the 16th century it was said that the earl marischal could travel from Berwick to John o' Groats stopping each night on his own property (it was a two-week journey).

As a result of marriage to the heiress of Ackergill the Keiths moved into Caithness in the 14th century, where they became involved in a long and sanguinary feud with the Gunns (see Gunn).

At Bannockburn the successful performance of the Scots' cavalry, mounted on mere ponies compared with the great heavy horses of the English, reflected credit on the current marischal, Sir Robert Keith. His

Keith and Austin

Dunnottar Castle, on its spectacular and all but impregnable site, connected to the mainland by a narrow path only, was the last stronghold to surrender to Cromwellian forces during the 'Second' Civil War (1652).

great-grandson Sir William founded the castle of Dunnotar (later rebuilt) on its superlative site south of Stonehaven on the Kincardineshire coast.

In the 16th century at least three Scottish monarchs were entertained at Dunnotar, and during the civil wars the royal regalia were taken there for safe keeping. When the castle was besieged they were smuggled out, let down the cliffs to an old woman supposedly gathering kelp on the seashore and buried in a nearby churchyard.

The castle expanded, along with the influence of the Keiths, in succeeding generations. For in spite of what would seem to be the excessive dangers of such an office as marischal – attendance at all battles obligatory – the Keiths flourished until the 17th century. The Earl even survived Flodden, and his standard in that battle has survived to this day.

There is some confusion over the numbering of the earls marischal. The fourth earl (died 1623) is sometimes called the fifth. He was a firm Protestant, who had spent some time in his youth in Calvinist Geneva, and was one of the commissioners who arranged the marriage of James VI/I to Anne of Denmark. He founded Marischal College, Aberdeen. His grandson William, the seventh earl (died 1661), was a leading Covenanter and opponent of Huntly, but later supported the royalists and invaded England with Hamilton in 1648.

Naturally, many of the earls marischal gained a reputation in the military field (they were not so good at sea: William, fifth earl, was also Admiral of Scotland, but 'wold never boate'). James, a younger son of the eighth earl marischal, was 'out' in the Jacobite rising of 1715 and afterwards became a distinguished mercenary, fighting in the service of Spain, Russia and most notably the Prussia of Frederick the Great, who made him a field marshal and erected a statue to him in Dresden after his death in battle in 1758. His brother George, ninth and last earl marischal, was also compelled to travel on the continent after his participation in the Fifteen. He became a close friend of Frederick the Great, his brother's commander-in-chief.

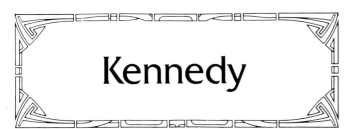

Kennedy

The Kennedys come from Carrick in Ayrshire and dominated that district for many centuries. The earliest record of them dates from the reign of King William the Lion. A Henry Kennedy was reported to be involved in a rebellion in Galloway in 1185.

A branch of the Kennedys who found their way to the Highlands about the 15th century were known as *Ceannaideach*.

The Kennedys of Carrick were probably connected genealogically with the old Celtic lords of Galloway. John Kennedy of Dunure, recognised as chief of the Kennedys by King Robert II, married an heiress of the old Carrick earls and was established in Cassillis (where the present Kennedy chief still maintains a seat), which he had possibly acquired as a result of an earlier marriage. His grandson James Kennedy of Dunure married a daughter of King Robert III, bringing the Kennedys to a prominent place on the national stage. Their son Gilbert became the first Lord Kennedy (1457) and was one of the numerous regents during the minority of King James III. A kinsman, Sir Hugh Kennedy, fought with Joan of Arc against the English.

The most famous member of the clan in the Middles Ages was a brother of the first Lord Kennedy, James, Bishop of St Andrews from 1441 to his death in 1465, Chancellor of Scotland and one of the most effective statesmen of his time. He is regarded as a co-founder of St Andrews University, originated by his predecessor. A younger son of the first Lord Kennedy was the poet Walter Kennedy (died c. 1508), best known for his participation in William Dunbar's *Flyting*, a battle of wits between the two poets.

Few of the early Kennedy chiefs died peacefully: the third Lord Kennedy, created Earl of Cassillis in 1510, died at Flodden, the second earl was murdered by Campbell of Loudon in 1527 and the third was captured at Solway Moss and died in mysterious circumstances in Dieppe when returning from the

Kennedy

wedding of Mary Queen of Scots to the Dauphin.

His son the fourth earl, known as 'King of Carrick', was a Protestant who nevertheless fought for Queen Mary at Langside. Described as 'ane werry greedy man', he is best remembered for literally roasting the Abbot of Crossraguel at Dunure Castle in 1570 in an attempt to persuade him to renounce title to the abbey's lands, which had been appropriated while the earl's uncle was abbot. The unfortunate man was rescued by the Kennedys of Bargany. They were engaged in a feud with the senior house which ended in their virtual extinction in the time of the fifth earl (died 1615), a lord high treasurer of Scotland.

The childless fifth earl was succeeded by his nephew John (1595-1668), 'the grave and solemn Earl', who was a strict Presbyterian and a leader of the Scottish resistance to Charles I. According to a probably false tradition the heroine of the ballad 'The Gypsie Laddie' can be identified with the sixth earl's first wife, who was Jean, daughter of the Hamilton Earl of Haddington. The gypsy hero was Johnnie Faa, Sir John Faa of Dunbar, the name borne by the gypsy king acknowledged by King James V long before but not known to history in this later identity. The countess was in love with him; he carried her off, but was caught by the outraged earl who hanged Johnnie from the Dule Tree in front of her eyes and kept her captive the rest of her life.

The seventh earl gave his support to the Glorious

Revolution of 1688. The eighth earl had no children and the title passed to the Kennedys of Culzean, descended from a younger son of the third earl. The subsequent history of the Kennedy chiefs is less romantic and more honourable. The eleventh earl was a notable admiral whose son was created Marquess of Ailsa, the title held by his descendants.

The famous home of the chiefs since the end of the 18th century is Culzean Castle, perhaps the most remarkable of the sham castles built by Robert Adam in his later years (and now owned by the National Trust for Scotland). Its rugged neo-Gothic exterior conceals rooms of exquisite delicacy, from which one may contemplate the splendours of a stormy sea from a position of the utmost graciousness and security.

Culzean, Robert Adam's impressive sham Gothic pile built in the 1770s and 1780s, incorporates a medieval stronghold of the Kennedys. A massive tower on the seaward side has no defensive pretensions but contains a magnificent saloon with dramatic marine views.

Kerr

The name Kerr, variously spelt, was fairly common in the Borders at an early date and possibly not all its bearers come from the same stock.

By tradition the Kerrs were of Anglo-Norman origin, though the name may be British or Norse, and its earliest known bearer was described as a 'hunter', of Swinhope, in the reign of King William the Lion.

The governing theme of the Border Kerrs is the long rivalry between the two chief branches, said to have descended from two brothers, Ralph and John, resident near Jedburgh in the early 14th century. The Kerrs of Ferniehurst were descended from Ralph, the elder brother, the Kerrs of Cessford from John. (The rivalry was even reflected in the name, the Kerrs of Ferniehurst usually preferring the spelling Ker).

One or other of these two, whose homes were only

Kerr

a few miles apart, usually held the title of warden of the Middle March – Sir Andrew of Ferniehurst was appointed in 1502, Sir Andrew of Cessford held it after Flodden – and although they sometimes combined against the English, their frequent brawling between themselves brought much violence and destruction to Teviotdale.

The rivalry took on a national political dimension in the 16th century when the Kerrs of Cessford supported the pro-English policy of the Douglases (led by the Earl of Angus and his wife Margaret, the Tudor widow of King James IV), while the Kerrs of Ferniehurst adhered to the party of King James V.

At the siege of the Castle of Ferniehurst by the English the attackers claimed that its defence was assisted by 'spirits' and even the devil himself. Fearful atrocities were committed there when the castle fell. On its recapture from the English in 1549 great efforts were made to take prisoners alive so that they could be slowly tortured to death, in revenge for the rape of Kerr womenfolk by the English.

The dispute between the two Kerr houses continued. Besides warden of the Middle March, they contended for the office of provost of Jedburgh. Sir Walter of Cessford was against Mary Queen of Scots, Sir Thomas of Ferniehurst for her. Eventually the feud died down. The union of the Scots and English crowns reduced the importance of the Border clans, and the final solution was the marriage in 1631 of Anne Kerr of Cessford to William Kerr of

Ferniehurst, who inherited the title Earl of Lothian formerly held by the Cessford branch. Their son became the Marquess of Lothian in 1701.

The first Earl of Roxburghe (created 1616) was a descendant of Sir Andrew Kerr of Cessford, Warden of the Middle March a century earlier. The fifth earl was a strong supporter of the union with England (1707) as a result of which the grateful government made him a duke. The title was later inherited by Sir James Innes of that ilk, twenty-fifth Chief of Innes, who adopted the name Kerr.

Lamont

Clan Lamont was a relatively small and therefore not very powerful clan with the misfortune of formidable neighbours – the Campbells – but their history is well documented. A fine history of the Lamonts by Hector McKechnie was published in 1938.

When the Scots came from Ireland to Dalriada one district, Cowal, was named after King Comgall (died 537) and the Lamonts who made their home in Cowal were probably descended from the same family. In the late 12th century Ferchar was a chief in Cowal and his grandson Lauman, or Ladman, was the ancestor from whom the clan took their name. The Gaelic name of the chief was *Mac Ladhmainn Mór Chòmhaill uile* (great son of Lamont of all Cowall).

A famous relic of the Lamonts is the Lamont harp now in Edinburgh, which was made about the middle of the 15th century. It is said to have travelled to the Robertsons in Perthshire with a Lamont daughter who married a Robertson.

The original home of the chiefs was at Inveryne on Loch Fyne, but their main stronghold from the 15th century was Toward Castle, the ruins of which can still be seen.

The clan was virtually destroyed in the 17th century in a notorious episode for which the chief himself was partly to blame.

The civil wars offered plenty of opportunities to pay off old scores, but because fortunes tended to change with dramatic swiftness, those who took advantage of such opportunities laid themselves open to future retribution.

Sir James Lamont of Inveryne sympathised with Charles I in the religious quarrel of the 1630s, which put him on the opposite side from his powerful neighbour, Campbell of Argyll. Sir James was a man of some ability, who established a school at Toward in

Lamont

1643, one of only two in Argyll. He was anxious to escape Campbell thraldom and recover lands in Cowal which the Campbells had taken. Nevertheless he was compelled to fight on Argyll's side, and was taken prisoner, to his relief presumably, by Montrose at the battle of Inverlochy, a resounding defeat for Argyll. Montrose soon released him, with a commis-

sion to act against rebels, which in Lamont's case meant the Campbells. Together with some of Montrose's Irish MacDonalds the Lamonts ravaged the Campbell country, undoubtedly committing atrocities in the process.

After Montrose's defeat the Campbells took a terrible revenge. They besieged and destroyed Toward Castle and the other main Lamont base at Ascog and slaughtered the Lamonts without mercy in spite of having granted a safe conduct. The women and girls were killed first, the men kept prisoner for a week, then massacred in Dunoon churchyard, where thirty-six 'chiefs and special gentlemen' were hanged on the same tree before being cut down and buried alive. Sir James himself was kept a prisoner for five years in Dunstaffnage Castle without being able to change his clothes. A memorial to the dead was erected at Dunoon by the Clan Lamont Society in 1906.

Subsequently the Lamont chiefs lived at Ardlamont, but the property was sold in the 19th century. The chiefship has twice passed to different branches of the clan, the current one being resident in Australia.

The Lamonts of Knockdow were an old cadet branch, descended from a younger son of the 15th-century chief. Sir Norman Lamont, fifteenth Laird of Knockdow, left the estate in trust for the clan.

Sunset over Cowal, the scene of strife between Campbells and Lamonts.

Leslie

The lands of Leslie in Aberdeenshire were granted to a Fleming named Bartolf in the 12th century. His son Malcolm took his name from the lands, but the question of who among later Leslies were descendants of this line is impossible to answer.

Sir Andrew Leslie was one of those who signed (more strictly, sealed) the Declaration of Arbroath in 1320, and his descendant was created Earl of Rothes by King James II. The chiefship of the Leslies remains with the earls of Rothes today.

William, third Earl of Rothes, was killed at Flodden and George, fourth earl, fought in France with King James V. His son Norman, Master of Rothes, also fought in France and was killed there in 1554. Earlier, he had made a name for himself by taking part in the assassination of Cardinal Beaton.

The Leslies are famous for producing soldiers of fortune: at one point in history there was a General Leslie on active service in three European countries (including Scotland).

Although there was no recognised chief the Leslies individually gained their greatest fame in the 17th century. Alexander, son of George Leslie of Balgonie and a member of the family of Leslie of Balquhain, fought under Gustavus Adolphus in the Thirty Years' War and returned to Scotland in 1638 as a field marshal to command the Scots in the impending Bishops' War. He was an ardent Covenanter, but in the course of the next few years it was sometimes difficult to say exactly where his true loyalties lay (the same could be said of many others in those difficult times). Although 'Sandy' Leslie was small and 'somewhat deformed' in person, he was an excellent commander who was able to enforce discipline on turbulent Scottish nobles. The king made him Earl of Leven in 1641, and he retained his command until he was in his seventies (he died in 1661, aged over 80), finally relinquishing it in favour of David Leslie. He was succeeded as Earl of Leven by his grandson, but after the deaths of the latter's two daughters, both Countesses of Leven in their own right, there was a dispute over the succession between John Leslie, Earl (created duke in 1680) of Rothes and the Earl of Melville. Rothes's death in 1681 decided the matter and Melville, a great-grandson of 'Sandy' Leslie, became Earl of Leven and Melville.

David Leslie, who succeeded Leven as Lord Gen-

Leslie

eral, was a grandson of the fifth Earl of Rothes. He ended the legend of Montrose with a convincing victory at Philiphaugh (1645) but was later defeated, though not disgraced, by Cromwell at Dunbar and Worcester. After the Restoration he became Lord Newark.

The Leslies of Balquhain were perhaps the most distinguished branch. They held that barony in the early 14th century, and were long involved in a feud with the Forbeses, in the course of which Balquhain Castle was destroyed and rebuilt. The Walter Leslie who assassinated Wallenstein in the Thirty Years' War came from this family, of whom the most notable member was John Leslie, Bishop of Ross during the Reformation, a staunch supporter of the Roman Catholic Church against Knox and later of Mary Queen of Scots. While in England he was involved in the Ridolfi plot and spent some time as a prisoner in the Tower of London. He used the time profitably in gathering material for his history of Scotland, published (in Latin) in 1578.

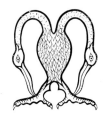

Lindsay

Lindsay

Lindsays are now spread all over Scotland, not to mention other countries, and, thanks perhaps to the high proportion of literary talent for which the name is famous, their early history is quite well known.

The Lindsays were of Lowland origin, and the first known member of the family was a Norman, Baldric de Lindesay, who held lands in England and Normandy and took his name from the district south of the Humber. Early in the 12th century Sir Walter de Lindsay was a member of the council of Prince David, Earl of Huntingdon, who became King of Scots in 1124. Sir Walter's successor acquired the lands of Crawford in Clydesdale and married an English heiress: the family continued to hold lands on both sides of the border.

Sir David Lindsay, who died on crusade in 1268, had served as Regent and later Chamberlain of Scotland, but his descendants were torn between two loyalties. His son Sir Alexander had been knighted by Edward I of England but nevertheless became a supporter of Wallace and Bruce, losing his English properties as a result. His son and successor Sir David

The 16th-century tower of Edzell Castle, once the home of a prominent branch of the Lindsays who were descended from a younger son of the third Earl of Crawford.

was taken prisoner, but survived to become one of the signatories of the Declaration of Arbroath, the Scottish declaration of independence, in 1320. His great-grandson, yet another Sir David, was created Earl of Crawford in 1398. He is thought to have been the organiser of the famous battle of the Clans at Perth in 1396.

The first earl was a famous champion who fought a duel against the English champion Lord Welles at a tournament on St George's Day in front of the king of England. He unhorsed his opponent so easily that the spectators suspected he was somehow fastened to his saddle, which he disproved by leaping to the ground and back into the saddle – no mean feat in full armour.

By this time the Lindsays of Crawford had acquired lands in Angus through marriage, and made their home there. The earls of Crawford were one of the mightiest families in Scotland, overlords of a vast area which included Strathnairn. By the end of the Middle Ages there were about one hundred landed Lindsay families of varying note in Scotland, especially in Angus and adjacent counties, and most of them acknowledged the Earl of Crawford as their chief.

The Lindsays were involved in some spectacular feuds in Angus, notably with the Ogilvies and with Lyons of Glamis, both near neighbours.

Generally the Lindsays remained loyal to the Stewarts. The sixth earl fell at Flodden, the tenth supported Mary Queen of Scots, and the sixteenth fought for Charles I (though the Lindsays of Edzell were Covenanters). Despite their reputation as 'the lightsome Lindsays', not all the members of the chiefly family were amiable gentlemen. The fourth earl, known as 'Earl Beardie', was a ferocious character, and Alexander, heir to the eighth earl, was known as 'the Wicked Master', having failed in an attempt to murder his father. He was disinherited, but later regained the title after the death of his cousin, a Lindsay of Edzell, who had replaced him. From his younger son descended the earls of Balcarres (created 1651), who in the 19th century inherited the chiefship and the Crawford title and became earls of Crawford and Balcarres.

Sir David Lindsay (1490-1555), a courtier and Lyon King of Arms in the reign of King James III, was author of *Ane Satyre of the Three Estaits*, in the Scots vernacular, a play that attacked national, religious and court vices. It has recently been revived with great success at the Edinburgh Festival. The witty if unreliable historian Robert Lindsay of Pittscottie (died c. 1565) was his contemporary. The playwright belonged to a branch of the family descended from Lord Lindsay, a younger son of a 14th-century laird of Crawford, whose successors became earls of Lindsay (1633).

Livingstone

The name comes from what is today a somewhat blighted 'New Town' in West Lothian, and the Lowland spelling of the name generally omits the final E. The town itself probably took its name from a Saxon named Leving, whose grandson, 'of Livingstone', is named in a charter of King William the Lion. His descendant Sir William Livingstone was taken prisoner fighting in northern England in 1346 with King David II, from whom he acquired the forfeited barony of Callandar, marrying the Callandar heiress into the bargain. A number of landed Livingstone families descended from Sir William's grandson Sir John Livingstone of Callandar (died 1402).

One of these grandsons was Sir James Livingstone of Callandar, who became first Lord Livingstone in the mid-15th century. His descendant Alexander, fifth lord, was one of the guardians of the young Mary Queen of Scots before the battle of Pinkie, and his son

Livingstone

fought for the queen at Langside. The seventh lord was created Earl of Linlithgow in 1600, but the title was forfeited after the fourth earl joined the Jacobites in 1715. A branch descended from the first earl who had become earls of Callendar suffered the same fate.

Some writers refer to a member of this Lowland family, Sir James Livingstone of Stirling, who as a result of a royal grant settled in Lismore, at the entrance of Loch Linnhe, in the 17th century and gave his name to his tenants. However, the origin of the Highland Livingstones is surely much earlier than this.

They were originally named MacLeay, an anglicised version of the Gaelic *Mac an Léigh*, meaning 'the son of the physician', and they were at one time connected with the famous hereditary physicians to the lord of the Isles, the Beatons. They were also found in Kintyre and Appin – as followers of the Stewarts. They adopted the name Livingston because of similarities in sound and meaning: *Léibhe* (whence *Léigh*) = Living; *Mac* = s(t)on.

The holy isle of Lismore had once been the home of St Moluag (died 592), who had left behind him his bishop's staff, known as the *Bachull Mór* or *Bachull Buidhe* (yellow staff) because for a long time it was cased in copper. Of this sacred relic, which is associated with highly unChristian rites performed at Hogmanay, the MacLeays were hereditary keepers, and that office is held to this day by the chief of the Livingstones.

The remains of the bishop's palace at Achinduin on the island of Lismore, essentially a rough, rocky ridge (though with some pockets of fertile soil) at the mouth of Loch Linnhe, a Livingstone base (Clan MacLeay) from the mid-17th century. The name Lismore is believed to derive from the Gaelic for 'the Great Garden', the soil being very fertile.

The great explorer David Livingstone (his father spelt the name without the final E), was descended from the Livingstones of Argyll. His grandfather had been a tenant farmer on the island of Ulva, west of Mull, but he was evicted in 1792 and came to the Glasgow area to find work. His famous grandson was born in a miserable tenement beside the mill at Blantyre.

Logan (MacLennan)

A man wearing the Logan tartan. Detail of a painting by the Highland artist, R. R. McIan.

Although they are usually grouped together, there is probably no connection between the MacLennans of the Highlands and the Lowland Logans.

According to ancient and demonstrably unreliable tradition the Lobans or Logans were led by a chief named Gilligorm in a feud with the Frasers in Easter Ross somewhere about 1200 (too early for 'Frasers' or 'Logans' of course). In a battle at Drumderfit, the Logans' seat, Gilligorm was killed and his widow carried off by the Frasers. She later gave birth to Gilligorm's posthumous son, called *Crotair* (hump-

Logan

backed) MacGilligorm. His disability was due to the Frasers breaking his back when a baby to prevent him taking revenge on them when he grew up. He went into the Church and had a son (priests in the Celtic Church were not barred from marriage), called *Gillie Fhinnein* (disciple of St Finnan) and MacLennan is the anglicised version of this name.

There was a saying, 'as old as the Lobans of Drumderfit', and they were still in residence in the early 18th century. At the house they kept a wooden figure of the legendary Gilligorm, but it was unfortunately destroyed (along with the house) in the wake of the Jacobite rising of 1715.

There were, and are, many MacLennans in Ross. They were connected with the MacRaes and were standard bearers to the Seaforth Mackenzies – two MacLennans died in defence of the standard at the battle of Auldearn (1645) – but there is little record of

them as a clan, and no one has appeared to claim the chiefship in modern times.

The name Logan appears in the south at an early date. The 'Good Sir James' Douglas was accompanied by two knights of that name when he set out to take Bruce's heart to the Holy Land. They died fighting alongside him in Spain in 1329.

Sir Robert Logan of Restalrig, near Edinburgh, married a daughter of King Robert II and was Admiral of Scotland in 1406. This family held Fast Castle on the coast of Berwickshire, but they fell from favour and the last known Logan of Restalrig died an outlaw. Fast Castle ('Wolf's Crag' in Scott's *The Bride of Lammermoor*) passed into the possession of the Homes.

In relation to the history of the Highlands, and of tartan in particular, few names are more honoured than that of James Logan, author of *The Scottish Gael* (1831). This was the first serious effort to record the history of Highland dress, predating the fascinating but dubious work of the extraordinary Sobieski Stewart brothers. He gave details but not illustrations of about fifty tartans and most scholarly work on the subject starts with him, Gaelic sources notwithstanding.

MacAlister

The MacAlisters of Loup descended from Alasdair, younger son of Donald of Islay, grandson of the mighty Somerled. They were thus a branch of Clan Donald – the senior branch in fact – though some of the MacAlisters were later vassals of the Campbell earls of Argyll and survived Campbell hegemony in their homelands with more success than most.

Alasdair *Mór* died in battle against his cousin, the MacDougall Lord of Lorne, in 1299 and his descendants settled mainly in Kintyre. Charles MacAlister was appointed steward of Kintyre by King James III in 1481; his headquarters were at Dunaverty Castle. By about this time branches of the MacAlisters were also settling in Arran, where they were to give bonds of manrent to the Hamiltons, and in Bute.

Charles's son was known as 'John of the Lowb', or 'Loup', from a Gaelic word meaning bend or curve and apparently referring to the shape of the coastline of MacAlister territory. Subsequent chiefs have retained this appellation and the Gaelic title *Mac Eoin Duibh* (son of Black John).

The MacAlisters of Tarbert belonged to a cadet branch of the MacAlisters of Loup. They became hereditary constables of the royal castle of Tarbert, on behalf of the earls of Argyll, hereditary keepers. A 'tarbert' is a place where a boat can be dragged overland from one shore to another (in this case the neck of land linking Kintyre and Knapdale), and it was by this trick that King Magnus Barefoot of

MacAlister

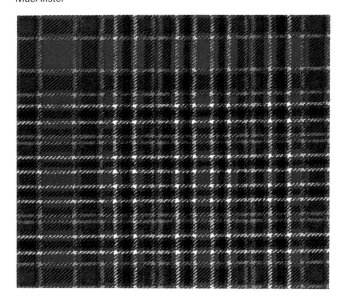

Norway in 1093 defined the fertile and therefore desirable peninsula of Kintyre as an island – and thus part of Norway's possessions, not Scotland's. It consequently passed into the domain of the lord of the Isles until the Campbells took over in the 17th century.

Another branch of the clan, who took the name Alexander (equivalent to Alasdair), settled at Menstrie in Clackmannanshire, as vassals of the Earl of Argyll, in the 16th century. In 1603 William Alexander of Menstrie (1567-1640), poet and courtier, accompanied King James VI to London. He was knighted by the king, an admirer of his poetry, and later created Viscount, then Earl of Stirling. He was acknowledged as chief of the clan by the MacAlisters of Tarbert, presumably impressed by these honours, but not by the MacAlisters of Loup.

Another family of Alexanders, claiming descent from the house of Menstrie, settled in Ireland in the 17th century and became earls of Caledon. Their most famous descendant was Field Marshal Lord Alexander of Tunis.

The MacAlisters of Loup, the senior house, were supporters of the royal house of Stewart. Alexander, eighth of Loup, fought at Killiecrankie with Bonnie Dundee and took part in King James VII/II's ill-fated campaign in Ireland which ended with the battle of the Boyne (1690). His brother, who succeeded after the early death of his son, married the daughter of Lamont of that ilk.

In the late 18th century their grandson made a more fortunate marriage than this, to Janet Somerville, an heiress who brought him the estate of Kennox in Ayrshire. Thereafter the chiefs of Clan MacAlister, styled MacAlister of Loup and Kennox, maintained their seat in Kennox.

The Tarbert family went bankrupt in 1745, losing their lands and castle, but they survived to produce a famous principal of Glasgow University, Sir Donald Macalister of Tarbert (1854-1934).

MacAlpine

The name MacAlpine is fairly common today, but there is little trace of a Clan MacAlpine and although there is a modern tartan there is no chief. It is said that former MacAlpine chiefs had their seat at Dunstaffnage Castle in Argyll, an early capital of Kenneth MacAlpin. The name means 'son of Alpin' and the original MacAlpin was of course Kenneth

MacAlpin himself, that rather mysterious figure who was the founder of the Scottish kingdom in 843.

The main question about Kenneth MacAlpin is: How did he do it? A hundred years earlier the Picts had practically wiped out the Scots of Dalriada, and had defeated them again less than ten years before, yet Kenneth MacAlpin's victory was so conclusive that even the Pictish language soon disappeared. He was helped by having a claim to the Pictish throne through his mother, and he appears to have helped himself in a misty episode in which the seven Pictish earls of Alba were apparently murdered at a stroke during a conference at Scone where they were

Dunstaffnage Castle said to have been the seat of Pictish and Scottish princes and early MacAlpine chiefs. The present castle is largely 13th-century.

MacAlpine

supposed to be discussing the question of the succession with MacAlpin. Probably the decisive factor was the attacks of the Vikings: the Norsemen were responsible for the Scots' drive towards the centre (to escape Norse depredations in the west) and, on the other hand, the attacks of the Danes, with whom MacAlpin may possibly have been in league, explained the current weakness of the Picts.

Kenneth MacAlpin died in 860 and his descendants reigned as kings of Alba or Albany (i.e. Scotland) for many generations. The following nine kings all died violent deaths.

A great many clans and families can claim indirect descent from the royal house, but those particularly associated with *Sìol Ailpein* (descendants of Alpin) were the MacGregors, Grants, MacNabs, Mackinnons and MacAulays, all of whom have the pine tree as their badge. *Sìol Ailpein* was never an effective confederation of clans, like Clan Chattan. Nevertheless, there was a strong tradition of friendship, particularly between the MacGregors and the Grants, on the face of things unlikely allies. The name MacAlpine is associated with the MacGregors especially. Among the Grants, when a famous laird of Rothiemurchus was adopted into Clan Gregor because of the good services he had rendered them, he took the name of MacAlpine.

MacArthur

Several old Gaelic sayings testify to the ancient origins of the MacArthurs. For instance, things are said to be 'as old as the hills, the MacArthurs and the Devil'.

The MacArthurs themselves claimed as their progenitor the legendary King Arthur of the Round Table. This would place the semi-mythical British leader not in Cornwall but in southern Scotland, where of course the Celtic Britons were established (though hard-pressed by the Picts and Scots to the north and west and by the Anglo-Saxon Northumbrians to the south and east) in the post-Roman era when, it is generally agreed, the prototype of King Arthur actually lived. Arthur's Seat, the hill in Edinburgh, would presumably provide more evidence to support King Arthur's northern origin although the name is generally assumed to be a corruption of 'Archer's'.

Argyll is the homeland of the MacArthurs, and in the 13th century a MacArthur married the heiress of Duncan MacDuibhne or O'Duin who in a royal charter of the following century is acknowledged as the progenitor of the Campbell lords of Lochow (Loch Awe).

The Campbells are also called *Ua Duibhne*, and as their modern surname had not yet been generally adopted in Argyll, there is some reason to suppose that the MacArthurs and the future Campbells belonged to the same stock. The hereditary pipers to

MacArthur

the MacDonalds were named MacArthur, and so were the armourers of MacDonald of Islay.

The MacArthurs of Loch Awe supported Bruce during the wars of independence and they were rewarded with, at the expense of the MacDougalls who unwisely opposed Bruce, considerable lands in Lorne together with the keepership of Dunstaffnage Castle.

This was the peak of their prosperity, and it did not last very long. When King James I returned from his long exile in England and launched his fierce campaign to re-establish the authority of the Crown by crushing all – from the Regent Albany downwards – who threatened it, one of those who suffered was Iain MacArthur, Chief of Clan Arthur. 'A great prince among his own people and leader of a thousand men', he was executed in 1427 and his lands, or most of them, forfeited. For practical purposes this was the end of the clan.

Later bearers of this name who were of Scottish origin include John MacArthur (1767-1834), who arrived in New South Wales in 1790 as a soldier. He was one of the first men to raise sheep in Australia, and as he is said also to have planted the first Australian vineyard, he must be regarded as one of the founders of that country's prosperity. His first home, Elizabeth Farm in Parramatta, survives to this day.

The American General Arthur MacArthur, father of the more famous General Douglas MacArthur (responsible for the victory over the Japanese in the Second World War), was the son of an emigrant from Strathclyde.

MacAulay

There were two Clans MacAulay, who were unconnected by blood and occupied widely separated regions.

The MacAulays of Ardencaple were in Dumbartonshire at an early date. Sir Aulay MacAulay of Ardencaple appears in a roll of landlords in 1587, as a vassal of the Earl of Lennox. Although separated by rather a long period, it is reasonable to assume he was a descendant of *Amhlaidh Mac Amhlaidh* (i.e. Aulay MacAulay) who lived in the late 13th century and was possibly the son or grandson of Aulay, a younger son of the Earl of Lennox, whose name appears in charters somewhat earlier. The

Lennox connection would give the MacAulays ancestors among the royal house of Munster.

The MacAulays considered themselves as members of *Sìol Ailpein* (their badge is a pine tree) and thus connected with the MacGregors. MacAulay of Ardencaple gave a bond of manrent to MacGregor of Glenstrae in 1591 in which he described his own family as a branch of MacGregor's house (which would throw some doubt on the Lennox connection). This was at a time when kinship with the MacGregors was something for the sensible man to keep quiet about, and the motive for MacAulay's acknowledgement of the MacGregors may have been his need for friends in a feud provoked by the murder of a MacAulay by the Buchanans at Dumbarton the previous year.

However, the MacAulays escaped the fate which overtook the MacGregors in the 17th century despite the enmity of the Campbells, who were accused of attempting to murder their chief in 1602. They remained in possession of Ardencaple until 1767, when the bankrupt twelfth chief was compelled to sell out to the Campbell Duke of Argyll. The Campbells turned the castle into a typical Victorian Scots-baronial hall in the 19th century before selling it to Colquhoun of Luss. It is now a ruin.

The second Clan MacAulay were to be found in the island of Lewis in the Outer Hebrides. The derivation of their name is different, meaning 'son of Olaf', though there is some doubt as to the Olaf in question. He is presumed to have been Olaf the Black, King of Man and the Isles (including Lewis), who died in 1237. An early ancestor was Donald *Cam* (crooked), who lived around 1600 and is the subject of heroic folktales. Sir Iain Moncreiffe suggested that these MacAulays originated on the mainland (Ullapool means Olaf's Palace), where they were certainly

quite numerous in later times. These mainland MacAulays regarded themselves as a sept of the MacAulays of Lewis.

The northern MacAulays produced a notable line of Presbyterian ministers. Zachary Macaulay (1768-1838), a famous opponent of slavery and one-time governor of Sierra Leone, came from this line. His son was Thomas Babington Macaulay (1800-59), the great historian and essayist, who was created Lord Macaulay in 1857 but had no descendants to continue the line. Macaulay was born in Leicestershire and had little affection for his Highland heritage (see his 'A Jacobite's Epitaph').

MacBean

Like so many names derived from Gaelic – and there are several possible Gaelic originals – MacBean poses a number of problems. MacBain and MacVean are common variations. MacBeath or MacBeth, McVane, etc. also occur. The 19th-century Gaelic scholar Alexander MacBain stated that the clan name *Mac Bheathain* (MacBean) would in earlier times have been MacBeath. It has also been suggested that the name may derive from *Bàn*, meaning fair-headed perhaps unlikely.

According to tradition the MacBeans came from Lochaber with Eva, a Clan Chattan heiress, when she married Angus Mackintosh of Mackintosh. A MacBean with his four sons settled in Petty, near Inverness, in the 14th century and came under Mackintosh protection, engaging in a feud with the

MacAulay

MacBean

A detail of a portrait of a warrior of Clan MacBean, by the Highland artist R. R. McIan, published in his *Clans of the Scottish Highlands*.

be merciful. The dragoons trampled him under their horses' hooves and left him for dead, but he somehow managed to crawl to a farm where the farmfolk covered him with straw and, when he died, buried him under a lathe stone.

Echoing this achievement, William MacBean, who enlisted in the Sutherland Highlanders and eventually rose to command the regiment, gained the Victoria Cross for an incident at Lucknow (1858) in which he single-handedly killed eleven of the enemy.

The MacBeans of Tomatin, who were in business, survived the difficulties of the late 18th century and held on to their lands in Strathdearn, but the chiefly family of Kinchyle was less fortunate. The chief himself was forced to join the army, and in his absence Kinchyle had to be sold. The chiefship continued among his descendants in Canada and in 1958 passed to an American businessman, Hughston MacBean, who repurchased part of Kinchyle and founded the MacBean memorial park east of Dores.

MacCallum (Malcolm)

The name MacCallum means 'son of Colm', i.e. (it is said) St Columba, but a thousand years divides St Columba from the earliest mention of the MacCallums in documentary records.

The MacCallums were settled in Lorne, Argyll. Legend tells us that their original seat was at Colgin, near Oban, where the chief lived with his three sons. They spread in the following manner (it's a familiar tale, in one form or another). On their father's

MacCallum

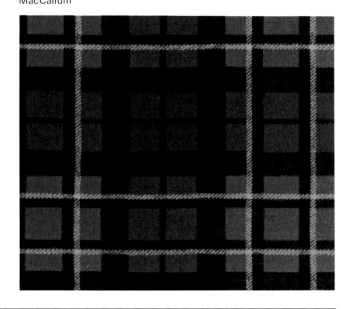

Red Comyns and killing his steward, though whether the steward's death was the cause or effect of their Mackinstosh alliance is unclear. Many MacBeans are said to have died at 'Red' Harlaw in 1411, when Mackintosh supported Donald, Lord of the Isles, in his claim to the earldom of Ross.

The MacBean territory was established around the northern end of Loch Ness, the senior family in Kinchyle, and with heavy concentration in Dores, site of the modern MacBean memorial. The surname does not appear in historical records until the 17th century, although thanks to the form of patronymic name-giving (X son of W, son of V, etc.), a series of MacBean chiefs can be traced to the 15th century.

The MacBeans were powerful warriors. Aeneas MacBean of Kinchyle served with the Mackintosh in the Jacobite rising of 1715 and his brother, the mighty Gillies, was one of the heroes of Culloden. A major in the Clan Chattan regiment, he was felled by a bayonet but rose and retreated as far as a stone wall, where he was overtaken by dragoons and infantry. Broadsword in hand, he placed his back against the wall and fought with such courage and tenacity that he won the admiration of the chivalrous Earl of Ancrum, who tried to call his men off. But Gillies had killed fourteen of them and they were not inclined to

Loch Etive, looking north towards the ridges of Buchaille Etive Mor and Buchaille Etive Beg, the Big and Little Herdsman of Etive. The MacCallums held land in this region from various Campbell overlords but retained their clan integrity. The MacDonalds and the MacIntyres also held land here.

direction each son went out with a donkey loaded with panniers to settle wherever the panniers slipped from the donkeys' backs. In the case of the eldest son they fell off before he had left the parental homestead. The panniers of the two youngers sons slipped off at Glenetive and Kilmartin, where they accordingly founded their cadet houses.

As Sir Thomas Innes remarked, a 'more definite account . . . from documentary sources would be preferable' to this tale. Documentary sources may be meagre, but we do know that in 1414 Sir Duncan Campbell granted lands in Craignish to Ranald MacCallum, whom he also made hereditary Constable of Craignish Castle. The MacCallums of Poltalloch can be dated from 1562, when by a charter of Duncan Campbell of Duntrune that property was bestowed on 'Donald McGillespie vich o Callum', i.e. Donald son of Gillespie (Archibald), son of the descendants of Callum. Both Poltalloch and Duntrune thus became MacCallum property.

In 1647 Zachary MacCallum of Poltalloch, a man renowned for his strength, died in a famous fight. Like all his line he was an adherent of the Campbells, and at Ederline he encountered a party of MacDonalds. He killed seven of them and was fighting the redoubtable Alasdair MacColla (Sir Alexander Mac-

Donald) when treacherously attacked from the rear by a man wielding a scythe. This enabled MacColla to kill him.

A later Zachary MacCallum, fifth MacCallum of Poltalloch (died 1688), inherited Corbarron from his kinsman, who was the last of the line of Ranald MacCallum, Constable of Craignish.

The MacCallums of Poltalloch have held the chiefship since the time of Donald MacGillespie. In the 18th century they changed their name to Malcolm, which also occurs as an earlier variant, apparently because it was simpler. John Malcolm, fifteenth Laird of Poltalloch, was member of parliament for Argyll in the late 19th century and was subsequently raised to the peerage as Lord Malcolm of Poltalloch. The title expired with him in 1902. The home of the present Malcolm of Poltalloch and chief of the clan is Duntrune Castle, a venerable but more amenable house than Poltalloch. (See also Malcolm.)

MacDonald

Clan Donald, as any MacDonald will tell you, is the oldest and greatest of the Highland clans. Originally a single clan, some branches later became substantial independent clans. The Gaelic name of which Donald is an anglicisation is *Domhnall* (world ruler), and

MacDonald

and built up his own principality which included Arran and Bute. By marriage to a daughter of King Olaf of the Isles, backed up by force, he acquired the Southern Isles (Bute to Mull), leaving the Norse king (now son of Olaf) in possession of the Outer Hebrides, which were traditionally Norse.

The kings of both Norway and the Scots were Somerled's nominal overlords, but he was effectively an independent ruler, of considerable military and naval might. However, in challenging the King of Scots he overreached himself. The great fleet which he led up the Clyde to attack the heart of the Lowlands was defeated in 1164 and Somerled was assassinated.

His lands, according to Norse custom, were divided between his three sons. Dugall, presumably the eldest and the ancestor of Clan Dougal, received the mainland possessions plus some adjacent islands; Ranald (Reginald) received Kintyre and Islay and Angus received Bute (which, by the marriage of his granddaughter, eventually passed to the Stewarts).

Ranald had two sons who in turn divided their father's inheritance between them. Donald, founder of the MacDonalds, held part of Kintyre and some of the Southern Isles, including Islay, the future heart of the lordship of the Isles.

some clans adopted the spelling MacDonell, which is the same as MacDonald, i.e. son of Donald, and rather closer to the Gaelic form. It is worth noting that the name MacDonald (or MacDonell, or most other clan names), did not come into general use as a surname until about 1500.

The original progenitor of the MacDonalds was Donald, son of Ranald, son of Somerled (died 1164).

In spite of his Norse name (or nickname?), Somerled was a Gael on his father's side: both his father and paternal grandfather had Gaelic names. He ended Norse dominance on the mainland of Argyll

A peaceful scene in Moidart, MacDonald country.

Donald's possessions were small compared with those held by his descendants, but they were soon to increase. The MacDonalds did not benefit particularly from the administrative reorganisation of 1266 which followed the defeat of the Norwegian King Haakon at Largs and the secession of the Norse kingdom of the Isles to Scotland. The main beneficiary then was the Earl of Ross, whose territories were extended to Skye and Lewis. However, during the wars of independence the MacDougalls of Mull who as sons of Dugall were senior to the MacDonalds of Islay, were allies of Balliol and, after Bruce became king, fought on the side of the English. As a result they were forfeited and the MacDonalds of Islay, under the leadership of Angus *Mór* (son of Donald) and his son Angus *Òg*, received Mull, in line with Bruce's policy of bestowing forfeited lands on near-relations to avert future resentment. Loyalties were complex in these years: Angus *Òg* was actually a younger son; his elder brother Alexander was allied by marriage with the Red Comyns, enemies of Bruce, and he too was forfeited to the benefit of Angus *Òg*.

Angus *Òg's* territories thus extended from Ardnamurchan to Islay, including a section of Lochaber on the mainland. This, however, was only about a fifth of the territory of the lords of the Isles, the first of whom was Angus *Òg's* son and heir John (or Iain or Eoin).

MacDonald of the Isles

MacDonald of the Isles

In spite of his father's support for the Bruce (it was probably Angus *Òg* who sheltered and supplied Bruce after the battle of Methven in 1306), John of Islay did not feel bound to obedience to Bruce's successor King David II, who, however, brought him round by granting him the island of Lewis. Greater acquisitions were made through marriage. John's wife was the sister and heiress of Ranald MacRuari, descended from a younger son of Ranald, son of Somerled. On the murder of Ranald MacRuari John of Islay acquired the southern half of the Outer Hebrides (North and South Uist, Barra, etc.), Rum and adjacent isles, and the district of Garmoran (Moidart and Knoydart, where you can now shoot deer for £700 a day) on the mainland. He kept these extensive possessions although not his wife, divorcing her in 1350 to marry the daughter of the future King Robert II, the first Stewart king. This second marriage brought him Kintyre and much of Knapdale after the accession of his father-in-law to the Scottish throne.

John of Islay was now the ruler of territories much larger than those held by the old Norse kings of the Isles. Moreover, his castle of Finlaggan on Islay was strategically a much better capital than the Norse Isle of Man. In 1354 he bestowed on himself the title *Dominus Insularum* (Lord of the Isles). The Gaelic title was *Buachaille nan Eileanan* (Shepherd of the Isles).

The first Lord of the Isles had a son by each wife. Ranald was the elder, but by agreement the second son, Donald, the nephew of the king of Scots, succeeded as Lord of the Isles, while Ranald was given the MacRuari inheritance, as a vassal of his younger brother.

Donald, second Lord of the Isles, married the sister of the Earl of Ross, whose territories were in extent second only to his own. When the earl died his legal successor was his daughter, but she was set on a religious life and the Regent Albany secured the earldom for her maternal uncle, the Earl of Buchan, who happened to be Albany's son. This led to one of the most famous campaigns of the lords of the Isles, since it was clear that Donald's wife had a prior claim as sister of the late Earl of Ross. Full of wrath, Donald gathered his men, including such famous subordinate chiefs as the MacLeod chief, Red Hector of the Battles, and swept across Scotland towards Aberdeen. They were met at Harlaw (1411) by the Regent's army, commanded by the Earl of Mar (Alexander Stewart, who was Donald's cousin, both being grandsons of King Robert II). The fight was ferocious, Red Hector was killed, and neither side could claim a victory. But Donald was forced to withdraw to his own territories, though he did not withdraw his claim to the earldom of Ross.

When opposed to the king of Scots it was natural

Like the earlier Norse kingdom the lordship of the Isles depended largely on maritime communication. Shipbuilding must have been a problem in the Outer Hebrides, timber being scarce even then.

though ultimately dangerous for the lords of the Isles to seek alliance with England, which treated them as the sovereign lords they were in fact if not in law (the king of Scots being their overlord). This alliance had been renewed as recently as 1408, but the English provided no assistance at Harlaw and subsequently made peace with Albany.

Donald died in 1423 and was succeeded by his son Alexander, who eventually acquired the huge Ross earldom, for which his father had fought, by grant of King James I.

The lordship of the Isles now reached its greatest extent. Perhaps it was too large: the lord of the Isles confronted similar problems to the king of Scots in asserting his authority in distant and inaccessible regions.

The lordship of the Isles, spoken of by its enemies as if it were an association of savages, was a centre of Gaelic culture which to some extent went into an irreversible decline when the lordship ceased to exist.

The lords of the Isles governed with the advice of their council from Finlaggan. The administration of justice was good: local judges existed in every major district and the lord's council acted as a court of appeal. Although the great chieftains were the lord's feudal vassals, this was essentially a Gaelic state in which ties of kinship were strong. As long as it existed

the rivalries and feuds of the developing clans were at least contained if not always prevented. In this respect and in others, the destruction of the lordship was a disaster.

From a wider, nationalist viewpoint, however, the lordship was always a potential and sometimes an actual menace. King James I was determined to assert the authority of the Crown and in 1427, having summoned the Highland chiefs to parliament, he arrested forty of them, including Alexander, third Lord of the Isles. Some were executed, including at least one of the Lord's kinsmen, and on his release he promptly raised a rebellion and burned Inverness. But he was later defeated and imprisoned again. The result of this was another western rising, led by Alexander's cousin Donald Balloch, though again it was suppressed after early success. King James I then sensibly changed his policy, releasing Alexander who was restored to the lordship and soon afterwards succeeded to the earldom of Ross on the death of his mother.

Nothing was permanently solved thereby, and in

1462 the fourth Lord, John, together with the Earl of Douglas and others, was involved in a conspiracy with the English to divide the country between them. The terms of this treaty of Ardtornish (or Westminster) soon became public knowledge, and in 1476 the Lord of the Isles was deprived of much of his territory, including Kintyre and the earldom of Ross.

This was unacceptable to Angus Òg, illegitimate – and ferocious – son of John, who was married to a daughter of the Earl of Argyll, and the result was a serious split, with Angus Òg and his father on opposite sides. The MacDonalds themselves were willing to follow Angus Òg, but the non-MacDonald vassals, notably the MacLeods and Mackenzies, remained loyal to the fourth Lord. At the battle of Bloody Bay (Mull) in 1480 Angus Òg was victorious, capturing his father as well as two MacLean chieftains. He was about to execute MacLean of Ardgour on the spot but was prevented by MacDonald of Moidart, who protested, 'If MacLean were gone, who should I have to quarrel with?'

Angus Òg was murdered by his own harper in 1490, but almost immediately the conflict was renewed. The Islesmen's leader now was Alexander of Lochalsh, nephew of the fourth Lord of the Isles, who captured Inverness and ravaged the lands of the Mackenzies until defeated by them at Park.

John of the Isles was now an old man and though he had played no active part in the recent rebellion, he had been once again intriguing with the English. The lordship of the Isles was therefore annexed to the Crown in 1493, and John, fourth and last Lord of the Isles, died in a Dundee boarding house a few years later.

Unfortunately, this was not the end of the matter. For many years afterwards efforts were made to restore the lordship, most notably by Donald *Dubh* (Black Donald), son of Angus Òg. The young Donald was captured in 1506, not long after the Islesmen had yet again burned Inverness, but after almost 40 years in prison he escaped in 1545 and, though he must have been ill-fitted for warfare then, at once rose in rebellion in alliance with Henry VIII of England. With MacLean assistance he raised a force of 8,000 men and 180 galleys against the King of Scots. Loyalties die hard in the Highlands, as the descendants of Donald *Dubh*'s men were to prove exactly 200 years later.

Donald *Dubh* died in 1546 and the rebellion fizzled out amid mutual recriminations. The western clans held together by the lords of the Isles had now become quarrelsome and independent units, though they were at last prepared to forget their heritage as 'auld enemys to the realme of Scotland' and to acknowledge the Stewart dynasty as their rightful sovereigns.

MacDonald of Sleat

After the downfall of the lords of the Isles the individual clans which had come into being during the lordship became effectively independent. Their chiefs were tenants of the Crown, holding their land on leases rather than as vassals of the lord of the Isles. The chiefship of Clan Donald, disputed between various rivals, was no longer a force for union, rather the reverse, and since the Crown was initially unable to supply the authority of the forfeited lordship clan feuds were a frequent cause of disorder.

Alexander, third Lord of the Isles, had three sons, including his successor John. The youngest of them was Hugh, who inherited the barony of Sleat, on Skye, as his share of his father's estate. He lived until 1498, i.e. after the abolition of the lordship.

The remains of his castle at Dunskaith can still be seen, although it was abandoned in the 16th century by his descendant Donald *Gorm* in favour of the

MacDonald of Sleat

impregnably situated Duntulm, near Kilmuir.

The MacDonalds of Sleat were known as *Clann Uisdein* (children of Hugh) and sometimes as Clan Donald North, to distinguish them from the MacDonalds of Islay (Clan Donald South). The early chiefs were invariably – and later chiefs often – called Donald, which is apt to cause confusion. Donald *Gorm*, fifth of Sleat, was involved in an attempt to recover the lordship of the Isles in 1539. He drove the MacLeods out of Trotternish and invaded Kintail, but

while besieging the Mackenzie castle of Eilean Donan during his attempt to recover the earldom of Ross he was killed by a chance arrow.

After the death of Donald *Dubh* the MacDonalds of Sleat represented the senior male line of Clan Donald. Donald *Gorm Mór*, seventh of Sleat, was last in the direct line from Hugh and a still more formidable warrior than his earlier namesake. He assisted the Irish rebels against Elizabeth of England with a force of 500 men and at a later date, offering his aid to the same queen, he described himself as 'Lord of the Isles of Scotland and chief of the whole Clan Donald Irishmen wheresoever'. By that time he had made peace with King James VI, whose government secured his release after he had been captured while raiding the MacLeans of Mull. Although there were a

few little upsets in this new relationship, Donald *Gorm Mór* appeared in Edinburgh together with other Highland chiefs in 1610 and agreed to accept certain limitations on his household.

Thereafter the MacDonalds of Sleat were generally loyal to the Stewarts. They supported Mary Queen of Scots, fought with Montrose during the civil war and under Bonnie Dundee for King James VII/II at Killiecrankie. As a result of their support of the Jacobite rising of 1715 the estates were forfeited, but later restored. In 1745, however, the current chief, Sir

Above: Duntulm Castle on Skye, one of the many castles in the Western Isles built by the MacDonalds, their allies or enemies.
Below: Armadale, in the 'garden of Skye' as this part of Sleat has been called. The mansion house was built by Lord MacDonald in the early 19th century.

Alexander MacDonald of Sleat, who was influenced by Forbes of Culloden and also appalled by the prince's lack of preparations, refused to bring his men out, despite his natural sympathies. He was in poor health anyway, dying in 1746.

The first baronet, created in 1625, was Sir Donald MacDonald, nephew and successor of Donald *Gorm Mór*. Sir Alexander, ninth baronet, was created Lord MacDonald in 1796. As a result of his marriage his successor became heir to the Bosville estates in Thorpe, Yorkshire, in 1832. By an arrangement which had to be ratified by act of parliament, his eldest son inherited the Bosville estates, adopting the Bosville name, while the chiefship and the MacDonald peerage went to a younger son. However, in 1910 Bosville's grandson regained the chiefship of MacDonald of Sleat, although Lord MacDonald, descendant of the third lord, remained Chief of the Name, i.e. of Clan Donald. This unusual arrangement was confirmed by the Lyon Court in 1947.

MacDonald of Clan Ranald

MacDonald of Clan Ranald

The progenitor of the MacDonalds of Clan Ranald was Ranald, son of John, first Lord of the Isles. For about four centuries Clan Ranald's stronghold was the dramatic fortress of Eilean Tioram which commands Loch Moidart from its rocky island below Ardmolich. Ranald was the Lord of the Isles's eldest son, but the title went to his young half-brother whose mother was a daughter of the High Steward (later King Robert II), while Ranald received the MacRuari inheritance from his own mother (see MacDonald of the Isles).

Clanranald was a loyal vassal of the Lord of the Isles, and it was a member of his house, Donald Balloch, who attempted to rescue Alexander, Lord of the Isles, from imprisonment in the fortress of Tantallon.

The history of the clan in the 16th century was notably turbulent. Dugall, the sixth Clanranald, was killed by his own kin for unspecified 'cruelties', and replaced as chief by his uncle, Alastair. When Alastair died in 1530 he was succeeded by his illegitimate son, John of Moidart (*Ian Mùideatach*), who fell foul of the royal government and was imprisoned along with other chiefs during King James V's visit to the Hebrides in 1540. An attempt was then made by the Frasers to assert the claims to the chiefship of a candidate amenable to them, Ranald *Gallda* (the

Stranger), who was son of the fifth chief by a Fraser wife and had been fostered by the Frasers. He proved unacceptable to Clan Ranald, and the controversy eventually led to one of the bloodiest battles in Highland history, *Blar-na-Léine*, 'the battle of the Shirts' (1544).

The Frasers had approached with a powerful alliance led by the Earl of Huntly, but the Earl of Argyll, in his official capacity as the king's lieutenant in the west, intervened to prevent the battle. On their way home the Frasers unwisely separated from their allies and were ambushed by Clan Ranald on the

The castle of Tantallon on the coast of Lothian (near North Berwick) was built in the 14th century.

Glen Lochy, scene of one of the most famous battles in Highland history. Though it is remembered as *the* occasion when the combatants discarded their plaids, that practice must have been a common one. Wielding a claymore or a Lochaber axe was sufficiently demanding without contending with yards of potentially obstructive cloth.

north side of Loch Lochy. As it was a hot day both sides abandoned their plaids and fought in their shirts.

Legends have accrued around this famous conflict. It is said that over 300 Frasers were killed, including their chief, Lord Lovat, his son and Ranald *Gallda* himself, and that only five surivived – also that all eighty of the Fraser 'gentlemen' who fell left pregnant widows who later without exception gave birth to sons! Clan Ranald are said to have suffered even worse casualties, with a dozen or so survivors out of

500, but among them was John of Moydart. Though Huntly returned to exact revenge, John of Moydart survived that as well and lived to gain royal recognition as chief of Clan Ranald and, surprisingly, the friendship of the next Lord Lovat. He died in 1584. His grandson Sir Donald, tenth chief, was knighted by King James VI.

Powerful and prosperous, retaining possession of their lands while others were losing theirs, Clan Ranald played an important part in the internecine conflicts of the 17th and 18th centuries, their activities recorded, not without understandable bias, in the *Leabhar Dearg*, the Red Book of Clan Ranald.

John, eleventh Clanranald, supported Montrose in 1644-45. Some 700 MacDonalds of Clan Ranald fought at Killiecrankie and the thirteenth Clanranald

MacDonell of Glengarry

The MacDonells of Glengarry were a cadet branch of Clan Ranald, descended from Donald, son of the founder of Clan Ranald. Their castle at Invergarry overlooking Loch Oich is today a grim, intimidating ruin.

The Gaelic name of the chief, *Mac Mhic Alasdair*, derives from the fourth MacDonell of Glengarry.

The sixth Glengarry married Margaret, daughter of Sir Alexander MacDonald of Lochalsh, the senior surviving line of the lords of the Isles, and this gave his successors a questionable claim to the chiefship of Clan Donald. Since Margaret was not the sole heiress of Lochalsh, it also led to a long and bloody feud with the expanding power of the Mackenzies over that desirable property.

A number of Glengarry chiefs adopted a high-handed attitude to the world at large which was excessive even by Highland standards. One example was Angus, ninth Glengarry, created Lord MacDonell and Aros at the Restoration (1660), who attempted to dictate humiliating terms to the burgh of Inverness after two of his men had been killed in a brawl in the marketplace in 1665 (he did later obtain substantial damages).

Generally, Glengarry loyalties were the same as Clan Ranald's, and the future Lord MacDonell had earned his promotion by fighting with Montrose in 1644. His successor, Alasdair *Dubh* (he did not inherit the title as he came from another branch, MacDonell

MacDonell of Glengarry

was killed at Sheriffmuir (1715). He was succeeded by his brother, who died in exile at the Jacobite court. The future seventeenth chief was one of the first to rally to Prince Charles in 1745, and many members of Clan Ranald played prominent roles in the ensuing campaign.

The estates were forfeited after Culloden but later restored. Sadly, Clan Ranald's luck ran out when the seventeenth chief's grandson succeeded in 1794. This wretched fellow preferred the frivolity of Regency society in London and Brighton and managed to squander his vast resources (rents alone brought him the enormous sum of £25,000 a year) to such an extent that practically all the Clan Ranald territories were sold out to sheep-raising landlords. The clan disintegrated.

of Scotus), fought for King James VII/II in 1688-89 and carried the royal standard at Sheriffmuir.

According to General Wade, in 1716 Glengarry could put 500 men in the field, but rather more than that were present among Prince Charles's forces in 1745, under the chief's son Angus Òg. Unfortunately, Angus was killed when the musket of a MacDonald of Clan Ranald went off while being cleaned – the unfortunate perpetrator being also killed according to the rough Old Testament precepts accepted in the Highlands. Dispirited by the loss of their leader, many Glengarry men deserted (the incident did not improve the morale of Clan Ranald either) though there remained 500 of them in the MacDonell regiment at Culloden under the command of the 18-year-old younger son of the chief, who himself took no part in the fighting though he was afterwards imprisoned along with his son.

It is said, though not in front of a MacDonell, that the thirteenth chief subsequently changed sides, acting as a spy for the government among the Jacobites in France.

In the 1790s the Glengarry Highlanders, mostly remnants of a company of militia raised to ease their poverty, received assistance to emigrate to Canada, where they founded Glengarry, Ontario, each family naming their homestead after their old farm in Glengarry. In the war of 1812 with the United States, they were summoned by the fiery cross to combat an American raid. The Glengarry immigrants were perhaps the most influential in rooting the idea of clanship in Canada, where it has prospered to this day.

The headstrong behaviour noted in an earlier chief was also unfortunately evident in the notorious fifteenth chief, the friend of Scott and subject of

Above: A frosty morning in Glen Garry. But the frost never nipped the MacDonells as fiercely as did changing economic circumstances.
Above right: A detail from Raeburn's portrait of the combative Colonel Alasdair MacDonell of Glengarry.

Raeburn, Colonel Alasdair MacDonell of Glengarry. At a time when his clansmen were close to economic extinction he strutted about with a 'tail' of attendants in the manner of a Highland chief of an earlier and very different period. This 'tiresome poseur', as a recent historian of the Highlands described him, put every possible obstacle in the way of Telford's Caledonian Canal project in spite of receiving enormous compensation for the very small part of his estates through which it ran, and also carried on an endless argument over precedence with Clanranald.

His successor, beset by debts and worried by evictions, sold out and emigrated to the Antipodes.

MacDonell of Keppoch

The MacDonells of Keppoch were descended from Alastair *Carrach* (the Warty) third son of John, first Lord of the Isles, who was a grandson of King Robert II. Their lands were on the mainland, in Lochaber, and they were sometimes known as Clan Ranald of Lochaber. Their history is decidedly eventful.

Alastair *Carrach* was responsible for the burning of Elgin, one of the most plundered cities of the north, in 1402, only 12 years after the notorious assault of the Wolf of Badenoch. Alastair *Carrach* spared the

The remains of Elgin cathedral today. After the collapse of the tower in 1711 it was allowed to disintegrate, but the ruins were preserved by a local cobbler, John Shanks.

cathedral, or what the Wolf had left of it, in memory of which act of forbearance the Little Cross was erected in Elgin. In 1411 the chief fought at 'Red' Harlaw with his brother, Donald of the Isles. For his part in the rebellion led by Donald Balloch on behalf of the imprisoned third Lord of the Isles he was forfeited and some of his lands in Lochaber given to the Mackenzies, leading to a rancorous feud. His son Angus, second MacDonell of Keppoch, lost the lordship of Lochaber, and John, fourth chief (or captain, the older name preferred by many of Clan Donald) was deposed because he had agreed to hand over a clansman to the Mackintosh. He was succeeded by a cousin, Donald *Glas*, who built the old castle of Keppoch. His son Ranald, who fought in the battle of the Shirts with the MacDonalds of Clan Ranald, was executed as a rebel in 1547 along with Cameron of Lochiel by the Earl of Huntly. The ninth MacDonell of Keppoch, also Ranald, spent most of his life as an outlaw. His son, tenth chief, was father of the ancestor of the Canadian line of MacDonells, *Seigneurs de Rigaud*, in Quebec.

The murder of Alastair, twelfth chief, in 1663 is commemorated at 'the Well of the Heads' near Invergarry. The heads of seven of his murderers were washed by the clan bard Iain *Lom* MacDonell and presented to Glengarry, who had failed to respond with the requisite spirit of vengeance (exacted later by MacDonald of Sleat). The sculpture commemorating the event was erected in the 19th century by Colonel Alasdair MacDonell of Glengarry.

The last clan battle in the Highlands was fought between MacDonell of Keppoch and Mackintosh of Mackintosh in 1688. The Mackintosh had obtained what Highland chiefs sometimes scornfully called a 'sheepskin charter' for the lands of Glenroy. The affronted MacDonells met the Mackintoshes in a pitched battle in Lochaber, defeated them, and captured Mackintosh himself, who was forced to surrender his claim to Glenroy.

However, times had changed, and MacDonell's lands were subsequently ravaged by government troops with Mackintosh assistance. The fifteenth chief, known as 'Coll of the Cows', held on to his lands by the sword for 40 years, evading all attempts to capture him. Together with his son Alexander, he fought for the Jacobites at Sheriffmuir.

The MacDonells of Keppoch provided many heroes in the Jacobite risings of the 18th century. Though an elderly man by 1745, the sixteenth chief was one of the first to join Prince Charles. He intercepted the government force at Highbridge on their way to the gathering of the clans at Glenfinnan, where the prince raised his standard, and thus initiated the first action of the Forty-five. Keppoch had only 200 men with him at Culloden and like many others, including Lord George Murray, he doubted the wisdom of giving battle at that time and place (he was practically the only Highland chief with military experience, having fought in France). He fell during the retreat and was left for dead, but his son Angus *Bàn* found him and, calling some of his men, carried the old chief in his plaid to a nearby bothy, where he breathed his last. The estates of Keppoch were subsequently forfeited. The last chief in the direct line from Colonel Alexander MacDonell died in 1889.

MacDonald of Glencoe

The MacDonalds came to Glencoe when a brother of John, first Lord of the Isles, settled in Lochaber in the early 14th century. His name was Iain *Abrach*, and the chiefs of the MacDonalds of Glencoe were subsequently known as MacIain. By the 17th century they were a small, more or less independent clan, who were notorious cattle thieves. Despite the proximity of the powerful and perhaps understandably hostile Campbell of Glenorchy, they were survivors, their men renowned for brawn, and secure in their natural fortress of Glencoe.

They are, of course, chiefly remembered for the disaster that overtook them on the night of 12-13 February 1692.

After the resistance in the Highlands following the flight of King James VII/II and the accession of William III and Mary II, a free pardon was promised to all chiefs who took an oath of submission to the Crown before 1 January 1692. The elderly MacIain MacDonald set off in reasonable time to perform this, but he was delayed by snowstorms and then found when he got to Fort William that he would have to go on to Inveraray. As a result he was six days late, but nobody appeared troubled by this and he returned home feeling perfectly secure. He was not even

The rugged hills south of Glencoe, heartland of the MacDonalds of Glencoe.

MacDonald of Glencoe

campaign and on other occasions, appears to have had no idea of what was afoot and later condemned the massacre.

The intense unpopularity of the Campbells in many parts of the Highlands was certainly exacerbated (there are still old men who will spit on the floor at the mention of the name Campbell, though perhaps only in front of tourists), and they were unjustly blamed for the deed itself. The troops were commanded by Campbell of Glenlyon (a minor sept), who was in fact related to MacIain by marriage. His men came from Argyll's regiment but that does not mean they were Campbells; most apparently had other names.

The order to carry out the massacre was signed by Campbell's superior officer, Major Duncanson, and given only a few hours in advance. Moreover, it seems not to have been carried out with great efficiency. So many escaped chiefly because the additional troops (not Campbells) assigned to block the glen on the night did not arrive in time (snowstorms again). But some of Campbell of Glenlyon's men dropped hints to their hosts, and others made sure their approach was noisy enough to give the victims a chance of escape.

A government inquiry was later held into the affair but not surprisingly it failed to probe too deeply. Stair was removed as Secretary of State but later received an earldom. The MacDonalds of Glencoe were not exterminated but survived to fight in MacDonell of Keppoch's regiment in the Forty-five.

suspicous when a company of troops was billeted on him at the end of the month.

After a fortnight's amicable residence the soldiers attacked their hosts in the middle of the night. MacIain was shot dead in his bed and his wife thrown naked into the snow where she died hours later. Altogether thirty-eight men, women and children were killed, and probably more died in the snow. The remainder, fewer than 150 in all, escaped up the glen.

As the orders had been to massacre the entire clan, the operation cannot be called successful. Moreover, it gave rise to a feeling of horror and revulsion not only in the Highlands but throughout the British Isles and even in Europe.

Such a massacre was not unique in Scottish history; it was not even particularly uncommon. What made this incident so shocking was that it happened at a date when clan wars and feuds had virtually disappeared, that it was perpetrated not by a rival clan but by the forces of the government under orders approved at the highest level, and that it was carried out in such a particularly treacherous manner. Who was responsible?

The chief villain was undoubtedly the Master of Stair, Lord Advocate and William and Mary's Secretary of State. He wrote down quite plainly the intention 'to extirpate that set of thieves', adding, 'Let it be secret and sudden'. (Stair wished to annihilate the MacDonells of Glengarry as well but was discouraged by the formidable defences of Invergarry Castle.) King William signed the order and although he may not have understood exactly what was intended, he cannot be excused on that account. His public denial of all foreknowledge was clearly a plain falsehood. Campbell of Glenorchy, first Earl of Breadalbane, who had suffered from the activities of the MacDonalds of Glencoe during Montrose's

MacDonald of Kingsburgh

This family was not a clan, scarcely even a sept of Clan Donald, but it achieved fame at the time of the last Jacobite rising. The MacDonald of Kingsburgh tartan is said to be copied from a waistcoat given to Prince Charles during his flight after Culloden by Alexander MacDonald of Kingsburgh.

When Prince Charles arrived in Scotland he no doubt expected the great chiefs of Skye, MacDonald of Sleat and MacLeod of MacLeod, to rally to his banner. But, influenced by Forbes of Culloden (who had once done him a good turn in suppressing awkward facts about a group of alleged 'emigrants', tenants of Sleat, who were apparently forced on to the ship after being evicted), Sir Alexander of Sleat held aloof, as did MacLeod. Nevertheless it was to Skye that the prince came during his dramatic flight after the final defeat.

While there may be doubts about the chief, his wife, Lady Margaret (a daughter of the Earl of Eglinton) was a very popular figure in Skye, though not a fervent Jacobite (nor were the others involved in this romantic episode).

One of Sir Alexander's tacksmen or lessees was his relative Hugh MacDonald of Armadale, whose wife was connected through an earlier marriage with the MacDonalds of Clan Ranald. Her daughter by this marriage was Flora MacDonald (1722-90), who was to marry (in 1750) Allen MacDonald of Kingsburgh. Allen's father, Alexander of Kingsburgh, was factor to MacDonald of Sleat.

In 1746, when the prince was wandering westward, Hugh of Armadale was in Hanoverian service in South Uist in the Outer Hebrides, where Flora was able to visit him without arousing suspicion. The

MacDonald of Kingsburgh

her Irish maidservant, 'Betty Burke'. If this tale were fiction, one would scoff at such unlikely plotting, but 'Betty Burke' arrived safely and was conducted to Sleat, where at that moment Hanoverian soldiers were quartered. Lady Margaret and the laird's factor were drawn into the business, and the prince spent the night at Kingsburgh's house. A great many other people must have known what was going on by the time Prince Charles said goodbye to Flora at Portree, but no one talked.

Both Flora and Alexander of Kingsburgh were imprisoned after their activities had been uncovered, but both were fairly soon released. Flora married Alexander of Kingsburgh's son Allen and they later emigrated to North America. Allen fought for the government in the American War of Independence and was taken prisoner. Flora returned to the Hebrides in 1779 (her husband following later) but the Kingsburgh property had gone and they were poor. Fortunately they had five sons, one of whom became a successful military engineer.

MacDougall

The MacDougalls are an example of a race that once held great, indeed royal, authority who survived the vicissitudes of the early modern period, although in reduced circumstances, and still hold a small part of their ancient lands in Lorne.

The MacDougalls were senior to Clan Donald, since their progenitor Dugall was son of Somerled by the daughter of the Norse King Olaf of Man, who held

Flora MacDonald, a somewhat enigmatic heroine in spite of vivid romantic writings. The portrait, undated, is by Richard Wilson and is in the Scottish National Portrait Gallery.

prince arrived there in due course, but the trail was getting hot and he was warned by Hugh, despite the latter's official allegiance, that the island was no longer safe. It was decided by a family conference that he should travel with Flora to Skye, disguised as

Argyll and Lorne, Mull, Jura and other Hebridean islands. He was the senior sub-king of the Isles under the king of Norway. His son was known as Duncan 'of Argyll' and that name was used by his immediate descendants.

The MacDougalls were a considerable sea power, with great fortresses on several islands. Their main bases, however, were Dunstaffnage, which later passed to the Campbells, and Dunollie Castle, which

Left: MacDougall

Below: Gylen Castle on Kerrera not far from Oban, 'a tall grey tower perched on a cliff above a bay rude with rocks and cliffs'.

still overlooks Oban Bay and still belongs to the MacDougall chief. Sir Iain Moncreiffe pointed out its similarity in design to the castle of Bergen in Norway.

The son of Duncan, Ewen of Argyll, Lord of Lorne and third chief, was faced with a difficult decision in 1263 when King Haakon of Norway made his cruise through the Western Isles in an attempt to re-establish Norwegian sovereignty. He decided to support Alexander III, King of Scots, but first requested permission from his Norwegian overlord and formally surrendered the lands he held of him. Such feudal gallantry was not very common, but it proved wise, since Haakon was repulsed at Largs and the MacDougall King of Argyll remained in full possession.

Events during the wars of independence brought changes from which the MacDougalls were never to recover. Alasdair of Argyll, Lord of Lorne and fourth MacDougall chief, married an aunt of the Red Comyn, who was killed by Bruce in the church at Dumfries in 1306. As a result the MacDougalls were involved in the blood feud between the Comyns and Bruce, and became Bruce's most dangerous opponents. At one moment they almost captured him in the Pass of Brander: he escaped but left the MacDougalls in possession of his cloak pin, 'the Brooch of Lorne'. Later, however, the MacDougalls were defeated, Dunstaffnage captured, and the estates forfeited.

The sixth chief partially retrieved the position. He married a granddaughter of Bruce and regained the lordship of Lorne from King David II. He had no sons and the lordship passed to the Stewarts through the marriage of his daughters to two Stewart brothers. The chiefship passed to his cousin Iain, son of Duncan, the fourth chief's brother, who had taken the opposite side in the wars of independence and had gained Dunollie Castle as a result of his support for Bruce. In 1451 the Stewart Lord of Lorne confirmed the then MacDougall chief (the first, incidentally, to be known as MacDougall) in the possession of lands around Oban and the island of Kerrera in the Firth of Lorne.

The MacDougalls did not lose hope of regaining their former lands, and for a brief period following the attainder and execution (in 1686) of the Earl of Argyll, it looked as though they might succeed. However, the Campbells were soon back in favour and the MacDougalls had to remain content with Dunollie. They nearly lost that during the Jacobite rising of 1715, when the twenty-first chief fought with the Jacobites while his wife successfully defended the castle against siege. It had undergone an earlier siege in 1647 when, as in 1715, the estates were temporarily forfeited.

MacDuff

MacDuff

In the days before the clan system had come into recognisable existence the MacDuff earls of Fife were the greatest family in Scotland. They represented the ancient Celtic royal house to which the MacBeth and Lady MacBeth known chiefly through Shakespeare's play both belonged. The MacDuff of that play, however, who assists Malcolm (IV) to defeat MacBeth, is fictional, though something similar may well have happened.

The wife of King Malcolm III (*Ceann Mór*) was an English princess. They had five sons, four of whom became kings of Scots in their turn. Strangely enough, the one who did not was the eldest, although the reasons why he was passed over are no longer apparent. His name, no doubt chosen by his English mother, was Aethelred. He is the first historically documented Earl of Fife and was also hereditary Abbot of Dunkeld (perhaps this office barred him from the throne). His wife was a granddaughter of Queen Gruoch (i.e. Lady MacBeth) and sister of the King of Moray (Malcolm's authority had not advanced into that region).

So far as is known Aethelred, or *Aedh* as he was called in Gaelic, caused no trouble, though the men of Moray, i.e., more or less Clan MacDuff, rose on several occasions in attempts to gain the throne for his son before they finally accepted the status quo.

The earls of Fife, first subjects of the king, enjoyed particular privileges known as the Law of Clan

MacDuff. Chief of these was the right to enthrone the king of Scots on the Stone of Scone at his coronation. They also included the right to lead the vanguard in battle (a dubious honour, we 20th-century cowards might suppose), and the right to be absolved from a charge of homicide by taking sanctuary at the Cross of MacDuff (north of Newburgh) and paying a fixed fine. This extended to fairly remote kindred.

The first chiefs of Clan MacDuff of whom anything is known for certain were successive earls of Fife named Constantine and Gillemichael MacDuff, who lived in the early 12th century. They were probably brothers, and possibly grandsons of Aethelred (their father having predeceased their grandfather).

The centre of MacDuff power was the kingdom of Fife, but they also held extensive lands in the north-east and in the Lowlands, south of the Forth. A number of clans claim descent from them and there are many families named Duff or MacDuff who may have originated in some branch of the ancient royal house. The name MacDuff was not generally used as a surname, and there is no proof that the modern earls and (since 1889) dukes of Fife were related to the old Celtic earls, whose line came to an end in the 14th century. The earls of Wemyss were recognised in the 18th century as representing the ancient line, with reasonably authenticated descent from Gillemichael MacDuff, the 12th-century Earl of Fife. The Wemyss family is still resident in what used to be known as 'Wemysshire' in Fife because of its former size.

MacEwen

MacEwen

Since the Clan MacEwen was 'broken' in the 15th century, little is known of its history. In the records of the parish of Kilfinnan, Argyll, an entry from the end of the 18th century remarks on the remains of a building on a rocky promontory of Loch Fyne below the church which was called 'MacEwen's Castle', after a MacEwen who was the chief of a clan and held a district called Otter, which means a spit of land. It is clear that practically all memory of the MacEwens in their homeland had been lost by this time.

According to a 15th-century genealogy the MacEwens were connected with the MacNeills and MacLachlans as member of Siol Gillevray, all of them being neighbours in Cowal and allegedly sharing a common ancestor. They seem to have been fairly numerous. The name is fairly common today although there are no certain links between contemporary MacEwen (or Ewing and other possible variants) families and the old Clan MacEwen of Otter.

The first recorded chief of the clan was Ewen of Otter, probably the source of the patronymic, who held land on Loch Fyne in the early 13th century. About a century later Gillespie was the fifth chief from Ewen, and the names of his successors are known down to Swene, ninth and last chief.

The manner in which he lost the clan territory suggests that he was a victim of the Campbell facility in exploiting the law to their own benefit and the detriment of their simpler neighbours. In 1432 Swene granted land to Sir Duncan Campbell of Lochow and surrendered the barony of Otter to King James I. He received it back from the king but with remainder to Campbell's heir. Thus the MacEwen chief signed away his territory to the Campbells, who took over on Swene's death. In 1493 the grant of the lands to the second Earl of Argyll was confirmed by royal charter.

What happened to the MacEwens? Probably a large proportion of them became followers of the Campbells. The hereditary bards of Campbell of Argyll and Campbell of Glenorchy were MacEwens, and in 1602 a number of them were listed as vassals of the earl of Argyll, who was to be responsible for their good behaviour. Some apparently followed the MacLachlans, their kin; others scattered across the Highlands and, eventually, the Lowlands: groups of MacEwens were later to be found in Dumbarton and Galloway, Loch Tayside, Comrie and Crieff.

The name often appears in criminal records, a sadly inevitable result of the loss of a clan's territory. According to General Wade, 150 MacEwens crossed to the mainland from Skye to take part in the Fifteen, but whether these men were connected with the MacEwens of Otter it is impossible to say.

MacFarlane

MacFarlane

The soft glens and lochs of the Trossachs on a summer day present a lovely and peaceful scene, as millions of visitors would testify, but things were not always so: 'a land of savage hills, swept by savage rains, peopled by savage sheep, tended by savage people', said Burns. The savage sheep sound a little unlikely, but the people – certainly.

Clan MacFarlane is well documented. They were a branch of the family of the old Celtic earls of Lennox, descended from Gilchrist, younger brother of Earl Malduin (a common name in the ancient royal house of Munster, from which the earls of Lennox were probably descended). Gilchrist received from his brother the lands of Arrochar, north of Loch Long and west of Loch Lomond, territory expanded through

'Towards the north end of [Loch Lomond] the scene becomes very different . . . bold and rugged mountains [whose] bare and serrated tops [are] often enveloped in mist and clouds, and for a great part of the year covered with snow' – MacFarlane country.

marriage in the 14th century. The clan name was derived from *Pàrlan* (Bartholomew), the descendant of Gilchrist and accounted fourth chief. The seventh chief's possession of Arrochar was confirmed by a charter of 1420. A predecessor, Malduin, third chief, was a supporter of Bruce during the wars of independence. Later chiefs were killed at Flodden (1513) and Pinkie (1547).

The Lennox earls came to an end when the last of them, Duncan, was executed in grisly circumstances by the vengeful King James I in 1425. The MacFarlane chief, as senior male descendant, claimed to be his heir, but the earldom was subsequently conferred on Sir John Stewart of Darnley, descended from a daughter of Earl Duncan. This might have caused serious trouble, but it was averted by the marriage of Andrew MacFarlane of Arrochar to the Stewart Earl's daughter. Thereafter, the MacFarlanes remained loyal subjects of the Stewarts.

The murder of Mary Queen of Scots' husband (and cousin) Lord Darnley (as he is generally known today) in 1567 turned the MacFarlanes against the queen, as their first loyalty was to the Earl of Lennox, Darnley's father. Moreover, they had become Protestants. Their action against her at Langside, after she had escaped from captivity in Loch Leven Castle, is said to have been decisive in the final defeat of that unfortunate lady.

The MacFarlanes were a notably warlike clan, frequently raiding their neighbours by the light of 'MacFarlane's lantern', i.e. the moon. Their pipe tune is appropriately called 'Lifting the Cattle'. They were involved in ferocious feuds at various times with the Buchanans, Colquhouns and other neighbours on Loch Lomond. (The gruesome revenge taken on a Colquhoun chief who had seduced MacFarlane's wife is mentioned under Colquhoun.) In 1594 some MacFarlanes were listed among the 'broken' clans.

Walter MacFarlane of MacFarlane, sixteenth chief, fought under Montrose during the civil war and was subsequently fined by the Covenanters. His castle of Inveruglas, a small island in Loch Lomond whose remnants are overlooked by the modern power station, was twice besieged by Cromwellian forces and on the second occasion destroyed by fire. The chief moved to a house at Arrochar (later rebuilt).

The twentieth chief, also Walter (died 1767), was a famous antiquary, one of the few people before the 19th century who made a serious effort to preserve the Scottish heritage by collecting and transcribing documents. He was a friend of Boswell, who recorded that General Wade, the famous builder of roads in the Highlands after the Fifteen, had addressed the chief as 'Mr MacFarlane' since, in English custom, plain 'MacFarlane' would have been discourteously

informal. The chief was incensed. 'Mr MacFarlane', he said, 'may with equal propriety be said to many; but I, and I only, am MacFarlane.' He was succeeded by his brother William, who was an Edinburgh doctor.

The arrival of a black swan among the MacFarlane's white swans was a grim omen, since that had been forecast as presaging the loss of Arrochar. Not long afterwards the twenty-first chief was forced to sell the lands. The twenty-fifth chief, who died in 1886, was the last of his line.

MacGillivray

The MacGillivrays are of ancient origin and according to one account sat on the council of the lord of the Isles. Mull is usually suggested as their original homeland, but at some point in the 13th century, probably as a result of King Alexander II's campaigns in Argyll, they split up. Some remained in the west, becoming followers of MacLean of Duart, but in about 1268 protection was sought from the Mackintosh chiefs on behalf of his people by Gillevray, the presumed progenitor of Clan MacGillivray (that the progenitor was Gillebride, or Gillivray, the father of

The MacGillivray memorial stone at the Well of the Dead on the field of Culloden marks the spot where the MacGillivray chief died.

MacGillivray

as many. When he fell, with many wounds, he managed to drag himself to a well, where he died as he drank. A stone marks the spot today.

Times were hard after Culloden and Alexander's successor was forced to enlist in the army. He died in 1783 and was succeeded by his son, John Lachlan, chief for nearly 70 years, who when he died bequeathed his capital and lands to his tenants. A fine gesture, but after numerous legal disputes, the estates were broken up.

MacGregor

Somerled, seems rather far-fetched). There was no connection by blood so far as we know, the MacGillivrays and the Mackintoshes being of different racial origin, and the association seems to be an early example of a small, independent clan joining what was to become the great confederation of Clan Chattan. During the 15th century the MacGillivrays became established in what was to be their home for four centuries, Dunmaglas in Strathnairn. Possibly the first MacGillivray of Dunmaglas (the patronymic was not yet in use) was one Iain *Ciar* (the Brown), mentioned in Mackintosh documents of the 15th century.

They prospered and increased, forming many cadet branches and becoming one of the major constituents of Clan Chattan. Three MacGillivrays signed the Clan Chattan bonds of union in the early 17th century, when the clan was probably at its height. The name crops up frequently in the accounts of the many disputes in which Clan Chattan was involved, and also, more pleasantly, in unlikely tales of ladies kidnapped by fairies and retrieved by magic.

The MacGillivrays were prominent in the Jacobite risings of the 18th century. In 1715 the two sons of the current chief were officers in the Clan Chattan regiment, and in Prince Charles's rising Clan Chattan was led by Alexander MacGillivray of Dunmaglas, appointed to the command (consisting mainly of Mackintoshes, Farquharsons and MacBeans, besides MacGillivrays) in the absence of the Mackintosh, who had remained loyal to his commission in government service. At Culloden they made a famous charge which all but annihilated Cumberland's left wing before they were pushed back, tearing up stones from the heather to hurl at the enemy. Their casualties were frightful. Iain *Mór* MacGillivray killed twelve men before he died, the red-haired Dunmaglas about

The motto of the MacGregors is translated 'Royal is my blood', and the original Gregor is said to have been the brother or son of King Kenneth MacAlpin. More probably the patronymic derives from an early 14th-century chief, but no one would dispute that the MacGregors were the principal members of *Sìol Ailpein*.

Their original home was Glenorchy and adjacent glens, and it was the loss of this land that led to their dreadful persecution in the 17th and 18th centuries. There is no doubt that the MacGregors were violent and troublesome (so, inevitably, were other landless clans), but it would be hard to prove that they were any worse than others, at least until circumstances forced them into a life of outlawry.

The original chiefly line descended from Iain, the first known chief, and ended when his descendant died leaving only daughters. As a result of their marriages the Campbells established a foothold in the

MacGregor

MacGregor lands in the early 14th century, which by one means or another they were able gradually to extend.

The new line of MacGregor chiefs descended from a younger son of Iain and included Gregor 'of the Golden Bridles', from whom the clan is thought to have taken its name. Unwilling to submit to another chief, the MacGregors held on to their lands by the sword for as long as possible. The Campbells, with or without justification, continued to foment trouble by attempting to undermine the authority of the MacGregor chiefs (their feudal tenants) among their clansmen, and in 1519 they set up their own nominee as overall Chief of MacGregor. He was a junior chieftain who had married Campbell of Glenorchy's daughter (despite having begun his courtship by raping her). However, the landless MacGregors, 'the children of the mist' (a name which, it has been waspishly remarked, might equally be translated as 'the fog folk') continued their lawless existence, in which even the imposed chief became involved, and several commissions of fire and sword were issued to neighbouring chiefs, including the much-injured Colquhoun of Luss. The latter feud culminated in the battle of Glenfruin, when the Colquhouns were massacred in large numbers.

King James VI, furious at this latest example of the failure of his policy of pacification in the Highlands, then issued the Privy Council edict in which Clan Gregor was proscribed (it was practically his last act before leaving for London in 1603). This made it illegal even to bear the name MacGregor, and the

clansmen were compelled to adopt pseudonyms (often, ironically, Campbell) to the confusion of later genealogists. They were not allowed to carry weapons, except a blunt-ended knife to cut their meat, and no more than four were allowed to gather in the same place. The chief and a number of leading clansmen were executed in Edinburgh, and by a new commission issued to Argyll against them in 1611 the women were to be branded in the face with a red-hot key.

Such laws could not be, and were not, effectively enforced, but they remained current, with brief intervals, until 1774. At times MacGregors were hunted down with bloodhounds, though at other times they were largely left alone.

Many of the Highlanders were sympathetic to them, notably the Grants and the Mackenzies, and were prepared to aid and shelter them even at considerable risk to themselves. At one time a merger was discussed between MacGregors and Grants, though it foundered on the question of the chiefship. Huge fines were levied against those who succoured the MacGregors, the proceeds going straight into Argyll's coffers.

MacGregors fought with Montrose for Charles I and for his son at Worcester (1651), and as a result the proscription of the clan was lifted at the Restoration (1660), but it was reimposed after the rebellions against William III. Some MacGregors fought in the Jacobite risings of 1715 and 1745 and one of the Seven Men of Glenmoriston, the outlaws who sheltered the prince in 1746, was named Gregor MacGregor.

The laws against the MacGregors were finally lifted in 1774, and when the Honours of Scotland were paraded before George IV in Edinburgh in 1822 the MacGregors held a place in the guard of honour.

Sir David Wilkie's painting of George IV's arrival at Holyrood in 1822, an event marking the start of a tartan extravaganza and a quasi-Celtic revival in which the kilt was accepted as Scottish national costume.

MacGregor (Rob Roy)

The tartan known as Rob Roy is the oldest of the MacGregor tartans and its simple sett of red and black dice was no doubt worn in the 18th century, though whether by Rob Roy himself it is impossible to say.

Rob Roy, the famous outlaw romanticised by Sir Walter Scott, was born in 1671. His father was Donald MacGregor, fifteenth chief of the 'children of the mist', and his mother was a Campbell. At that time the penal laws against the MacGregors had been temporarily lifted, following the Restoration of Charles II and the disgrace and execution of the MacGregors' enemy, the Marquess of Argyll. Nevertheless Rob Roy, an exceedingly powerful young man although not tall, probably learned the MacGregor techniques of lifting cattle and extracting blackmail. However until he fell out with the Duke of Montrose he seems to have been a law-abiding figure.

In 1693, the year in which the penal acts were renewed, or thereabouts, Rob Roy, whose father had led the MacGregors in the Jacobite forces in 1689, became acting head of the clan, probably by sheer force of character. He had to go into hiding in 1712, adopting his mother's maiden name of Campbell, to avoid arrest on a charge of defrauding Montrose. This charge seems to have been false, at least in a moral if not strictly legal sense, and Rob Roy nursed his resentment.

In the Jacobite rising of 1715 he led a collection of Buchanans and others in the Jacobite cause and captured Falkland Palace in an independent action. Thereafter he was mainly engaged in his depredations against Montrose and those who could be considered his allies. Stories of his exploits are numerous, and no doubt a few of them are more or less true. He was captured twice, but effected a dramatic escape, and eventually made some sort of truce with Montrose through the mediation of Argyll, who, of course, was no friend to Montrose and may well have assisted Rob Roy on certain occasions. In 1722 he submitted to General Wade, commander in Scotland. In his later years he lived quietly at Balquhidder, adopting Roman Catholicism and dying peacefully in 1734, practically a national hero. He had five sons, at least three of whom were convicted of treason after the Forty-five, though only one was executed.

Scott's Rob Roy may be a highly romanticised figure. Nevertheless, the man was romantic enough in actuality, the hero of excellent yarns of derring-do, an outlaw and brigand who was also a man of fine sensibilities, excellent education and a considerable musician.

There are almost as many pictures of Rob Roy as there are stories, but authenticity in both cases is sometimes hard to establish. As with other Highland characters and incidents, history is for ever coloured by the romantic imagination of Sir Walter Scott.

MacGregor (Rob Roy)

MacInnes

One of the few things that can be said with reasonable certainty about Clan MacInnes is that they had no connection with the Inneses of the north-east. We can also be sure that they were of ancient Celtic origin; their ancestors were probably among the earliest settlers of Dalriada (the original kingdom of the Scots

MacInnes

Another group was to be found on the Jacobite side in the 18th century. They were followers of the Stewarts of Ardshiel and are assumed to have split away from the Kinlochaline branch in about the 15th century. They were probably among the force of 300 'men of Appin', led by Stewart of Ardshiel (standing in for the Appin chief, who was a child) at the battle of Culloden.

MacIntyre

from Ireland). They were probably members of Siol Gillebride, or Gillevray, and a 17th-century MacDonald historian wrote that in the 12th century Morvern (the peninsula bounded by Loch Sunart and Loch Linnhe) was inhabited mainly by MacInneses and MacGillivrays 'who are the same'. A traditional tale has the MacInneses being congratulated and promised future favours for their good service by the lord of the Isles or, in one version, by King Somerled himself. He is said to have addressed them as *Mac Aonghais*, i.e. son of Angus, their Gaelic name, and their chief as Kinlochaline, the castle of which the MacInneses were apparently hereditary constables. A MacInnes was still in command, it seems, when the castle, today a picturesque ruin, was beseiged by Alasdair MacColla, the leader of Montrose's Irish MacDonalds, in 1645.

The clan was probably dislocated by the campaign of King Alexander II in Argyll in the 13th century, when they are said to have been among the worst hit. Or the murder of a MacInnes chief in the late 14th century may have been a decisive factor. At any rate, at that time or later the clan came under Campbell protection. They were first associated with the Campbells of Craignish, and in the conflicts of the 17th century they followed the Marquess of Argyll, supporting the Covenanters, while in the Jacobite risings they chose to adhere to the Hanoverian party.

However, this appears to have been true of only one part of *Clann Aonghais*. A family of hereditary bowmen to the chief of the Mackinnons were named MacInnes, said to have been descended from Neil *a' Bhogha*, who is claimed as an ancestor by the MacInneses of Rickersby. Whether this family was connected with the MacInneses of Kinlochaline is, however, not certain.

MacIntyre is perhaps more correctly spelt Macintyre. The Gaelic name *Mac an t-Saoir* means 'the Carpenter', and thus was probably applied to others not connected with the clan, which was settled in Glenoe, near Bonawe on Loch Etive, in the 14th century.

The MacIntyres were closely associated with the MacDonalds, though their war cry 'Cruachan!' is the same as the Campbells', and according to one unlikely tale their ancestor was actually a MacDonald who acquired his nickname 'the Carpenter' when he cut off his thumb to plug a leak in his boat so that he might

MacIntyre and Glenorchy

wave his arms to summon help. Alternatively, it has been suggested that the name came from a MacDonald who held lands in Kintyre.

Another, perhaps older tradition, says that the MacIntyres came to Lorne from the Hebrides in a galley, bringing with them a white cow, the significance of which is now obscure.

The MacIntyres were notable for other crafts besides carpentry. They were hereditary foresters to

The magnificent mountains of northern Argyll, between Loch Awe and Loch Etive, are dominated by the great summit of Ben Cruachan, which is associated with the MacIntyres and the Campbells.

the Stewart lords of Lorne and later to the Campbells. They were also hereditary pipers to the Mackenzies and produced one of the most famous Gaelic bards of the 18th century, Duncan *Bàn* MacIntyre (1724-1812), born in Glenorchy where he was a Campbell forester. His works were published in Edinburgh in his lifetime, and there is a monument to him there in Greyfriars churchyard.

There was once a Black Book of Glenoe which would have been informative on MacIntyre genealogy, but it is lost, and the Glenoe chiefs are generally numbered from Duncan, who died in 1695, although there were many generations before him. His descendant Captain Donald MacIntyre died in London in 1808. The lands of Glenoe had been lost shortly before this.

Things had never been the same since the MacIntyres' landlord, Campbell of Glenorchy (Breadalbane), had commuted their rent of a snowball to a cash payment.

With the loss of the clan territory a large number of

the MacIntyres of Glenoe emigrated to the United States, the chiefship going with them.

There were also MacIntyres in Clan Chattan, and a sept of the Glenoe clan at *Camus na h-Eiridh*, which traces its descent from Duncan in the 17th century, still exists (the 16th chieftain being Alastair Macintyre, the Scottish broadcaster).

Mackay

The Mackays, who for many centuries held a large dominion in the north-west corner of the Scottish mainland centred on Strathnaver, were called *Clann Aoidh*, or alternatively Clan Morgan (*Morgund*). They claimed descent from the old royal house of MacEth, mormaers (earls) of Moray. It has been said that 'Morgan' was a son of King Magnus of the Northern Isles and that *Aodh* (Hugh) was his grandson, but this seems unlikely.

Assuming the Mackays did originate in Moray, they probably reached Strathnaver when King Malcolm IV drove them 'beyond the Scottish mountains' in the 12th century. Clearly they prospered there. It was said that in 1427 the chief of Mackay, Angus

Dubh (died 1429), could command 4,000 fighting men.

The Mackays are noted both for the martial qualities of their men and the beauty and intelligence of their women. The historian of the chiefs of Mackays, Ian Grimble, has pointed out that up to the 17th century every traceable marriage of a Mackay chief was with a member of the old Celtic aristocracy. The most notable of these marriages was that of Angus *Dubh* to a daughter of Donald, second Lord of the Isles. He had possibly met her while he was the lord's prisoner, for he had opposed Donald's attempt to gain the earldom of Ross which culminated in the famous battle of 'Red' Harlaw (1411).

In 1626 Donald, chief of Mackay, created Lord Reay in 1628, took a regiment of 3,000 men to fight on the Protestant side in the Thirty Years' War, a memorable episode commemorated in well-known prints of 1631 which provide useful evidence of Highland dress at that time (vast plaids and floppy bonnets), and by an account of the expedition which was published in 1637.

Another famous warrior was Hugh Mackay of the cadet branch of Scourie, who served in Holland and accompanied William III to England in 1688. He commanded the army defeated by Bonnie Dundee at Killiecrankie (1689) and was killed in a later engagement.

Strategically the Mackays' country appears well placed to avoid the problems faced by clans nearer the centre of government, but from the 14th century if not earlier they were frequently hard pressed to preserve their lands from the earls of Sutherland. Early in the 16th century that earldom passed to the Gordons of Huntly and by the end of the century the chief of Mackay was a vassal of the Gordon Earl. Subsequently the Mackays became involved in the efforts of the Gordons to expand their power in the far north at the expense of the Sinclair earls of Caithness.

As Whigs and Protestants the Mackays survived

The Pass of Killiecrankie. The battle in which General Hugh Mackay, commanding government forces, was defeated by Graham of Claverhouse, Bonnie Dundee, in 1689, was actually fought beyond the pass, Mackay's men being ambushed as they emerged.

Bagpipe played by George Mackay at the battle of Waterloo (1815) and by James Mackay on George IV's arrival in Edinburgh in 1822. The Highland bagpipe or 'Great Pipe' has a chanter, on which the tune is played, and three 'drones', each playing a single note.

Mackay

the 18th-century troubles comparatively unscathed. In the late 18th century the Earl of Sutherland (raised to a duke in 1833) was an absentee English millionaire – the largest landowner in Britain – with no feeling for the country or its inhabitants. The Sutherland Clearances in which vast numbers were removed from the interior to the coast (and beyond) are infamous: their effect is visible to this day.

The seventh Lord Reay sold his estates, including the House of Tongue, his ancestral home, in 1829. The old way of life, destroyed forever by the Clearances, was celebrated in the poetry of Rob Donn Mackay (1714-78), said to be the Gaelic poet most nearly comparable to Burns.

A younger son of the second Lord Reay, who was also a nephew of General Hugh Mackay, followed his uncle's example and entered Dutch service in the 17th century. His grandson, Aeneas (an anglicised form of Angus) married the heiress to a Dutch barony and his son, Barthold Mackay, was created a baron of the Netherlands in his own right. His nephew, another Aeneas, was Prime Minister of the Netherlands. The Dutch Mackays inherited the Mackay chiefship when the senior line died out in 1875.

Mackenzie

The Mackenzies were one of those Highland clans who prospered at the expense of their Gaelic neighbours by allying themselves with the English-speaking south.

Their origins are disputable. One tradition holds that their ancestor was an Irish chieftain who came over with his forces to take part in the battle of Largs, and was rewarded with lands in Kintail in Wester Ross. A more probable one asserts that the Mackenzies were descended from Gilleon of the Aird, a scion of the ancient royal house of Lorne, who lived about 1100.

The old Gaelic name is *Mac Cainnigh*, a name anglicised as Kenneth, and at least one early 15th-century Mackenzie chief was called *Cainnech Mór*. He could allegedly command 2,000 men in 1427.

His predecessor Murdoch is the first to appear in a

The Five Sisters of Kintail, a mountain range to the north-east of Glenshiel, flanking the road which leads from Glenmoriston to Eilean Donan Castle.

surviving charter, in 1362, and he is described as son of Kenneth, son of John, son of Kenneth, son of Angus, son of Christian, son of Adam, son of Gilleon of the Aird. He was confirmed in the lands of Kintail by King David II.

His descendant Alasdair (Alexander) of Kintail was among the chiefs summoned to parliament (with disastrous results for some of them) by King James I in 1427. He must have been a young man then, for he lived until 1488. He supported the Crown against the MacDonald Lord of the Isles and benefited immensely as a result, not least by gaining legal title to his land,

old and new, the lack of which created so many problems for other Highland clans. His son Kenneth defeated the MacDonalds in battle in 1491 but died soon afterwards and was succeeded by his son Iain.

Some Mackenzies fought at Flodden in 1513 under Iain who, like his grandfather, was a natural survivor.

Mackenzie

Opposite: A Mackenzie on the defensive – detail of one of the clan cameos of the 19th-century Highland artist, R. R. McIan.

Below: Loch Carron, a region disputed between the Mackenzies and the MacDonells of Glengarry.

Though at least one Mackenzie chieftain fell in that disastrous battle, the chief was one of comparatively few Scottish leaders who survived. Moreover he lived to fight again at Pinkie 35 years later and emerged from that battle unscathed also. His grandson Colin supported Mary Queen of Scots and was probably among her forces at Langside (1568), but he avoided retribution by making fairly prompt submission to the Earl of Moray, Regent for the young King James VI. Nevertheless the Mackenzies' loyal adherence to the Stewart dynasty, which assisted their rise, was eventually to become a serious disadvantage.

By this time the Mackenzies were becoming very powerful. They had benefited, first, from the decline of Clan Donald, while avoiding the usual concomitant of creating many dangerous enemies. In the reign of King James VI they bought out the Fife Adventurers, who had attempted to settle Lewis but had been thrown out by the affronted MacLeods. The Mackenzies, who had already absorbed MacLeod lands on the mainland, had more success and soon became dominant in Lewis too. They also prised

Lochalsh away from the MacDonells of Glengarry.

Their territories now extended in a wide swathe across Scotland from the Outer Hebrides to the Black Isle, in total acreage unchallenged by any clan except the Campbells. Kenneth of Kintail became Lord Mackenzie and his son by his Grant wife was created Earl of Seaforth in 1623.

So far the story had been one of constant expansion. However, the loyalty of the Mackenzie chiefs to the unlucky remnants of the Stewart dynasty was their undoing. The fourth Earl of Seaforth, one of the original Knights of the Thistle, died in exile with King James VII/II. The fifth earl took part in the rising of 1715 and was attainted, losing lands and title. He was also a leader of the abortive Spanish-assisted rising of 1719, being wounded at Glenshiel. Nevertheless, he was pardoned in 1726 thanks to the insistence of General Wade, the Commander-in-Chief in Scotland, who threatened to resign if this were not done. He regained some of his lands but not the title and died peacefully in Lewis in 1740.

The Mackenzies did not fight as a clan in 1745-46, although many cadet branches were 'out'.

For the fifth earl's grandson, who repurchased the family estates from the government, the earldom of Seaforth was recreated in 1771. In gratitude (it is said), the earl raised the Seaforth Highlanders in 1778, made up mostly of Mackenzies and MacRaes, old allies of the Mackenzies. They were sent to India in 1781 – a disastrous voyage on which one man in three died (mostly of scurvy).

The estates but not the title passed to another branch in 1784 and after that line had failed they passed through various heiresses, constantly diminishing, along with other Mackenzie families, though the foremost of them, the earls of Cromartie, hung on to at least a remnant. The Kintail estate today is owned by the National Trust for Scotland.

The decline of the house of Seaforth was foretold by the 'Brahan Seer' (Brahan was a Mackenzie castle near Dingwall, at one time chief residence of the Seaforths) in the 16th century. The details of this prophecy were written down before the events they foretold, and they cannot therefore be dismissed as the result of someone's memory reworking the prophecy to suit the circumstances. Their accuracy is certainly remarkable, and that some of the events forecast have yet to occur is more disquieting than consoling.

Mackinlay

This was not a common name in Scotland. It comes from the Gaelic *Mac Fhionnlaigh* (son of Finlay), which was the title of the Farquharson chiefs, deriving from Finlay, grandson of Farquhar, who was killed at the battle of Pinkie in 1547. It is probable that the Mackinlays, or some of them, came from the same stock as the Farquharsons of Braemar, for although the name was not known in that district, it may have been adopted by those who moved away. Finlayson is simply another form of the same name, and the small Clan Finlayson in Lochalsh also claimed descent from Finlay.

Mackinlay

The early 18th-century account by Buchanan of Auchmar ascribes to the Mackinlays a descent from a Buchanan chieftain named Finlay, and according to Sir Thomas Innes, 'there can be little doubt the country of this clan was in the Lennox district'; there was a colony north of Callandar. According to Buchanan of Auchmar some Mackinlays were to be identified with MacFarlanes.

Besides the septs of Farquharson and Buchanan, the Mackinlays have also been connected with Stewart of Appin.

Several variants of the name appear in the 17th century (McKandlay, McYndla, etc.), especially in Glenlyon and Balquhidder, and a family of Mackintoshes from Glenshee were described as 'alias Macinlies'.

There are possibly more Mackinlays, or McGinleys, in Co. Antrim than anywhere else, the result of the plantation of Ulster by Protestant Scots in the 17th century. From one of these David McKinley (whose ancestors spelt their name McKinlay), was descended a president of the United States, William McKinley (1843-1901). Mount McKinley in Alaska, the highest mountain in North America, was named in his honour.

Mackinnon

Mackinnon

The Mackinnons claimed kinship on the one hand with Kenneth MacAlpin, first king of a united Scotland, and on the other with St Columba, 'the apostle of Caledonia'. A more distinguished heritage would be hard to imagine. Although, as with other clans claiming membership of *Sìol Ailpein*, the descent there is speculative (it was said that the Mackinnons' ancestor was Fingon, younger brother of King Kenneth MacAlpin), there is little doubt of their kinship with St Columba.

In the 14th century the brother of the Mackinnon chief was Fingon, Abbot of Iona, known as the Green Abbot. His grandson (Celtic clergy were free to marry, despite Rome's disapproval), who was also called Fingon, was said to have made free with the monastery's property. A fine Celtic cross at Iona was erected by Lachlan Mackinnon, father of the last abbot, Iain Mackinnon, who died in 1500. His effigy has survived at Iona.

The original homeland of the Mackinnons was the Isle of Mull, at first apparently in the south, then from the 15th century, at Mishnish in the north. Although the clan was not a large one, it was of some note (and probably more numerous than generally supposed) during the time of the lords of the Isles.

The Mackinnons seem to have lost their original territory through some trouble created by the Green Abbot, described by the chroniclers as 'subtle and wicked', as a result of which the Mackinnon chief was executed and the lands in the south of Mull were taken over by the MacLeans.

By the 16th century the Mackinnons also held (probably as a result of a marriage with the MacLeods) Strathaird in Skye, comprising over 150 square miles and rather more significant than their lands in Mull, together with the isle of Scalpay. The ruins of the great Mackinnon castle of Dunakin still command the passage between Kyleakin and Kyle of Lochalsh on the mainland.

Mackinnon was one of the barons of the council of the lord of the Isles and held the hereditary duty of superintending weights and measures. He also had the equally challenging job of resolving disputes arising out of gambling debts, and according to an account of 1594 it was for undertaking this delicate office that he received Strathaird.

The Mackinnons took part in efforts to restore the lordship of the Isles after its suppression in 1493. Ewen Mackinnon of Strathaird was a member of Donald *Dubh*'s council during his last rising in 1545. The clan was regarded as troublesome by the govern-

A peaceful scene on Skye, where Clan Fingon and Clan Donald lived in relative amity. The Mackinnons acquired Strathairdale through marriage with the MacLeods, or through a grant from the lord of the Isles (perhaps both).

ment, and early in the 17th century the chief, along with other Highland leaders, submitted to the restrictions of the Statutes of Iona.

Subsequently the Mackinnons were loyal adherents of the Stewarts. Sir Lachlan Mackinnon, twenty-eighth chief, was knighted by Charles II before the battle of Worcester (1651). His successor John *Dubh* was 'out' in the Jacobite rising of 1715, his estates being forfeited but later restored, and again in 1745. After Culloden the Mackinnons of Mull were harassed by troops and the chief spent some time in prison at Tilbury. He was eventually released on account of his age and sent home. When the attorney general emphasised the king's generosity in so releasing him, Mackinnon replied, 'Had I the King in my power as I am in his, I would return him the compliment of sending him back to his own country'.

He died in 1756 and was succeeded by his son Charles, who had the melancholy experience of seeing the estates sold to pay off debts. His own son inherited nothing except the chiefship and died 'in humble circumstances' in 1808, the last of his line. The chiefship passed, via some convolutions, to a cadet branch.

Mackintosh

Mac an Tòisich means 'son of the chief' or 'thane', and some Mackintoshes are not connected with the famous clan whose chief became also the captain of Clan Chattan, the confederation of the Cat. The ancestor of the Mackintoshes, according to a tradition which has not been seriously questioned, was a younger son of MacDuff, ancestor of the old earls of Fife. He, or perhaps one of his immediate descendants, married the heiress of Clan Chattan, which was named after a 13th-century chief, Gilliechattan *Mór*.

Mackintosh is first referred to as captain (i.e. chief) of Clan Chattan in 1442. By that time he was established on an island in Loch Moy, Strathdearn, where the Mackintosh has his seat (albeit a fine modern house on the mainland) today.

Clan Chattan was a loose confederation of clans among whom the Mackintoshes were most often ascendant. Clan Chattan occupied a swathe of the Central Highlands which stretched roughly from the Forest of Atholl to the Moray Firth.

During the wars of independence the Mackintosh chiefs supported Bruce in spite of the dominance of the Comyn family, at feud with Bruce, in their district. They also chose the right side in 1411, fighting with the regent's forces at Harlaw under the Earl of Mar. Their lands in Lochaber were obtained in the 14th and 15th centuries at the expense of the Camerons and the MacDonells of Keppoch, which led to feuds that continued off and on for centuries.

No clan was more frequently embroiled in violent quarrels than the Mackintoshes, though that was probably due more to unavoidable circumstances, including their wide responsibilities, the difficulty of getting Clan Chattan to act together, and their complicated landholding arrangements, than to the alleged short tempers of the Mackintoshes. The feud with the Comyns (Cummings) over lands in Strathnairn may have lain behind the famous clan battle at Perth in 1396, a sort of mass duel witnessed by the king himself. Some mystery surrounds the precise identity of the participants, but Sir Ian Moncreiffe believed that they were the Mackintoshes and the Cummings.

An ultimately more dangerous opponent was the Gordon Earl of Huntly, who was feudal overlord for some Mackintosh lands in Badenoch, and had the advantage of government backing for most of his activities. It was probably through Huntly that the Shaws (members of Clan Chattan and kin to the

Mackintosh

remained loyal to his commission. However, the clan was raised by his young wife 'Colonel Anne', whose strategy was responsible for the 'Rout of Moy', when several hundred redcoats were repulsed by half-a-dozen Mackintosh retainers (see also Farquharson).

On the death of the twenty-third chief the chiefship migrated, first to a merchant in the West Indies, then to a Canadian businessman. But eventually it returned, and today the Mackintosh resides in the lands of his forefathers.

MacLachlan

Mackintoshes) lost Rothiemurchus to the Grants in the 16th century. The Mackintosh tried to get it back, at first by purchase and, when that was rejected by the Laird of Grant, by force – which was no more successful. One 16th-century Mackintosh chief was judicially murdered by Huntly. His successors had the satisfaction of taking part in the battle of Corriechie (1562) where the Gordon Earl was killed, and at Glenlivet (1594), where they fought less successfully for Argyll against the rebellious Catholic earls.

The feud with the MacDonells eventually came to a head in what is usually described as the last great clan battle, at Mulroy in 1688. Despite the assistance of a company of regular soldiers and contingents from their allies, the Mackintoshes were defeated.

In the 17th century Clan Chattan generally supported the Stewarts (though not King James VII/II in 1688-89) and that allegiance continued during the Jacobite risings of the 18th century. Lachlan (a favourite name among the Mackintosh chiefs) brought his men 'out' in 1715, but the most notable Mackintosh leader in that campaign was William Mackintosh of Borlum, known as 'Old Borlum', who had served in the French army. He led a Jacobite force into the Lowlands and, prevented from taking Edinburgh by Argyll, continued south as far as Preston in Lancashire, where he was forced to surrender. He was released in plenty of time to participate in the stillborn rising of 1719 and was captured again. While in prison he wrote a book on agricultural management.

The Mackintosh himself regained his estates and died in 1731. He had no direct heir and the chiefship passed to a cadet branch; not a single father-son succession occurred during the next hundred years.

Angus, twenty-third chief, was an officer in the British army at the time of the Forty-five, and

The MacLachlans have a good fairy, the Brounie, who has watched over them since ancient times, and it is said that when the first marriage between a MacLachlan and a Campbell (the first of many) occurred, the Brounie was so angry that he made the wedding feast laid out at Castle Lachlan disappear. This seems misguided, for it was largely through their alliance with the Campbells, the seat of whose chief at Inveraray was only a few miles away from the MacLachlan stronghold, that this clan preserved their lands and independence into modern times.

The descent of the MacLachlans from the Ulster royal family of O'Neill is as well attested as these things can be. According to the old Celtic genealogists five generations separated King Aodh O'Neill in the 11th century and Lachlan *Mór*, from whom the MacLachlans take their name. There is independent evidence from a charter of about 1238 of the existence of Lachlan *Mór*'s father, Gilpatrick.

In 1292 Gillescop, son of Lachlan, was named as one of the twelve barons whose lands formed the new sheriffdom of Argyll. His son (or grandson) of the same name supported Bruce, at least from his coronation, and attended King Robert's first parliament at St Andrews in 1308. The same chief made a grant to the friars of Glasgow, an example of the numerous connections of the MacLachlans with the Church in the Middle Ages.

The territory of the MacLachlans ran for about ten miles on both sides of Loch Fyne, extending in the west at one time as far as the Sound of Jura. Cadets held other estates; the MacLachlans of Craiginterve were established near the head of Loch Awe and were once physicians to the Campbells of Argyll, when they were sometimes called Leech. Another MacLachlan family held the castle of Inchconnel on Loch Awe in the 17th century.

MacLachlan

MacLaren

The MacLachlans' ability to stay on the right side of the Campbells did not extend to other neighbours in Cowal. With the Lamonts there were frequent feuds, though also alliances. They seem to have been involved in the dreadful massacre of the Lamonts by the Campbells in 1646. Subsequently, Lachlan MacLachlan of that ilk held office under the Protectorate, but despite the dominance of the Campbells, the chiefs of MacLachlan retained their freedom of action to such an extent that they were zealous Jacobites in the 18th century. They were with Bonnie Dundee at Killiecrankie in 1689 and in the rising of 1715 Lachlan MacLachlan was with Mar's somewhat stationary army at Perth. He died in 1719, possibly shot by Campbell of Ardkinglas.

In 1745 his son, accounted seventeenth chief and bearing the same name, was an early supporter of the prince, although he was able to raise only 180 men due to the Campbells all around. They joined the MacLeans at Culloden and most of them were killed, cut down by grapeshot and musket fire before they could engage the foe. The elderly chief, leading his men, died as he made his way forwards, shot off his horse by a cannon ball. His son, Prince Charles's aide-de-campe though hardly more than a boy, was already dead, killed by a chance shot before the charge began. It is said that the news of the terrible defeat was brought to Strathlachlan by the dead chief's riderless horse.

During the disgraceful harassment of the Highlands after Culloden, Castle Lachlan was bombed into ruins by a ship in Loch Fyne. The estates, though forfeited, returned comparatively quickly thanks to the good offices of the Duke of Argyll. A new castle was built in the 19th century in the Scots-baronial style. This slightly whimsical edifice is today the seat of the chief of the MacLachlans.

Unfortunately the history of the MacLarens is shrouded in Highland mists. Their origins are a matter for speculation: Sir Thomas Innes accepted that there were two distinct clans, the MacLarens of Perthshire and the MacLarens or MacLaurins of Argyll. Generally it is agreed that the homeland of the MacLarens was the Braes of Balquhidder, the district around Loch Voil. The war cry and the gathering place of the clan was *Creag an Tuirc* (the Rock of the Boar) near Achleskine, where the chiefly family resided, in Balquhidder. Heraldic evidence supports this (the MacLaren badge of a mermaid represents the water spirit of Loch Voil). The MacLarens were probably kin to the Celtic earls of Strathearn, who died out in the mid-14th century.

The MacLarens were at their height around the end of the Middle Ages, when they had spread beyond their original homeland throughout Strathearn and to other parts also. The disappearance of their former landlords, the earls of Strathearn, brought problems, but since the MacLarens never held their land by charter, they were perhaps fortunate to survive as long as they did.

About the middle of the 16th century they were overrun twice in the same generation by the MacGregors. A great many people died and the clan never really recovered, subsequently seeking the protection of Campbell of Glenorchy. It was probably at this time that clan records were completely destroyed.

The prominence of the MacLarens in foreign military service may have been partly due to difficulties at home, and the warlike reputation of the clan equally a necessary characteristic to preserve their existence (the chiefs were said to have been 'all grand, strong men'). There were MacLarens in French service in the 15th century, and they fought for the Swedes in the Thirty Years' War.

In later times many MacLarens followed Stewart of Appin. This resulted from a romantic marriage in the 15th century between a younger son of the Stewart Lord of Lorne and a notably beautiful daughter of a MacLaren chieftain. Their son, born out of wedlock but legitimised after his parents' marriage, became the founder of the Stewarts of Appin.

MacLarens fought alongside the Stewarts of Appin

MacLaren

MacLean

for the royal Stewarts in the civil war and in 1689, and they took part in the Jacobite risings of 1715 and 1745. One of their officers at Culloden was Donald MacLaren of Invernenty, who was afterwards captured and sent for trial at Carlisle. He made a dramatic escape in the mist at the Devil's Beef Tub in Annandale, hiding in a bog for several days and living off the flesh of a dead (long dead, apparently) sheep. He then made his way back to Balquhidder, where he lived for the next two years disguised as a woman. Scott made use of the episode in *Redgauntlet*, and it is said to have been some business connected with the MacLarens that first brought the great novelist, then a young lawyer's clerk, into direct contact with the Highlands.

By that time the clan had disintegrated, but the chiefship was later re-established and some of the original clan territory, including *Creag an Tuirc*, has been regained by purchase.

MacLean

The MacLeans became a powerful and prominent clan under the lords of the Isles, of whom they were loyal vassals. After the extinction of the lordship – few fought harder than the MacLeans to maintain it – the main divisions of Clan Gillean became virtually independent clans, at times feuding with each other as well as with the MacDonalds. Nevertheless, the MacLeans benefited territorially from the collapse of the lordship and probably reached their greatest power and influence in the 16th century.

The Gillean from whom the clan takes its name was Gillean of the Battle-Axe, who lived in the 13th century and is said to have fought at the Battle of Largs (1263). No doubt he was a warrior as fierce as he sounds, though his nickname arose from the peaceful use of that instrument: he became lost while hunting, and after wandering for days lay down to die, hanging his axe on a laurel tree where it was observed in time to save him. He was probably descended from the royal house of Lorne and therefore from the kings of Dalriada, the ancient kingdom of the Scots corresponding roughly with Argyll.

The original home of the MacLeans was probably Morvern, though they were soon spread more widely as a result of the favours of the lord of the Isles. The two senior branches, the MacLeans of Duart and the MacLaines (they preferred the phonetic spelling) of Lochbuie were descended from two brothers, Hector (Lochbuie) and Lachlan (Duart), whose grandfather had fought at Bannockburn. They were originally followers of the lord of Lorne but transferred their allegiance to the lord of the Isles in the 14th century probably after the marriage of Lachlan (see MacLean of Duart) to the daughter of the Lord of the Isles, reputedly a love match.

Besides Duart and Lochbuie, two cadet branches of the MacLeans of Duart came to be recognised as distinct clans.

The MacLeans of Ardgour, in Morvern, were founded in the 15th century by Donald MacLean, son of Lachlan, son of Red Hector of the Battles, son of Lachan the progenitor of the house of Duart. Donald wrested Ardgour from the MacMasters, whom he slaughtered to the last man, and since 'MacLean's Towel', the waterfall that descends the hillside at the back of (18th-century) Ardgour House has not yet run dry, his descendants are there still. Sir Fitzroy

Maclean of Strachur, traveller, writer, soldier (notably with Tito's partisans) politician and farmer, belongs to the Ardgour family.

The MacLeans of Coll were descended from Iain, brother of Donald of Ardgour. They quarrelled with the senior house of Duart in the 16th century and MacLean of Duart attacked them, taking over their lands and castle of Breacachadh, which, however, were restored after government intervention. 'Young Coll', the chief's son, was host to Samuel Johnson and James Boswell when they visited the island during their Hebridean tour of 1773 and was drowned soon afterwards. At that time the MacLeans of Coll also held land in Mull and Rum. The lands were sold in 1848 by the last MacLean of Coll, who emigrated to South Africa. In Johnson's time there were a thousand or so people on Coll. Two hundred years later there were fewer than 200, mainly of Lowland origin.

The MacLean of Duart hunting tartan is of particular historical interest because as long ago as 1587, in a charter of land in Islay, then held by a son of MacLean of Duart, a feudal duty was payable in cloth of white, black and green – the colours of the modern hunting tartan. The same colours were mentioned in 1630. In 1527, between the two dates, when the lands were temporarily held by a different landlord, the 'green' becomes 'grey'.

MacLean of Duart

MacLean of Duart

Fierce argument has waged over which brother, Lachlan, founder of the MacLeans of Duart, or Hector, founder of the MacLaines of Lochbuie, was the eldest and therefore which house is the senior. It is rather a pointless argument, since the old Celtic law made inheritance a family matter rather than an individual one, and it was quite in order for the chiefship to be inherited by a younger son, whose house subsequently became the senior line.

Lachlan, even if younger, was the more successful, mainly as a result of his marriage to the daughter of the lord of the Isles. This was effected by unconventional techniques, involving an affray in which the Mackinnon chief was killed and the girl's father kidnapped, but the Lord of the Isles was impressed by his future son-in-law's boldness and from then on the MacLeans were in high favour. At the expense of the Mackinnons they received a large part of Mull and other islands. A more modest version of the great dark fortress of Duart, commanding the Sound of Mull and

the Firth of Lorne, probably already existed at that time.

There was a certain amount of rivalry between the houses of Duart and Lochbuie from the first, but in major matters the MacLeans generally all acted together. They repaid the favour of the Lord of the Isles with loyal service in peace and war. Red Hector of the Battles, the second MacLean of Duart, was killed at Harlaw in 1411 fighting for the Lord in his attempt to gain the earldom of Ross. MacLean chieftains held many military (and especially naval) commands and administrative posts, including that of seneschal of the Isles and chamberlain of the household.

The fall of the lordship was no doubt inevitable but it was certainly assisted by the disastrous career of Angus Òg, son of the fourth lord, who was supported in his revolt against his father by the MacDonalds but opposed by the MacLeans and other clans who remained loyal to his father. In the gruesome sea battle of Bloody Bay in 1481 the MacLeans were defeated. Some fifty of them were butchered in cold blood after being smoked out of the cave in which they had taken shelter.

The MacLeans continued to support the lords of the Isles until the death of Donald *Dubh* in 1546, but thereafter came to terms with the Stewart dynasty. MacLean of Duart received royal confirmation of his lands and titles as early as 1496.

From the time of Angus Òg the MacLeans were frequently at odds with the various branches of Clan Donald. However, though not yet fully apparent, the ultimate winner of this particular power struggle was neither the MacLeans nor the MacDonalds, but Clan Campbell, waiting in the wings and not at all inclined to discourage their rivals' mutual animosity. The

MacLeans did intermarry with the Campbells on several occasions, but this did not affect the outcome. In one notorious case, instead of cementing MacLean-Campbell relations, it had quite the opposite effect.

Lachlan MacLean of Duart married Lady Catherine Campbell, sister of the Earl of Argyll, early in the 16th century. He grew tired of her and marooned her on the Lady Rock in the Sound of Mull, which is submerged at high tide. MacLean hastened off to inform his brother-in-law how his wife had met with an unfortunate accident at sea. He should have waited, for the lady had been rescued by some fishermen who restored her to her brother's house. Later, on a visit to Edinburgh, MacLean was surprised by Campbell of Cawdor, another brother, who stabbed him to death in his bed.

That was not the end of the Campbells' revenge.

while, Duart himself was fighting with Bonnie Dundee, and the ultimate defeat of the Jacobites in the 1688-89 rebellion gave Argyll the opportunity to invade Duart with a sizable army, driving the chief into exile.

Though now landless, the MacLeans of Duart were active in the Jacobite cause in 1715 and 1745. The last chief of the line was captured in 1745 and the clan was led at Culloden by MacLean of Drimmin.

The chief was allowed to return to the exile from which he had emerged to lead his men for Prince Charles, though he was not, of course, restored to his lands and castle.

Nevertheless, against the odds the MacLean did eventually return to Duart. Sir Fitzroy MacLean, a survivor of the Charge of the Light Brigade, regained possession in 1911 and set about restoring the castle, which the Campbells had allowed to fall into ruins. As

One way or another, not least by their efforts on behalf of the Stewarts during the civil wars, the MacLeans of Duart fell heavily into debt. Argyll, with characteristic ingenuity, and by brazen employment of public office in private interest, bought up all the outstanding claims and eventually obtained a judgment authorising him to take over Duart's territory (which his predecesor had briefly held during the civil war).

The MacLeans resisted by the only means available – force. English warships were brought in to bombard Duart Castle from the sea, but its massive walls, some 10 feet thick, resisted successfully. Mean-

Duart Castle stands on a cliff on the sharp, northward promontory projecting into the Sound of Mull opposite Oban. Besides its massive walls, the 14th-century castle was protected by a 'moat' carved out of the solid rock on which it stands.

he was 77 years old when he finally gained possession after a lifetime of endeavour to that end, he was not expected to enjoy his success for long, but he lived to pass his 101st birthday, and his grandson, twenty-sixth chief, flies his banner from the ramparts of Duart today.

MacLaine of Lochbuie

The rivalry between the MacLeans of Duart and the MacLaines of Lochbuie, descended from two brothers, gave rise to many tales of dark and dirty doings, of which the most famous concerns the temporary eclipse of the Lochbuie chiefs at the hands of their kinsmen and rivals.

Iain Òg, also known as Iain the Toothless, was chief of Lochbuie. He had a single son Ewen, who rebelled against him. Hector *Mór* of Duart supported the father, and Ewen was killed in a battle (his ghost, the Headless Horseman, makes his ominous appearance shortly before the death of a MacLaine of Lochbuie). Hector then imprisoned his now childless kinsman of Lochbuie on a small island, and so that he would not beget a new heir his only female companion was a hideous hag. However, in due course she gave birth to Murdoch *Gearr* (Stunted), who later sought refuge in Ireland, while Duart attached the estates of Lochbuie to his own.

After various adventures Murdoch *Gearr* returned and regained his inheritance by force. He was legitimised in 1538 and subsequent MacLaines of Lochbuie were descended from him.

Despite these little family difficulties the MacLaines of Lochbuie were generally allied with their kinsmen in national conflicts, just as they had been as vassals of the lords of the Isles (both Duart and Lochbuie sat on the Lord's council at Finlaggan). They fought with Montrose for Charles I, and 300 of Lochbuie's men took part in the victory of Killiecrankie under Bonnie Dundee, but they were not with MacLean of Drimmin in the Forty-five.

While Duart was lost, the MacLaines hung on to Lochbuie. By the time they were visited by Dr Johnson and Boswell the chief no longer lived in the castle but in a house nearby. Johnson was not impressed by the house, nor by the chief, whom he described as 'a true Highland Laird, rough and haughty, and tenacious in his dignity'.

The estates would undoubtedly have been sold for debt in the 19th century but for the fortune amassed by Donald, twentieth Chief of Lochbuie, as a merchant in Java. A century later, however, it was lost, ironically a few years after Duart had been regained. Subsequent chiefs have by no means lost hope of returning to Lochbuie.

MacLeod

The MacLeods were descended from Leod (said to derive from an old Norse word meaning ugly), son of Olaf the Black (died 1237), King of Man and the Isles. Leod acquired Harris, Lewis and part of Skye, including Dunvegan, by marriage to the heiress of the Norse seneschal, or steward, of Skye. His sons Tormod (often called, a shade incongruously, Norman) and Torquil were the founders of the two main branches of the clan, respectively the MacLeods of Harris, whose chiefs became known, as the senior line, as the MacLeods of MacLeod, and the MacLeods of Lewis. The two main branches, known

MacLaine of Lochbuie

MacLeod of MacLeod

Above: Dunvegan Castle, the famous home of the MacLeods and a treasure house of history and legend. The return of the laird to Dunvegan used to cause a big herring catch, while the departure of a lady to Harris led to a diminished haul. There is (or was) a hollowed ox horn holding two quarts (of wine?) which a MacLeod chief would drain in one draught to prove himself up to scratch.

Right: A portrait of Norman, 22nd Chief of MacLeod by Allan Ramsay.

as *Sìol Thormoid* (Tormod) and *Sìol Thorcail* (Torquil), indulged in an intermittent dispute over seniority, but the chief of *Sìol Thormoid* was widely acknowledged as paramount by the 16th century.

The motto of the MacLeods is 'Hold Fast', and it seems an appropriate one. They certainly held fast to Dunvegan Castle, at the head of the sea loch facing towards Harris, for it has remained the seat of their chiefs for about 700 years. This, the most famous clan chief's castle in the Highlands, could be entered only by the sea gate (built by Leod himself) until after the Forty-five, which signifies the importance of the sea in the history of the MacLeods. Thanks to this security of tenure, despite the absence of a charter until about 1500, the archives of Dunvegan are a treasure trove for historians of the Highlands, and the history of the

The remarkable tomb which Alasdair *Crotach* had made for himself in St Clement's church, Rodel, in Harris.

MacLeods is comparatively well documented. There is a fine modern history of the clan by the well-known Highland historian, the late Dr Isabel Grant.

Among other treasures at Dunvegan is the Fairy Flag, to be unfurled only in case of extreme danger, which is now thought to be a thousand years old and of Byzantine origin. MacLeod tradition says it was the gift of a fairy princess to Iain, fourth chief. Sir Iain Moncreiffe suggested with characteristic ingenuity that it is the banner brought back from Constantinople by King Harald of Norway which he left behind in the ships of an ally, a Norse ancestor of the MacLeods, after their defeat in 1066 at Stamford Bridge by King Harold of England (who later the same year fought less successfully against another invader, William of Normandy).

Sìol Thormoid supported Bruce in the wars of independence although they do not seem to have benefited significantly from doing so. Under Malcolm, grandson of the original Tormod, Glenelg on the mainland was confirmed by a charter of King David II in about 1343, the first official confirmation of any MacLeod landholding. Early chiefs were known as 'of Glenelg' rather than, as later, 'of Dunvegan'. They were vassals of both the king of Scots and the lord of the Isles, with whom there were disputes, though the sixth Chief of Glenelg fought with Donald of the Isles at 'Red' Harlaw (1411). His successor, the first to be described as 'of Dunvegan', was killed in the very nasty battle of Bloody Bay by Angus Òg's MacDonalds.

The eighth chief was the famous Alasdair *Crotach* (Hump-backed – the result of an accident), who had a charter of Trotternish (the northern peninsula of Skye, later lost to the MacDonalds of Sleat) and built the Fairy Tower at Dunvegan and the church of Rodel in Harris where his fine tomb can still be seen. He married the alleged tenth daughter of Cameron of Lochiel, the previous nine having all refused him because of his deformity. In desperate battles with Clan Ranald he was twice compelled to resort to the ultimate weapon – unfurling the Fairy Flag. He died in 1547.

Alasdair *Crotach* was probably the MacLeod chief who figures in a famous story: dining at the royal court, a snooty Lowland courtier patronisingly remarked that the simple Highland chief must be impressed by the grandeur of his surroundings. MacLeod contradicted, saying he had finer halls, tables and candlesticks at home. A wager was made and subsequently MacLeod entertained the court to a banquet on the flat-topped hills opposite Dunvegan known as 'MacLeod's Tables', lit by torches held by statuesque clansmen. The Lowlander conceded the bet.

The most celebrated chief of *Sìol Thormoid* was Sir

Roderick (knighted by King James VI), better known as Rory *Mór*, who commanded that high degree of devotion from his followers that many MacLeod chiefs have shared up to present times. He is remembered in the famous lament of Patrick *Mór* MacCrimmon, of the family of hereditary pipers at Dunvegan.

There was no better place for a Gaelic poet to live. After the collapse of the lordship Dunvegan became perhaps the chief centre of Gaelic culture (it is one of the few districts where Gaelic is still an everyday language). The MacLeod court, attended by the chieftains of numerous septs of *Sìol Thormoid*, was entertained by harpers (including the great Blind Harper of Dunvegan, Roderick Morrison), pipers and jesters, as well as bards. Some of the learned families of the Beatons came to Dunvegan, and Rory *Mór* and his descendants spent freely on social and economic improvements such as schools and roads. In years of bad harvests they imported grain for their tenants. They even maintained an Edinburgh post.

Though they were not active in Montrose's campaign the MacLeods of Harris and Dunvegan supported the Stewarts in the 17th century. They provided about 700 men for the battle of Worcester (1651), of whom about three-quarters were killed. After this disaster no MacLeod chief ever took the field on behalf of the Stewarts again. Some were 'out' in 1715, but in 1745 the chief not only held aloof (though there were many MacLeods in Glengarry's and other regiments), but raised a company in Hanoverian service.

He was not one of the most admirable of his line, having been implicated along with his brother-in-law MacDonald of Sleat some years earlier in forcibly deporting a group of his clanspeople to the American colonies. He had interests in a wider world than the Hebrides, and that was often an ominous sign in a Highland chief. Within the next generation much of his lands had to be sold. This did not happen, however, until after the visit of Samuel Johnson and James Boswell in 1773. They were 'so comfortably situated' at Dunvegan that they did not want to leave. Boswell rejoiced in the wine and venison and in 'the sight of a great Highland Laird surrounded by so many of his clan'. The distinguished visitors combined to dissuade Lady MacLeod from moving out of the castle into a comfortable house more suited to a lady of 18th-century 'sensibilities'.

In the 19th century, inevitably, the clan dwindled and scattered, though the chiefs generally did their best. In 1935 Dame Flora MacLeod of MacLeod became chief and revived the life and spirit of the clan in an extraordinary way, making Dunvegan a kind of miniature United Nations assembly.

MacLeod of Lewis

Sìol Thorcail trace their descent from Torquil, brother of Tormond, progenitor of the MacLeods of Harris and Dunvegan (Skye). There was some argument over which was the overall chief, but Tormond's descendants came to be recognised as the senior line. They were also more successful in holding on to their heritage. Today, *Sìol Thorcail* have no chief of their own.

By the reign of King David II the MacLeods of Lewis had gained, besides Lewis, Assynt in Sutherland, presumably by marriage. It was passed to a younger son and became one of several powerful (and quarrelsome) septs of the clan. A 17th-century chieftain, deep in debt, was responsible for betraying Montrose in 1650, but his reward, according to tradition, was nothing more than a few bags of sour meal, not enough to save his lands from his creditors.

Another cadet branch of the MacLeods of Lewis held the island of Raasay, between Skye and the mainland, from the 16th century.

Like the senior branch, the MacLeods of Lewis supported their overlord, the MacDonald Lord of the Isles, up to the final rebellion of Donald *Dubh* in 1545, but subsequently came to terms with the royal government. Soon afterwards, however, they became involved in one of the worst conflicts in Highland history, which resulted in the extinction of the chiefly house and the loss of their lands.

MacLeod of Lewis

Besides internecine quarrels, the main source of trouble was the Mackenzies who had a (phoney) claim to Lewis through the marriage of a Mackenzie lady to Rory MacLeod of Lewis. The MacLeods, like many other Highlands clans, were at a disadvantage in having no formal title to their lands. When this could not be produced King James VI granted Lewis to a Lowland commercial company called the Fife Adventurers, his object being to suppress the admittedly unruly MacLeods of Lewis and pacify the Hebrides by Lowland settlement. The MacLeods were not so easily dislodged. They resisted by force under Neil *Mór*, an illegitimate son of Rory, and sent the Lowlanders packing. The disillusioned Fife Adventurers then sold out to Mackenzie of Kintail. He had already acquired Gairloch and other MacLeod territories on the mainland, and he moved into Lewis in force. Neil *Mór* was executed in 1613, and the entire chiefly family was massacred.

The Mackenzies thus acquired virtually all the lands of *Sìol Thorcail* except for Raasay, whose chieftain subsequently represented the Lewis family. Trouble was largely avoided during the ensuing civil wars, though Malcolm of Raasay took part in the rising of 1745. In 1773 Samuel Johnson and James Boswell found him hale and hearty, 'yet his look was not fierce'. He was in fact a 'perfect representation of

Ardvreck Castle near the head of Loch Assynt in Sutherland, where Neil MacLeod arrested Montrose and handed him over to the government for eventual execution in 1650. The property passed to the Mackenzies ten years later.

a Highland gentleman'. Ominously, however, the young laird, his son, was £40,000 in debt. Nevertheless Raasay was not sold until 1846, when the chief and his family emigrated, as so many of their kinsmen had already done.

MacMillan

The name MacMillan comes from the Gaelic *Mac Mhaolain*, generally translated as 'son of the tonsured one', i.e. a monk, though it could conceivably mean merely bald. The tonsure in the old Celtic Church was different from the Roman one, requiring the whole front of the scalp to be shaved. Although there is no more substantial evidence, it is generally agreed that the ancestor of the MacMillans was a monk. In that case he would probably have been of high social rank

and would have been free to marry and beget heirs.

MacMillans were to be found in many different parts of the country and the connection between them, if there was one, would be hard to trace. The most eminent, chiefs of a substantial clan, were the MacMillans of Knap (Knapdale) in the late medieval/early modern period.

Earlier than this there were MacMillans around Loch Arkaig, in Lochaber. According to tradition they

Loch Arkaig in Lochaber, associated with the MacMillans at an early date, also with the Camerons. A 19th-century guidebook remarked that the scenery here, 'so little known', was hardly excelled 'or even equalled, by any of our Scottish lakes'.

were moved during the reign of King Malcolm IV to Crown lands by Loch Tay, though in fact they seem to have been still established in Lochaber centuries later. They are said to have bound themselves to the

MacMillan

Hunting MacMillan

Mackintoshes in the 15th century, probably in return for lands at Murlagan. They were thus rather awkwardly placed between the Camerons and the Mackintoshes, eventually transferring their allegiance to Cameron of Lochiel. There is a legend that Lochiel, having been wounded at Culloden, was carried from the field by two MacMillans. The Seven Men of Glenmoriston, who sheltered Prince Charles in a cave for a week, included for a time an eighth man named Hugh MacMillan.

The Macmillans of Knap, possibly descendants of the MacMillans of Loch Tay, acquired their extensive holdings in that peninsula by a marriage to an heiress of the MacNeils. They held a charter from the lord of the Isles which promised that the land should be theirs 'while the sea beats on the rock', a promise that was engraved on a rock beside Loch Sween. It has gone now, allegedly removed by the Campbells after they had acquired Knapdale in the 18th century. (Since the rock itself has disappeared, thrown into the sea by Campbell of Cawdor according to one story, the promise cannot be said to have proved false.)

There are other memorials of the MacMillans in the district still surviving: MacMillan's Tower at Castle Sween, and a fine Celtic cross in the churchyard of Kilmorie, which is carved on the reverse with a hunting scene, MacMillan himself (presumably) wielding an axe.

In the 18th century Duncan MacMillan of Dunmore was described as the representative of the vanished MacMillans of Knapdale. His estates subsequently passed to MacMillan of Laggalgarve, whose descendant is the present MacMillan of MacMillan, chief of the clan.

There were also MacMillans in Galloway and Ayrshire. The well-known publishing family originated in Arran and Ayrshire, gaining extra fame for the family and name when a political scion became British prime minister in 1951.

MacNab

The number of clan names with an ecclesiastical origin is not surprising when we remember that the higher ecclesiastical offices among the Celtic clergy were usually held by leading families and that the clergy, unlike those of the Roman Church, were allowed to marry.

Clann-an-Aba means 'children of the abbot', and the MacNabs were descended from the abbots of Glendochart, possibly from the 7th-century St Fillan, relics of whom are preserved in the Museum of National Antiquities in Edinburgh. Glendochart, west of Loch Tay, was the MacNabs' homeland.

The MacNabs, members of the ancient *Sìol Ailpein*, were traditionally connected with the MacGregors and Mackinnons, whom in a clan bond of 1606 they recognised as their kin.

During the wars of independence they supported the losing side and their lands were confiscated by the victorious Bruce. However, a feudal charter of 1336, restoring the barony of Bovain in Glendochart, shows that they were reconciled with King David II at that date.

Raeburn's famous portrait *The MacNab* shows a

MacNab

Strathfillan, in MacNab country. The chapel of St Fillan in the glen, an indignant Presbyterian remarked, was 'associated with monstrous popish superstitions'. In Glendochart, there were five hereditary Dewars, kin to the MacNabs, guarding relics of the saint.

figure of marked individuality, tough, uncompromising, eccentric; and the MacNab chiefs were renowned as men of forceful character. It is not hard to guess that a MacNab chief called Iain *Mìn*, or Smooth John, owed his nickname to the same spirit in which Robin Hood's comrade was called Little John.

The MacNabs were not a large clan and as they were never inclined to be dictated to their fortunes were decidedly mixed. Among their neighbours were the MacNeishes, a sept of Clan Gregor, whose base

Raeburn's magnificent portrait of the MacNab, Francis MacNab, 16th chief (1734-1816), wearing the uniform of Lieutenant-Colonel of the Royal Breadalbane Volunteers.

was on an island in Loch Earn. One of the most famous incidents in clan warfare occurred in 1612 when Smooth John, at that time not yet chief, led his eleven brothers against the MacNeishes, carrying their boat on a winter's night from Loch Tay over the steep hills to Loch Earn. Anyone familiar with that country would say such a feat was impossible, but in fact it was repeated by a party of Black Watch territorials in 1965. The MacNeishes, greatly reduced in numbers since a recent battle with the MacNabs, were surprised sleeping and slaughtered (except for the obligatory single survivor, necessary to tell the tale). The MacNabs carried their enemies' heads home in a sack. However, they were forced to abandon their boat in the hills.

During the 16th century the MacNabs expanded considerably, but by the end of the century most of

their lands were officially mortgaged to Campbell of Glenorchy, and they were listed among the 'broken' clans in 1594. Nevertheless, they were a considerable force by the time of Smooth John. As chief he joined Montrose in 1644 when the royalist commander arrived in Glendochart on his way to harry the Campbells, and he died fighting with his clansmen at the battle of Worcester in 1651.

The Campbells were then able to dispossess the MacNabs, but the estates were regained after the Restoration, when the Campbells were going through a rare phase of royal disfavour. In the risings of 1715 and 1745 the MacNabs were not eager Jacobites. Although the clan was 'out' for Princes Charles, the MacNab himself adhered to the Hanoverian government.

Francis, twelfth and last chief of his line (the subject of Raeburn's portrait), held considerable estates at the end of the 18th century, augmented by an inheritance through his mother. However, by the time he died in 1816, he had amassed large debts and although 'he left the MacNab country littered with bastards', he failed to produce a legitimate heir.

He was therefore succeeded by his nephew Archibald, hitherto better acquainted with the salons of Paris and London than the hills of Perthshire. One morning he went out for a walk with his dogs and gun and disappeared. His creditors traced him to London and he fled to Canada, where he attempted to set up a little feudal empire among the MacNabs who had emigrated earlier. His exploitation of his clansmen led eventually to criminal prosecution, but he later returned to settle in Orkney, for by that time the MacNab lands had all been sold to the Earl of Breadalbane (i.e. Campbell of Glenorchy). The descendant of one of the Canadian MacNabs, Sir Allan MacNab, became prime minister of Canada.

Part of the old MacNab lands were recovered over a century later, and the present MacNab lives in Kinnel House, which was the home of his predecessors in the 17th and 18th centuries (after the castle of Eilean Ran had been destroyed by Cromwellian troopers in 1654).

MacNaughton

The MacNaughtons (or MacNachtans, etc., 'sons of Nechtan') were of ancient Pictish stock, and their homeland was between Loch Awe and Loch Fyne in Argyll, in what was to become the heart of Campbell country. They were earlier established in Strathtay and were probably moved there from Moray by King Malcolm IV in the 12th century. Later MacNaughton chiefs held land in widely scattered districts.

Gillechrist MacNaughton, son of Malcolm, was made hereditary keeper of the royal castle of Fraoch Eilean in Loch Awe in 1267. He also held Dunderave, on Loch Fyne, which was the residence of the chiefs of MacNaughton for many centuries. When Argyll was formed into a sheriffdom in 1292 MacNaughton was one of the twelve barons of whose lands the sheriffdom was comprised.

As adherents of the MacDougall lords of Lorne the MacNaughtons supported Balliol against Bruce and after Bruce's victory lost many of their lands to the fast-rising Campbells. They changed sides later and received other lands from Bruce's successor King David II. Sir Alexander MacNaughton died fighting for James IV at Flodden in 1513.

Since they no longer held lands on Loch Awe, Dunderave became the home of the MacNaughton chiefs from the 14th century onwards. Relations with the Campbells at this time were apparently untroubled, and the MacNaughtons seem to have recovered the position they held in the 13th century.

But the chiefs continued in their loyalty to the Stewarts throughout the 17th century, which entailed periodic Campbell hostility. In 1689 the sixteenth Laird of MacNaughton fought under Bonnie Dundee at Killiecrankie, for which he then lost his estates.

A bad situation deteriorated beyond recall about 1700 when the next chief, John of Dunderave, seventeenth and last of his line, fell out (albeit in romantic circumstances) with Campbell of Ardkinglas, whose daughter he was to marry. There were two eligible daughters and MacNaughton's scheduled bride was, he thought, the younger one, with whom, as subsequent events proved, he was genuinely in love. His prospective father-in-law had slightly different plans, however. When MacNaughton arrived for the wedding he indulged himself unwisely during the pre-nuptial convivialities and, on recovering from an alcoholic daze, discovered that he had married the elder daughter. He thereupon promptly – and permanently – disappeared into the mists of Ireland, taking with him not his unwanted wife but her sister, whom he had intended to marry.

The upshot was that Ardkinglas gained possession of the forfeited MacNaughton estates, the chiefship became vacant, and the clan, chiefless and landless, virtually ceased to exist.

However, in the 19th century zealous MacNaughton genealogists discovered a direct descendant in the male line of Sir Alexander MacNaughton, who died at Flodden. His name was Edmund MacNaughton and he lived in Co. Antrim. He was recognised as chief by the Lyon Court in 1818, and the title is held by his descendants, still resident in Antrim.

MacNaughton

MacNeil of Barra

The MacNeils were confined almost exclusively to the smaller islands of the Hebrides, chiefly Barra, Gigha and Colonsay, and in the 16th century they made their living largely from piracy. A famous story relates how Rory the Unruly of Barra got into trouble in the late 16th century by attacking English ships, which provoked a sharp protest from Queen Elizabeth to her kinsman, King James VI. Mackenzie of Kintail was commissioned to bring in the culprit, which he accomplished by some sort of trick, and the king demanded of MacNeil, an amiable-looking old gentleman with a long white beard, what the devil he meant by harassing the Queen of England's ships. MacNeil replied that he had thought to do His Majesty a favour by annoying the woman who had murdered his mother.

The MacNeil chiefs, famous for being even

prouder than they were poor, claimed descent from Niall of the Nine Hostages, king – at least in name – of all Ireland about the end of the 4th century. This is about as far back as even the old Celtic genealogists could go. The MacNeils were of the same stock as the MacLachlans, Lamonts and MacEwens, and took their name from Niall, a descendant of Anrothan, the Irish prince who married into the royal house of Argyll in the 11th century.

Niall lived in about 1300, but the first O'Neill chief known from historical records is a century later. He had a charter of Barra from the Lord of the Isles in 1427. Kisimul Castle, on a rock in a land-locked bay on the south of Barra, was the home of the chiefs for many years. The mooring place for MacNeil's galley can still be seen in the rock on which the castle stands.

MacNeil of Barra

Kisimul Castle, longtime home of the MacNeil chiefs, perched on its rock opposite Castle Bay, Barra. The MacNeils held Barra of the Crown, then, from the time of Rory the Unruly, of Mackenzie of Kintail (who had been responsible for getting Rory to Edinburgh by 'liquefying' him first), then of MacDonald of Sleat.

An old ceremony said to have been conducted there illustrates the extraordinary self-importance of the old island chiefs, and also the amazing cultural exchanges that took place in those distant times – since the ceremony is believed to be of oriental origin and was presumably introduced by the far-sailing Norsemen. In the evening a trumpeter ascended the ramparts of Kisimul and blew his horn to all corners of the compass, before declaring, to all the nations, that since the great MacNeil of Barra had finished eating, the princes of the earth might now sit down to dine. Poor or not, the MacNeils of Barra lived at Kisimul in some style.

The MacNeils remained loyal to the lords of the Isles and, after their disappearance, to the Stewart dynasty. The chief was 'out' in 1688-89 for King James VII/II and in 1715 for his son. After the Forty-five Roderick, 'the dove of the west', was imprisoned for Jacobite sympathies although he appears to have taken no part in the events of 1745-46. His great-grandson, the last of his line, was forced to sell Barra in 1838. The chiefship continued in exile and in 1914 passed to Robert Lister MacNeil of Barra, an American who fulfilled a childhood dream by repurchasing Kisimul Castle and much of Barra. He restored the ruined castle, making many fascinating discoveries in the process, and endeavoured to restore prosperity to the islanders.

MacNeil of Colonsay

According to tradition the MacNeils of Colonsay (who generally spelt their name MacNeill) and the MacNeils of Barra descended from two brothers. Of their common origin there can be no doubt. Since their lands were much closer to the centre of Campbell power, however, the territorial history of the MacNeils of Colonsay is less stable.

Their ancestors were known as the MacNeils of Taynish and Gigha, and in 1449 Torquil MacNeil of Taynish was keeper of Sween Castle (it later passed to the MacMillans through marriage with a MacNeil heiress after the main line had failed). Torquil was the father of numerous minor branches, and the genealogy of the family of Tynish and Gigha is very complicated. Right up to modern times there was a great deal of exchanging of lands and responsibilities. It is said that on Sundays the children of the MacNeils of Colonsay were compelled to recite their genealogy backwards: one pities the poor creatures.

The island of Gigha was sold in 1554 but two brothers, descendants of Torquil named Neil and John Òg, revived the failing fortunes of their house and Gigha was repurchased from the Campbells before the end of the 16th century.

Torquil MacNeil of Gigha was described as 'Chief and principal of the clan and surname of MacNeils' by the Privy Council in 1530, but this seems to have been a temporary anomaly (and in any case it is not certain that he did belong to this branch).

Colonsay and adjacent Oronsay, where the MacNeils had been established since early times, were acquired by Donald MacNeil of Crear in exchange for his own estates from the Earl of Argyll in 1700. His descendant Alexander, sixth of Colonsay, sold it to his brother Duncan and himself acquired Gigha from his cousin – a characteristic MacNeil transaction, confusing to the historian.

The early 19th century was a time of prosperity in the islands thanks to the kelp industry and, on Colonsay, to the reforms of 'the Old Laird'. But prosperity was short-lived. After more complicated exchanges, the island was eventually sold to pay off debts in the late 19th century, while the chiefship passed to a New Zealander.

MacPhee

The probable Gaelic original of MacPhee, or MacFie, is *Mac Duibh-sidhe* (son of the black fairy), and MacDuffy was an early form of the name. The MacPhees were said to have had close contacts with the fairy folk, and the name has prompted speculation that this undoubtedly ancient clan sprang from pre-Celtic stock. Another legend ascribes the origin of the MacPhees to a union between a mortal and a mermaid, or seal-woman. The more recent association of MacPhee with the trade of the tinker tends to encourage the belief in their ancient association with the elves, though more realistically this was due to their misfortune in losing their lands and livelihood.

The original homeland of the MacPhees, as far as

MacNeil of Colonsay

MacPhee

can be traced, was the fertile island of Colonsay, with the adjacent isle of Oronsay, in the Inner Hebrides. They held these lands under the lord of the Isles and were hereditary keepers of the records of the lordship, which have sadly almost totally disappeared.

A MacPhee sat on the lord's council at Finlaggan in 1463, though apparently not earlier, and after the fall of the lordship the clan were active in support of efforts to restore it. A fine tombstone in Oronsay commemorates the death in 1539 of 'Murchardus' MacPhee, and he was presumably the same chief who had been charged with treason eight years earlier in connection with his support of the lordship. Later chiefs generally followed MacDonald of Islay, and Sir Iain Moncreiffe suggested that the 'elfin bolt' which killed the MacLean of Duart Chief when his clan invaded Islay in 1598 was fired not by a *dubh-shidh* (a black fairy) but by a *Mac Duibh-sidh* (a MacPhee). There is a story too, from about this time, of a MacPhee chief who was killed by one of the MacLeans.

A MacPhee was among the Highland chiefs who consented (under duress) to the Statutes of Iona (1609), an attempt by the government of King James VI/I to restrain the independence of the chiefs by generally conciliatory means which, however, included drastic reduction of their authority.

The MacPhees' support for the MacDonalds of Islay eventually led to their downfall. Malcolm MacPhee of Colonsay joined the MacDonald rebellion of 1615 with forty men, probably all the fighting men of his clan. Another Clan Donald chieftain, Alexander MacDonald, known as Colkitto from his Gaelic nickname meaning left-handed (he was the father of Alasdair MacColla, sometimes erroneously given the nickname of his father, who gained such a reputation with Montrose), acting on behalf of the Earl of Argyll, defeated and later killed MacPhee of Colonsay (the MacPhee chief had attempted to hide under a heap of seaweed). Colonsay passed into his possession, then to the Earl of Argyll, who exchanged it in about 1700 for the lands of Donald MacNeil of Crear, in Knapdale.

The MacPhees, deprived of their chief and of their lands, became a 'broken' clan. Some of them settled in Lochaber and became a sept of Cameron of Lochiel, fighting with notable courage at Culloden. Others remained with the MacDonalds of Islay.

In the 1840s Ewen MacPhee held out on an island in Loch Phee (since named after him) with his wife, as good a shot as himself, and their children for some years, paying no rent, acknowledging no authority, and keeping intruders at bay. The outlaw is said to have been expelled after, as an elderly man, he was caught stealing sheep.

MacPherson

MacPherson means 'son of the parson' and there may have been other sons of parsons so named who were not connected with the famous Highland clan.

The MacPhersons of Badenoch were important members of Clan Chattan, for a long time rivals for its captaincy with the Mackintoshes. Like them, they claimed descent from Gillechattan in the 13th century, but the origins of the MacPhersons have not yet been fully elucidated. Among other names, they were

known as *Clann Mhuirich*, after Muriach (or Murdoch), great-grandfather of Duncan (the) Parson (imprisoned at Tantallon Castle with the Lord of the Isles in 1438), hereditary parson of Kingussie, and descended from Gillechattan.

They are also known as the Clan of the Three Brothers, who were sons of Ewen, a 14th-century chief said to have been son of Muriach. There are problems in fitting all these ancestors together chronologically however. Of these three brothers, Kenneth was the ancestor of the Cluny MacPhersons, who eventually came to be recognised as overall chiefs, Iain of the MacPhersons of Pitmain and Gilles the MacPhersons of Invereshie.

The conflict between the Mackintoshes and the MacPhersons was particularly unfortunate in view of the proximity of powerful neighbours, by no means friendly. The Comyns (Cummings) were their overlords until destroyed by Bruce in the early 14th century; then the Stewarts, among them the notorious Wolf of Badenoch whose principles, if fortunately not typical, were not far removed from other self-important lords, and finally the Gordon earls of Huntly, generally backed by royal commissions and not averse to exterminating their opponents if an opportunity presented itself. Huntly naturally exploited the Mackintosh-MacPherson rivalry on the time-honoured principle of 'divide and rule'.

Loch Laggan in Badenoch, MacPherson country. The MacPhersons lived for some time in this district without legal title. The clan museum at Newtonmore contains many fascinating relics.

MacPherson

Hunting MacPherson

From the 15th to the 17th century there were occasions of which evidence survives when the paramount status of the Mackintosh chiefs was acknowledged by the MacPhersons, but on the whole there was little co-operation, and the MacPhersons were seldom eager to support the Mackintoshes in their feuds. Andrew MacPherson of Cluny, with other MacPherson chieftains, signed the Clan Chattan bond of union in 1609, but Cluny MacPherson's claim to the captaincy of the confederation of the Cat was reasserted in 1672, only to be overturned by the Privy Council, which pronounced the Mackintosh to be 'the only and true representer of the ancient and honourable Clan Chattan'.

Duncan of Cluny, the rejected claimant of 1672, had no sons and proposed to settle the chiefship on his daughter Anne, who was married to Sir Duncan Campbell (of the Cawdor house). This was opposed by William MacPherson of Nuid, the nearest male heir, and others, and their opposition prevailed. When Cluny died he was succeeded by Nuid's brother, Lachlan.

The MacPhersons were strong royalists during the civil wars of the 17th century, Ewen of Cluny leading a Badenoch contingent under Montrose. But, although they were an ancient clan and not insignificant numerically, they did not play a great part in national affairs (partly as a result of their own divisions) until the 18th century, when their record of zealous support for the Stewart dynasty continued. Sir Aeneas MacPherson of Invereshie, whose father died of wounds sustained in Montrose's campaign, was a Jacobite agent after 1688 and, following a spell in prison in vile conditions, departed under sentence of banishment to the Jacobite court in France. Duncan of Cluny was 'out' with his clan in the Forty-five, and the greatest of MacPherson Jacobite heroes, Ewen of

Cluny (son of William of Nuid who died in 1746), also made his reputation in that sad affair. He joined Prince Charles at an early stage of the campaign in 1745, bringing 600 men, and fought with great dash and bravado. Campaigning elsewhere, he arrived at Culloden too late to take part in the fighting.

Afterwards, with a large price on his head, he hid in 'Cluny's Cage', a specially constructed hide-out on Ben Alder in Badenoch, for nine years, protected and supplied by his men, even receiving rent regularly from his tenants. Eventually he escaped to France. His forfeited estates were restored to his son Duncan in 1784 and Cluny, which had been destroyed after Culloden, was rebuilt.

Duncan's son Ewen (died 1885) was one of those Victorian Highland chiefs who maintained the old style and traditions in an age when they had become sadly redundant. But in spite of difficulties Cluny was not sold until the 1930s. The clan museum at Newtonmore, opened in 1952, was the first of its kind.

James MacPherson (1736-96), who was born in Kingussie, caused a tremendous stir with his alleged translations of Ossian, the Celtic bard of the 3rd century. The work was in fact mostly his own invention, as many suggested at the time (including Samuel Johnson), and modern Gaelic scholars find it hard to understand how anyone could have believed otherwise. Nevertheless, his *Works of Ossian* is a considerable achievement. It gave a powerful impetus to the Romantic movement in Europe.

The MacPhersons have a red tartan but the grey hunting tartan is generally preferred, being of some antiquity. It is said to be identical with the 'grey plaid of Badenoch' copied in 1745 by Lady Cluny-Mac-Pherson, the chief's wife, from an old plaid then at Cluny, which makes it one of the oldest, perhaps *the* oldest, authentic clan tartan.

MacQuarrie

MacQuarrie

The MacQuarries were a very small clan, whose badge of the pine marked them as members of *Sìol Ailpein*. The name was derived from *Guaire*, meaning noble, the original *Guaire* being, tradition says, the brother of Fingon (beloved), ancestor of the Mackinnons.

When those articulate travellers Samuel Johnson and James Boswell visited Ulva, off Mull, in 1773 they found it 'an island of no great extent, rough and barren, inhabited by the *Macquarrys*; a clan not powerful nor numerous, but of antiquity, which most other families are content to reverence'. The chief impressed them rather more, with his intelligence and worldliness (they never quite overcame the presumption of Lowlanders and Englishmen that Highland chiefs were primitive savages).

The MacQuarries had been established in Ulva for centuries. They also held Staffa, later famous for 'Fingal's Cave', and part of Mull. The first of them to appear in historical records was Iain of Ulva, who lived in the mid-15th century and was probably a member of the council of the lord of the Isles. It is said that a former chief supported King Alexander II in his campaign in Argyll in 1249, and his successor fought under Bruce at Bannockburn. The MacQuarries were active in efforts to restore the lordship after its suppression, supporting the rebellions of Donald *Dubh*, and they were associated with MacLean of Duart.

The island of Staffa, associated with the Macquarries and their kin, the Mackinnons, is one of the geological marvels of Britain. Its strange basaltic architecture (this is the feature known in English as the Herdsman) was generally unknown until the late 18th century.

In 1609 the MacQuarrie chief was one of the Highland chiefs inveigled into agreeing to the Statutes of Iona by King James VI/I's emissary.

In the train of the MacLeans, the MacQuarries were caught up in debilitating feuds, and they never recovered from the disaster at Inverkeithing (1651) when the chief and many of his men died, along with Duart and many MacLeans, fighting for Charles II. The MacQuarries were also involved in resisting Campbell encroachments in Argyll in the 1670s and in Bonnie Dundee's victory at Killiecrankie in 1689.

Lachlan MacQuarrie of Ulva, the chief who entertained Johnson and Boswell, was forced to sell his lands a few years later. He himself entered the army, at the alleged age of 63, and died in Mull in 1818, when he would have been 103 if the records are correct. He was the last of his line and there have been no MacQuarrie chiefs since, although no doubt some family from North America will one day succeed in establishing their claim (the MacQuarries, scarce in Scotland, are numerous in the New World).

The most famous member of the clan was a cousin of the last chief, Lachlan MacQuarrie (1762-1824), a soldier who was governor of New South Wales from 1810 to 1821. His brand of benevolent despotism (he was fortunate in having his own regiment, the 73rd, with him) plus his passion for building, turned a chaotic penal settlement into a substantial, even prosperous colony. He is remembered with affection and respect, and commemorated in numerous place-names (many of them bestowed by himself).

MacQueen

There are numerous, often highly dissimilar derivations of this name, the principal one of which is from the Gaelic *Suibhne*, meaning 'going well'. Preceded by Mac, the S is aspirated, giving rise to something very like 'MacQueen'. Some writers suggest that the origin is *Mac Cuinn* (son of Conn, i.e. the semi-legendary Conn of the Hundred Battles), but this was denied by George Black (*The Surnames of Scotland*, 1946). The Gaelic name is in turn perhaps derived from the Norse *Sweyn*.

At any rate, the Macqueens were of Hebridean origin, and were associated with the MacDonalds (in 1778 Lord MacDonald of Sleat wrote in a letter to the Macqueen chief that the Macqueens 'have been invariably attached to our family, to whom we believe we owe our existence'). It is therefore at first sight

MacQueen

surprising that the clan of this name should have been a member of the confederation of Clan Chattan. They were known as the Macqueens of Corribrough (the chiefly family) or alternatively as Clan Revan.

According to the traditional explanation the Clan Chattan Macqueens came from Moidart on the west coast early in the 15th century when Mora MacDonald of Moidart married the Mackintosh, bringing with her the usual train of kinsfolk. Among them was Revan, ancestor of the Macqueens of Corribrough, who settled in Strathdeath. Revan apparently fought with the Mackintoshes against the Lord of the Isles at the battle of Harlaw in 1411.

The first Macqueen known to be styled as 'of Corribrough' was Donald, who signed the Clan Chattan bond of union in 1609, taking responsibility also for Macqueen of Little Corribrough and Sweyn Macqueen of Railbeg.

The Macqueen lands appear to have been lost in the late 18th century, when a great number of the clan emigrated. A later chief followed their example and the chiefship is now in New Zealand.

There were Macqueens and MacSweens also in Argyll (MacSweens held Sween Castle in the 13th century), and the Hebrides, notably at Garafad in Skye. The Rev. Donald MacQueen, who in 1773 so impressed Dr Johnson ('There must be great vigour of mind to make him cultivate learning so much in the isle of Skye, where he might do without it'), was the fourth generation of Macqueen ministers of the church at Snizort.

Robert MacQueen, Lord Braxfield, the late 18th-century judge notable for the savagery of his prejudices and his sentences, came from a Lanarkshire family whose connection with the clan, if any, no one is particularly anxious to make.

MacRae

The name *Mac Rath* means 'son of grace'. MacRae is one of many anglicised forms, which include Macrea and the Irish form Magrath, which is closest to the original. It is basically a forename (like MacBeth), and may or may not have something to do with the number of MacRaes who entered the Church in the early modern period.

When surnames first became common in Scotland at the end of the Middle Ages MacRaes cropped up in various parts of the Lowlands and modern MacRaes are not necessarily related to the clan for ever associated with Kintail and the castle of Eilean Donan.

The original home of the MacRaes was near Inverness. They had a long-standing association with the Frasers, and there was once an inscription above the gates of Lord Lovat's castle asserting that no MacRae should wait without while there was a Fraser within. However, by the end of the 14th century they were established on the other side of the country in Kintail, Wester Ross, and attached to the rising star of the Mackenzies. Later a branch of the MacRaes acquired Inverinate from the Mackenzie Earl of Seaforth.

Eilean Donan Castle, of which the MacRaes were constables. Originally built by Alexander II in 1220 as a defence against Scandinavian raids, it was largely destroyed during the Jacobite rising of 1719 and rebuilt in this century.

MacRae

They became constables of Eilean Donan castle – not a hereditary office since it was sometimes held by others – more-or-less permanently. They also held other honoured posts under Mackenzie of Seaforth, whose chamberlain was at various times a MacRae, and were ministers of surrounding parishes. In the 17th century the same man was constable of Eilean Donan and minister of Kintail. This was Farquhar MacRae (1580-1662) of Inverinate, whose grandson Duncan of the Silver Cups compiled the invaluable Gaelic poetry anthology known as the Fernaig Manuscript, which contained works by himself and other MacRaes.

The MacRaes' loyalty to the Mackenzies and their stout defence of Eilean Donan castle, commanding the entry to Loch Duich and the route to the Isles, earned them the name 'Mackenzie's shirt of mail'. In 1539 when Donald *Gruamach* of Sleat was besieging the castle (at that time commanded by a Matheson), in his effort to restore the lordship of the Isles in his own person, Duncan MacRae, son of a previous constable, shot him in the knee with an arrow fired from the battlements. The wound might not have been so bad but Sleat impatiently wrenched out the arrow, and the barbs fatally ripped an artery. There are other tales of the individual military prowess of 'the wild MacRaes', one of whom, when Cromwellian troops occupied Eilean Donan, slew a soldier with one stroke of his sword.

During the unsuccessful Jacobite rising of 1719 Spanish troops who landed with the exiled Mackenzie chief were billeted at Eilean Donan, and the castle was subsequently blown up. It was restored in the 1930s to its present picturesque state, and it remains in the hands of descendants of the MacRaes of Conchra, an important branch of the clan since the 17th century.

Malcolm

It is said that the names Malcolm and MacCallum are interchangeable, and since an 18th-century Chief of the MacCallums, Alexander of Poltalloch, changed his own name to Malcolm solely, it appears, for 'aesthetic reasons', assuming them to be identical. However, there is an argument that the two were really quite different. Malcolm means 'servant' or 'devotee of Colm' (Columba). The Gaelic *Maol*

Malcolm

('shaven-headed', therefore 'monk') is similar, as a prefix, to the more familiar 'Gille-'. The 'devotee' of Colm is not the same as the 'son of Colm' (i.e. MacCallum), and the implication is clearly that no such blood relationship existed. The argument is strengthened by the paucity of evidence that, before the 18th-century MacCallum chief, the two names were used interchangeably. However, it must be said that this evidence is not altogether lacking, and also that it would be surprising if it could be found in convincing quantity, whatever the situation was. According to the famous work of Dr George Black (*Surnames of Scotland*, New York, 1946), MacCallum is a version of *Mac Gille Chaluim*, of which there are 15th-century examples, which means 'son of the devotee of Calum'. This seems to weaken the original argument. It is true, however, that as a surname Malcolm is comparatively recent (see MacCallum).

There is, anyway, both a MacCallum and a Malcolm tartan. Take your pick.

Matheson

The name comes from the Gaelic *Mac Mhathain*, though Mathesons in the south were 'sons of Matthew' and not connected with the northern clan. The clan was traditionally descended from Gilleon of the Aird, a scion of the royal house of Lorne who was also the ancestor of the Mackenzies.

The first known Matheson chief was Cormac (now regarded as the second chief), who fought with the

Matheson

Earl of Ross against Haakon of Norway, harrying the Norse Hebrides, possibly fighting at Largs (1263) and receiving twenty cows from the earl for services rendered. He held land in Lochalsh, the ancient home of the Mathesons.

Subsequently the Mathesons supported the Lord of the Isles, who became Earl of Ross in the 15th century. They were present at Harlaw in support of the lord's claim to the Ross earldom, and their chief was captured in that battle. This man, Alasdair, or his successor, was among those arrested at Inverness by King James I in 1427. At that time he was said to have 2,000 fighting men at his call, which would have made the Mathesons equal in strength to the Mackenzies. However, the Mackenzies were to expand while the Mathesons, as allies of the MacDonalds, were to contract. Their precarious hold on their lands was further weakened by clan feuds.

However, as noted already, the Mathesons were kin to the Mackenzies and at times they appear to

have held Eilean Donan castle (more often the prerogative of the MacRaes) on behalf of Mackenzie of Kintail. A Matheson chief, Iain *Dubh*, was killed in 1539 while defending the castle against MacDonald of Sleat, who was himself killed by a MacRae arrow on the same occasion.

Iain *Dubh*'s grandson was Murchadh (or Murdoch) *Buidhe*, from whom many branches of the Mathesons claim descent. Among them were the Mathesons of Bennetsfield in the Black Isle who included a hero of Culloden. This man's grandson was the historian of the clan, and his descendants became the present chiefly family.

Meanwhile a branch of the clan had settled in Sutherland in the 15th century, their leading family being the Mathesons of Shiness. They suffered grievously during the Sutherland Clearances, and many emigrated.

By the early 19th century practically all the Matheson lands had been lost, but fortune was restored to the name by two merchant princes, James Matheson and his nephew Alexander. They belonged to the Mathesons of Shiness; Alexander's father, however, had married into the Lochalsh Mathesons. Both amassed fortunes in the Eastern trade which they invested in property. Alexander gained Lochalsh, the old clan homeland, spending about a million pounds on purchase and subsequent land improvements. Sir James bought Lewis in 1844 and spent generously to alleviate the famine that struck the inhabitants on the failure of the potato crop in the following year.

Maxwell

The first leader of this famous Border clan of whom we have record was Maccus, son of Underweyn, who lived in the 12th century. He was probably of English origin (some say Norse) and gave his name to Maccuswell (*wael* meaning 'pool' in old English), near Kelso on the Tweed. His grandson, John of Maccuswell (Maxwell) was Chamberlain of Scotland about ten years before his death in 1241 and he was probably the first to hold the great Maxwell stronghold of Caerlaverock, whose impressive ruins stand today in the marshy fields of lower Nithsdale. He was succeeded as chamberlain by his brother Sir Aymer, from two of whose sons, Herbert and John, many of the numerous branches of the Maxwells descended.

The position of Border lords like the Maxwells

'between the hammer and the anvil', was not an easy one, though on the whole they tended to make the most of it. During the wars of independence Caerlaverock was besieged and changed hands on more than one occasion. Herbert, son of Aymer, recognised John Balliol as king and his grandson, Sir Eustace, held Caerlaverock for the English in 1312. But he subsequently dismantled the fortifications – before Bruce knocked them down – and was one of those who signed the Declaration of Arbroath, sometimes called Scotland's declaration of independence, in 1320. The castle was rebuilt on a triangular plan in the 16th century. Sir Eustace reverted briefly to (Edward) Balliol in 1322 and Sir John Maxwell, his brother and successor, accompanied King David II on the expedition which ended at Neville's Cross in 1346. Maxwell was captured and sent to London.

The Maxwells became increasingly important in the 15th century after the eclipse of the Black

Left: **Maxwell**

Below: Caerlaverock Castle, held by the Maxwells for four centuries. Earlier fortifications date back to the 13th century. It was largely ruined after a siege by the Covenanters during the Civil War.

Douglases. The chiefs bore the title Lord Maxwell from 1424, and as the leading power in the district often held the office of warden of the Western Marches. After Flodden (1513), where John, fourth Lord Maxwell, was killed fighting for the king, this office became almost a Maxwell monopoly.

Thanks to feudal ties, the power of the Maxwells was considerable; they were also supported by the many branches of the clan, and surviving bonds of manrent show them to have been particularly successful in securing loyalty and support by that means.

It was never an easy task, however. John Maxwell of Terregles, brother of the fifth Lord Maxwell (who later became Lord Herries through his wife's inheritance), resigned as warden in 1553 because he could not deal with proliferating local feuds. Later, however, he resumed the office. Meanwhile his brother had served briefly as regent during King James V's absence from the kingdom and was later captured by the English at Solway Moss (1542).

The Maxwells were naturally involved in feuds themselves, notably with the Johnstons, who also at times held the office of warden of the Marches. The rivalry was particularly fierce towards the end of the 16th century, and in 1593 the sixth Lord Maxwell, who had become Earl of Morton after the execution of the Douglas holder of that title in 1581, was killed in a battle with the Johnstons near Lockerbie. The seventh lord eventually gained revenge, killing Johnston of that ilk in 1608. Afterwards he fled abroad, but unwisely returned a few years later and was executed in 1613.

By this time the union of the Scottish and English Crowns had brought to an end the perpetual wars on the Borders and the Maxwells, along with other great Border families, lost their traditional role. Nevertheless, they did not retire into obscurity. Robert, eighth Lord Maxwell, was created Earl of Nithsdale – the earldom of Morton having been returned to the Douglas family – and on the death of his son without issue the title passed to Lord Herries, descendant of the first Lord Herries mentioned above.

The fifth Earl of Nithsdale embraced the Jacobite cause and was captured at Preston in 1715. He was tried for treason and sentenced to death, but his wife, a lady of some mettle, secured his escape from the Tower of London disguised as a maidservant. They got away to Rome where the earl died in 1744.

Among the prominent branches of the Maxwells were the Maxwells of Monreith, the barony held in the 15th century by a grandson of the first Lord Maxwell. Sir Herbert Maxwell (1845-1937), writer, statesman and expert salmon fisherman – and father of the writer-naturalist Gavin Maxwell (1914-69) – belonged to this line.

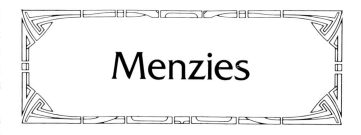

Menzies

The name Menzies is of Norman origin. It probably comes from Mesnières, and the English version of the surname is Manners. An early spelling in Scotland was Meyners, and the name is usually still pronounced (and sometimes spelt) Mingies.

The family was apparently first settled in Lothian, but in the reign of King Alexander II Robert de Meyners, who was the Royal Chamberlain, held Culdares (Culdair). A charter from him (regarded as the first chief of the Atholl Clan Menzies) to Sir Matthew Moncreiffe of that ilk, confirming him in the lands of Culdares and Duneaves (Glenlyon) is still in the possession of the Moncreiffes.

Sir Robert's son Alexander held Weem, Aberfeldy, Fortingall and Glendochart in Breadalbane as well as Durisdeer in Nithsdale. His son supported Bruce and was rewarded with further territories, making the family one of the largest landholders in the southern Highlands. In the early 15th century a David Menzies was governor of Orkney and Shetland under the king of Norway.

Sir Robert Menzies, descendant of the first Sir Robert, had his properties erected into a barony by King James IV, and at about this time the great Castle Weems (it was later renamed Castle Menzies) was built.

The Menzies were involved in various feuds. There was trouble with the Campbells despite various bonds and marriage alliances, and in a quarrel with

Hunting Menzies

the Stewarts of Garth, who had taken over the former Menzies property of Fortingall, the 'place of Weems' was burned early in the 16th century. The castle was rebuilt later on the Z-plan, designed for effective fire against raiders. During the 19th century it was enlarged and embellished with the usual turrets, etc., though without obliterating the original structure. Later it fell into ruins, but it has been partly restored by the Clan Menzies Society and remains the clan headquarters.

During the various civil conflicts of the 17th and 18th centuries Menzies were to be found on both sides. The Weems family were allied with the Campbells but the Pitfoddels branch fought with Montrose.

The senior house was again active on behalf of William III, but Pitfoddels was 'out' in the Fifteen for James Edward. During the Forty-five Clan Menzies, or some of them, were raised by Menzies of Shian, though it was said that the summons of the fiery cross was not obeyed with great enthusiasm by the clansmen.

The last member of the Pitfoddels family is remembered for founding the Roman Catholic college of Blairs, on Deeside.

A member of the senior line of Weems was the first, or one of the first, to introduce what is now a characteristic Highland tree, the larch, from the Tyrol, in 1737.

The Menzies of Menzies, chief of the clan, whose Gaelic title is *Am Mèinnearach*, is a member of a branch of the Culdares family, the senior line having ended in 1910.

The tartan illustrated below is a so-called mourning tartan. The Menzies also have a red tartan of the same sett (their war cry is 'Up with the White and Red!').

Moncreiffe

The name Moncreiffe comes from a Gaelic placename, *Monadh Craoibhe*, meaning 'hill of the sacred bough', or 'tree', which overlooks the valleys harbouring Scone and other centres of the ancient Pictish kings. The late Sir Iain Moncreiffe of that ilk, a notable Highland historian, surmised that the Moncreiffes themselves were descended from these Pictish kings in the female line.

Very few of Scotland's ancient families have remained ensconced in their original home and district for so long; there were Moncreiffes of Moncreiffe at the time of the earliest surviving records, and they are still there today.

Sir Matthew of Moncreiffe, brother-in-law of one of the regents of Scotland, had a royal charter of that estate in 1248, and a year later another charter from Sir Robert Menzies (founder of the Highland clan of that name) for the lands of Culdares and Duneaves, in Glenlyon.

For such an ancient and distinguished family the Moncreiffes did not play a major part in national affairs generally, which no doubt helps to explain why they have managed to hold on to their patrimony. Though various conflicts could hardly be avoided, the Moncreiffes, as Sir Iain wrote, 'have always had a firm reputation of loyalty to the Sovereign's person.' One was chamberlain to King James III and two fell at Flodden. However, one took part in the murder of Rizzio, Mary Queen of Scots' secretary.

Black and White Menzies

Moncreiffe

In 1312 Sir John Moncreiffe of that ilk, who is said to have once sheltered Wallace in a cave on Moncreiffe Hill, gave Easter Moncreiffe to his younger son Matthew, founder of that house. In 1592 Easter Moncreiffe was erected into a free barony, giving the laird the same powers of life and death as those of the Laird of Moncreiffe himself, but in the late 17th century it was acquired by Thomas Moncreiffe of Moncreiffe, who as the first baronet later became Sir Thomas.

The old tower house of Easter Moncreiffe fell into ruins about this time, presumably because no one lived there, but a house was built to replace it early in the 18th century. It was much extended in Victorian times by Sir Robert, eighth baronet and twenty-first Laird of Moncreiffe. Later it was the home of the ninth Duke of Atholl, from whom it was acquired by Sir Iain, a cousin of the twenty-third Laird of Moncreiffe. He also gained the old tower and the barony (no longer with powers of life and death, however).

The House of Moncreiffe was built in the late 17th century to replace a medieval tower house by Sir William Bruce, who went on to build Holyrood Palace. It was destroyed in a terrible fire in 1957 in which the twenty-third laird lost his life. Bruce's doorway is incorporated in the new house which, though of more modest scale, owes much to its predecessor.

The three main branches of the Moncreiffes are distinguished by the way the name is spelt. The Moncreiffs of Tulliebole have produced many distinguished churchmen. A number of other cadet branches, descended from the lairds of Moncreiffe, are called Moncrieff. They include the Scott-Moncrieffs, one of whom gained great literary fame as the translator of Proust.

The Moncreiffe tartan is a recent one, designed by Sir Iain Moncreiffe of that ilk, who chose a simple diced pattern of the kind which seems to have been common in the days before tartans became popular emblems. Previously Moncreiffes wore the Murray of Atholl tartan, having been closely connected with the Murrays for centuries.

Montgomery

Montgomery is a conspicuously Norman name. Roger de Montgomerie (died 1094) was one of those left in charge while the Duke of Normandy was absent on

Montgomery

other business in 1066. The following year he came to England and was made Earl of Arundel.

The first in Scotland was Robert de Mundegumri (died c. 1177), a grandson of the Earl of Arundel, who arrived with Walter fitzAlan, Steward to King David I. He received Eaglesham in Renfrewshire, which remained the property of his descendants until the 19th century. His descendant John Montgomerie of Eaglesham was a warrior of great renown for his feat at the battle of Otterburn (1388), where he fought single-handed with Henry Percy (Hotspur) and defeated him. He is said to have built the castle of Polnoon with the ransom, and he also made a profitable marriage to the heiress of Sir Hugh de Eglinton. His grandson became Lord Montgomery and the second Lord Montgomery was created Earl of Eglinton (1507).

Hugh, second Lord Montgomery and later Earl of Eglinton, was one of those who conspired to replace the unpopular King James III with his son, and he fought at Sauchieburn (1488), where the king was wounded and afterwards killed in miserable circumstances. He held Brodick Castle and the Isle of Arran until replaced there by the Hamiltons. He was succeeded by his grandson Hugh, second earl (died 1546), whose son the third earl was a loyal supporter of Mary Queen of Scots and fought for her in the final battle at Langside. Thereafter he was imprisoned for a time and after his release endeavoured to secure

Hugh Montgomerie, twelfth Earl of Eglinton (1739–1813), in the uniform of the Black Watch, by J. S. Copley.

toleration for Roman Catholics in that unpromising time when Calvinism was rampant.

One of the longest private feuds in Scotland was that between the Montgomerys and the Cunninghams. It originated in some relatively minor dispute over jurisdiction, was several times apparently settled by legal judgment or government intervention, but on each occasion broke out once more after an interval. The Eglinton manor house was burned early in the 16th century and in 1586 the fourth earl was killed by the Cunninghams. Finally the royal government persuaded the rivals to shake hands in 1609, and three years later the fifth earl died childless, which no doubt helped to cool the ashes of the old conflict.

He was succeeded in his estate and title – though not without objections by various people, including for a time the king, who took his time in assenting to the necessary charter – by Alexander Seton, through his mother, Lady Margaret Montgomery (daughter of the third earl), who had married the Earl of Winton. Seton took the name Montgomery and became chief of the name.

His son, sixth Earl of Eglinton, was a Presbyterian who sided with the Covenanters in the civil war and subsequently supported Charles II. He was imprisoned for his royalist sympathies by General Monk in 1659 a matter of months before Monk himself took the initiative in restoring the monarch to his throne.

Of the later members of this family, the tenth Earl of Eglinton was shot by a poacher in 1769, and the thirteenth earl (from another branch, the Montgomerys of Coilsfield) was responsible for that ultimate piece of early Victorian medieval romanticism, the Eglinton Tournament (1839), an occasion somewhat spoilt by the pouring rain.

More (Muir)

According to Black's *Surnames of Scotland* (1946) More, Moor, Muir, Mure, etc. are all variants of the same name, originally deriving from the English word moor, a type of heathland. Early appearances of the name include de la More, del Moore and other forms indicating that the person concerned lived on or by a moor. However, one of the earliest of all appears as Dovenal le fiz Michel More de Levenaghes, and the absence of any genitive preposition suggests that this man's father, Michael More, was in Gaelic known as Michael *Mór*, meaning big or great, which was of course frequently applied to prominent warriors, chiefs, etc. It is significant that other common descriptions of this sort became surnames. For example, Ogg comes from the Gaelic *Òg*, meaning young, Bain comes from *Bàn* (white or fair), and Begg from *Beag* (little).

As *Mór* was probably the most common suffix of all, it would be rather surprising if all Muirs, Mores, etc. were descended from heath-dwellers and none from great or large ancestors. It has even been suggested that the *de* or *de la* often appearing in front of the name in the early examples may as often as not have been a slip of the scribe, who would have been accustomed to such forms.

The variants of spellings of the name do show some regional identity. Thus, Moir is said to be characteristic of Aberdeen, Moar of Orkney and Shetland, etc. Anyone with the slightest familiarity with registers of the 17th and 18th century will feel a certain scepticism, and in fact it is quite easy to find families who themselves employed several variants of the name interchangeably. It was probably only coincidence that when the spelling of names became standardised, a particular form was adopted in a particular district.

Among notable families of this name were the

Muir

Mures of Rowallan. They were sufficiently prominent in the 14th century for Elizabeth, daughter of Sir Adam Mure of Rowallan, to marry King Robert II in 1347. The family continued to prosper until the 17th century, and died out in the male line about 1700.

Sir William Mure was a notable 16th-century Scottish poet and religious propagandist.

The variant spelling Muir is probably most familiar due to the prominence of several learned men who bore that name. They included John Muir (1810-82), the orientalist who held the first chair of Sanskrit at Edinburgh University; his brother Sir William Muir (1819-1905) who shared his interests and was an expert on the early history of Islam; John Muir (1838-1914), the Scots-born US naturalist; Sir Thomas Muir (1844-1931), mathematician and educationalist; Ramsay Muir (1872-1941), author of a famous historical atlas and Edwin Muir (1887-1959), the poet and translator. Sir John Moore (1761-1809), who died at Corunna, was one of Britain's most able and popular generals.

Morrison

Morrison, 'son of Morris', is a name that crops up in many different regions in the period when surnames became common, and it is unlikely that all stem from a common source, although that has been asserted. Among notable families of this name were the Morrisons of Woodend in Kirkmichael, Dumfriesshire, the Morrisons of Dairsie in Fife and the Morrisons of Prestongrange, East Lothian.

The Morrisons of the Outer Hebrides may themselves have been of mixed origin – Gaelic and Norse – but among the ancestors of one branch were probably the Irish bards known as O'Muirgheasain, who settled in Mull in the 16th century. In the far northwest, where Morrisons are still numerous, the name is the anglicised form of the Gaelic *Mac Ghille Mhuire* (son of the servant of Mary).

The Morrisons were renowned as poets, musicians and scholars, and 'celebrated . . . for their independence of mind and sobriety of judgment'. For many generations they held the office of *Britheamh*, or brieve, a kind of local judge, in Lewis under the MacLeods, from whom they held Habost in the district of Ness, at the northern end of Lewis. We know that a whole network of these judicial officials existed under the lord of the Isles, but the Morrisons are the only ones known by name. The first recorded holder of the office was Uisdean, who lived in the 16th century (comparatively late).

A later brieve confessed on his deathbed that he

Morrison

was the true father of the supposed eldest son of MacLeod of Lewis, and it was by a Mackenzie marriage to this child of dubious parentage that the Mackenzies later justified their campaign for possession of Lewis.

The Morrisons, or this branch at least, seem to have supported the Mackenzies, and two of them, Iain *Dubh* Morrison the brieve and Malcolm his eldest son, were killed by the MacLeods early in the 17th century. However, the victory of the Mackenzies corresponded with the end of the brieve's authority, probably already in decline. When the Mackenzies gained a commission of fire and sword against the Morrison chief for resisting the Mackenzie takeover in 1616, he was described as the brieve, but there is no later reference to such an office.

The famous Blind Harper of Dunvegan, Roderick (*Ruaraidh*) Morrison, was born in Lewis about 1660 and died in 1712, and Morrisons were hereditary smiths to the MacLeods of Harris. John Morrison (*Iain Gobha*, the Smith), the religious poet who was an important figure in the Long Island in the 19th century, was a member of this family. There were several branches of the clan in Harris and also on the mainland in Caithness, where they were associated with the Mackays. According to legend the Caithness lands were bestowed by the local bishop on a Morrison of Lewis, who brought sixty families to settle there.

It is interesting that the Morrison tartan is the same

Above: West Loch Tarbert, in Harris. There are still Morrisons in Harris and Lewis today.
Opposite: A Munro piper, from an 18th-century engraving.

as the Mackays' with an additional red line, though not much historical significance should be read into this as the Morrison tartan is of recent devising.

Munro

The origin of the Munroes is a matter of speculation, but a likely tradition, espoused by W.J. Watson in *The Celtic Place-Names of Scotland*, traces them to the River Roe, which flows into Lough Foyle in Northern Ireland. In Gaelic the Munros are *Clann au Rothaich*, and a Munro is a *Rothach*, or 'Ro(e)man'.

In the 14th century they were already established in Ferindonald, as they called it after a supposed ancestor, the fertile land north of the Cromarty Firth, dominated by the mighty summit of Ben Wyvis. The home of their chiefs was, as it still is, Foulis, from whose high tower (the medieval castle has long since been replaced) a fiery beacon summoned the clansmen with their war cry, 'Castle Foulis aflame!'

The Munros held their lands from the old earls of Ross, in the 15th century from the lord of the Isles (as earl of Ross) and later from the Crown. Robert of Munro, Laird of Foulis, was killed in the earl's service in 1369. He was presumably the descendant of a Munro of Foulis said to have died in 1126.

From 1476 the Munros of Foulis were active in the king's service and in 1547 George Munro of Foulis was among the Scots killed at the battle of Pinkie. His successor Robert *Mór* was a Protestant (like his descendants) who held various royal posts in Ross and Invernesshire.

Hector Munro of Foulis, chief of the clan, despite a university education employed witches when he became ill in 1589 to transfer what seemed to be his approaching death to his half-brother, George Munro of Obsdale. The spell, which involved the chief's midnight 'burial', seems to have worked, for he recovered from his illness and George died the following year. Munro was subsequently charged with witchcraft but acquitted (he died in 1603). The unfortunate witch was burned to death. In a later generation the chiefship and estate of Foulis passed to the descendants of George of Obsdale.

Munro

The Munros have long been noted for their martial spirit, and Hector's son and successor Robert, known as the Black Baron, with many of his clan, went with Mackay's regiment to fight for the cause of Protestantism and the Winter Queen (sister of Charles I and wife of the king of Bohemia deposed by the Catholic, imperial forces) in the Thirty Years' War. The Swedish army is said to have included 27 officers above the rank of captain named Munro. The chief himself died of wounds in 1638, and another Robert Munro, of the Obsdale branch, wrote a famous account of the Scots' campaigning.

In the civil wars Munro loyalties were divided and since for a long time there was no strong leadership owing to the minority of the chief and the termination of the original Foulis line, they were to be found fighting on both sides. Robert of Obsdale, who became chief in 1651, served as Sheriff of Ross in the Cromwellian period, though the sons of his predecessor fought against Cromwell at Worcester in the same year.

During the Jacobite risings of the 18th century the Munros consistently supported the Hanoverian government. In an incident at the battle of Glenshiel (1719) Munro of the cadet house of Culcairn was felled by rebel snipers but saved by two of his men, one of whom threw himself across the prostrate chieftain while the other charged the snipers single-handed and routed them.

Sir Robert Munro of Foulis, who had commanded

the Black Watch at the battle of Fontenoy (where he successfully introduced new infantry tactics) in 1745, was killed in the following year fighting the Jacobites at Falkirk. He was assailed, it is said, by six Camerons, slew two of them, broke his sword on a third, and was then felled by a pistol shot. Munros also formed the advance guard of General Cope's force defeated at Prestonpans.

Soon after this the old Castle Foulis was burned down, and the present impressive building was erected by Sir Harry (son of the gallant Sir Robert) Munro of Foulis (died 1781).

Many Munros emigrated to the colonies and from their descendants (and from those of the Irish Munroes who sprang from the same stem) many notable leaders arose, including two Commonwealth prime ministers and a US president, James Monroe (1758-1831), whose father is believed to have descended from the Munros of Foulis.

Murray

The name comes from the great province, former kingdom, in north-east Scotland. Some families prefer the spelling Moray, as in the territorial name.

Presumably the Murrays were of Pictish ancestry, but the man they claim as their ancestor, Freskin, may have been a Fleming, one of those adventurers (rather like the Normans later) who saw an opportunity to gain lands for themselves by assisting the feudal Scottish monarchy to bring distant provinces under its control. Possibly he married a princess of the old royal house. His grandson was known in Latin charters as William de Moravia (of Moray), and he had lands from King David II in the province.

His descendants were to prove remarkably numerous and successful. For a couple of centuries they held lands in Scotland ranging from Sutherland to the Borders. (One 15th-century Murray chieftain had 17 sons, most of whom founded substantial cadet houses.) So many locally powerful families dispersed over so wide an area naturally did not encourage close clan feeling, and in the 18th century Forbes of Culloden was to deny that the Murrays were a true clan at all. However, apart from the men of Atholl, there was undoubtedly a genuine clan spirit uniting the Murrays. On two occasions in the late 16th century Murray chieftains from all over the country (including the laird of Moncreiffe, closely associated with the Murrays through marriage) came together in

a 'Bond of Association' in which they recognised Murray of Tullibardine as supreme chief and bound themselves to defend each other against 'the intrusions of Broken Men, and unthankful and unnatural neighbours'.

The eldest son of William de Moravia came into possession of large estates in Sutherland, and the Murrays (not, in any case, yet so called) who followed him there took the name of the 'South land', as the Norsemen called it, for their own (see Sutherland).

Although the Murrays were essentially Highlanders, the first family to feature prominently in Scottish history were lords of Bothwell in Lanarkshire. These estates were acquired through the marriage of William de Moravia's descendant Sir Walter, Chief of the Murrays, to an Oliphant heiress in 1253. (They later passed out of the family in the same way as they

Murray of Tullibardine

entered it, a Murray heiress carrying them with her marriage to the Black Douglas). Sir Walter, first Lord Bothwell, was co-regent of Scotland in 1255.

Sir Andrew Murray of Bothwell was the associate of Wallace in resistance to the English in the late 13th century. Though scarcely more than a boy, some say he was the better general, for while Wallace was a first-rate guerilla leader it was largely Murray who engineered the smashing victory of Stirling Bridge (1297). Unfortunately, Sir Andrew fell in that engagement, and thereafter Wallace never won a pitched battle.

His son, also Sir Andrew, fourth Lord Bothwell, was no less active in resistance to the English. He was regent after Bruce's death and died in battle against the English at Halidon Hill (1333).

After the death of the last Murray lord of Bothwell in 1360 there was some doubt as to where the chiefship resided, and it was not for many generations that the Murrays of Tullibardine were generally acknowledged. They were possibly descended from a younger son of William de Moravia, and they acquired lands near Auchterarder, Strathearn, by marriage, not long before the last Murray of Bothwell died. They were erected into a feudal barony in 1443 and in 1606 the twelfth laird was created Earl of Tullibardine.

There were numerous important cadets of this house, including the Murrays of Ochtertyre and the earls of Mansfield, who have the curious distinction of being earls of Mansfield twice over – of Mansfield in Nottinghamshire and of Mansfield in Middlesex – both titles held since the 18th century. The earl of Mansfield's seat is Scone Palace.

The Morays of Abercairney, an older house, were descended from Sir John Murray of the house of Bothwell, who acquired the property when he married a daughter of the earl of Strathearn in about 1320. (It was his daughter who, on her second marriage, carried the lordship of Bothwell to the Earl of Douglas.) Sir John's sons Maurice (killed at Neville's Cross, 1346) and Alexander were successively earls of Strathearn, and the latter would seem to have been heir to the chiefship of the Murrays, although this honour eventually passed to the house of Tullibardine.

Scone Palace, home of the Earl of Mansfield one of the senior cadet families of Atholl.

Murray of Atholl

William, second Earl of Tullibardine, married the heiress of the Stewart Earl of Atholl, and their son John was confirmed as Earl of Atholl in 1629. The earldom of Tullibardine passed to his uncle. The Murrays were now a great power in the land, their possessions rivalling those of the Campbells. More-over, the Campbells were about to go through a sticky patch, due to changing fortunes in the civil wars, and the Murrays on the whole benefited by supporting the Stewart dynasty against the Campbells. When the Campbells' position was restored after 1688 the Murray chief, now Marquess of Atholl, was unassailable. In 1703 the marquess became a duke.

In 1706 the duke raised 4,000 Athollmen in an effort to dissuade the Scottish parliament from assenting to its own dissolution, but his action was not imitated elsewhere so he disbanded his men, and to his great disgust the Act of Union was subsequently passed. However, in the Jacobite risings the duke remained loyal to the Hanoverian government, a fortunate decision for the future of his house but one

Murray of Atholl

that presented some awkward problems at the time as the majority of the Athollmen (many of them Stewarts) were firm Jacobites.

In both risings the Athollmen were 'out' under William, Marquess of Tullibardine, son of the first duke (died 1724) and elder brother of the second, who was created Duke of Rannoch in the Jacobite peerage. His younger brother was the famous Jacobite leader of whom it was said that if Prince Charles had stayed in bed for the rising of 1745-46 and left the conduct of military affairs to his able lieutenant he would have woken up as king of Great Britain.

Lord George Murray (1694-1760), fifth son of the first Duke of Atholl, was a professional soldier from the age of 18. He took part in the rising of 1715 under the Earl of Mar and was wounded at the battle of Glenshiel, which terminated the abortive Spanish-assisted invasion of 1719. He escaped abroad but was later pardoned and settled down at Tullibardine in the 1720s, serving as Sheriff of Perthshire. On the eve of the Forty-five he was approached by the Jacobite leader, the Duke of Perth, but was at first very reluctant to rise in the Jacobite cause, having accepted a pardon for his previous efforts on behalf of the exiled Stewarts. He is said to have been persuaded by a personal letter from James Edward.

He was a true Highlander who spoke Gaelic (unlike Prince Charles) and marched with his men, not all of whom, however, followed him with total satisfaction when summoned by the fiery cross. He was without doubt the most able Jacobite general of this or any previous campaign, and although he pressed for the retreat from Derby, at that stage the alternative, a dash on London, was probably impracticable. (Prince Charles, with whom his relations were never very warm, subsequently regarded him as little better than a traitor, but this was perhaps the reaction of a weak man seeking scapegoats.) During the retreat Lord George found himself in a position which summed up the divided loyalties which made the Forty-five such a poignant episode, when he laid seige to Blair Castle, his family seat, then in Hanoverian hands. (It had earlier been besieged by his brother Tullibardine; Lord George's siege was the last of a castle in Britain.) After Culloden Murray again escaped abroad. He died at Medemblik in the Netherlands, where his tomb may still be seen, in 1760.

Blair Castle was repaired and considerably altered on two occasions, the later one being largely an attempt to restore its original Gothic outward appearance – it remains luxuriously neo-classical inside. Its white walls, familiar to all tourists, contain many treasures of art and history.

The martial traditions of Atholl are still continued by the Atholl Highlanders, somewhat reduced in

Detail from a painting of the fourth Duke of Atholl and his family, by David Allan (1780). Blair Castle is visible in the distance.

number nowadays, whose duties since the Forty-five have been confined to ceremonial. They are, however, the last private army in Britain.

It is said that the modern Murray of Atholl tartan is very similar to one worn by Murray of Pulrossie in the 17th century, but continuity would be hard to establish.

Napier

This is an English name which derives from the official who was in charge of the royal napery, or linen. Napier tradition says that the family was descended from the ancient earls of Lennox, but it is not impossible that some early descendant of that family should also have been the court 'naper'.

It is in a charter of the Earl of Lennox that we first find mention of the family. John de Napier held lands from the earl in Dumbarton in 1280, and he was present 23 years later at the defence of Stirling Castle. Almost a century after that William de Napier was governor of Edinburgh Castle, and his son Alexander was a successful merchant in the wool trade (the Napiers seem to have been loath to relinquish their old association with textiles), who acquired the lands of Merchiston. His son, also Alexander of Merchiston, was wounded while helping to rescue the widow of King James I and her second husband James Stewart (the Black Knight of Lorne) from the hands of a faction led by Sir Archibald Livingstone and others. As a result of this service to the king's mother he acquired some former Livingstone property as well as the office of comptroller of the household.

A succession of Napiers perished on the battlefield in the 15th and 16th centuries. John Napier of Merchiston died, rather unluckily as casualties were few, fighting for King James III against the victorious rebel earls at Sauchieburn (1488). His grandson Alexander was killed at Flodden with King James IV in 1513, and Alexander's son fell at Pinkie.

The most famous member of this family is John Napier (1550-1617), eighth Laird of Merchiston, grandson of the casualty of Pinkie and son of Archibald (died 1608), who was master of the Mint under King James VI. He seems to have lived most of his life at Merchiston where, though physically inactive, he was not quiet, being deeply and fiercely involved in religious controversies (he abominated the papists). He also designed weapons of war, including an early example of a tank (horse-drawn), but for relaxation he indulged in mathematical studies. He was especially interested in methods of making mathematical calculations easier, and through this work he arrived at the invention of logarithms with which his name is for ever associated.

His son Archibald, first Lord Napier from 1627, was

Nicolson (MacNicol)

'Sons of Nicol' appear in feudal rolls as far back as the 13th century, but there is no reason to suppose that all of them belonged to the clan who, in modern Gaelic, are called *Mac Neacail*. The MacNicols of Portree in Skye anglicised their name to Nicolson, though there are many MacNicols in Argyll today.

MacNicol of Portree is said to have been a member of the council of the lord of the Isles (the number of chiefs who are said to have belonged to that body, even allowing for switching, appears to exceed the stated membership – sixteen – considerably). The

Napier

Nicolson

related by marriage to Montrose and was a keen royalist during the civil war, as was his son, the second Lord Napier, who died in exile in 1658. The third Lord Napier was the last of his line.

Since the 17th century the Napiers have been remarkable for outstanding military achievements, hardly exceeded by any other family. During the Napoleonic wars there were six generals and an admiral named Napier. They included General Sir William Napier (1755-1860), author of the outstanding history of the Peninsular war (in six large volumes).

Nicolson chiefs held the land of Scorrybreck for many centuries: legend speaks of over a hundred chiefs buried in Snizort churchyard.

Another tradition, supported by the old Celtic genealogists, traces the origins of the Nicolsons further back, to Assynt, on the northern-western mainland, and Ullapool. Assynt passed to the MacLeods when Torquil MacLeod married the Nicolson heiress. Presumably the clansmen then moved to Skye, although perhaps others of their descent were already there.

The name appears frequently in the history of Skye (one of whose modern historians is a Nicolson), and the Nicolsons of Scorrybreck were notable for producing churchmen and Gaelic bards (sometimes both combined in the same man). Donald of Scorrybreck was a famous minister in the second half of the 17th century who eventually retired in 1696 under pressure from Presbyterianism, which he could not stomach. A contemporary, Thomas Nicolson, was a Roman Catholic convert who worked in the Scottish mission, spent some time in prison, but survived to make the journeys which enabled him to compile a valuable record of the Hebrides at the end of the 17th century.

Donald MacNicol, appointed Minister of Lismore in 1766, made a valuable collection of Ossianic ballads, and his resentment of Samuel Johnson's derogatory remarks on Gaelic literature informed his *Remarks on Dr Samuel Johnson's Journey to the Hebrides.*

Sir Thomas Innes recorded a press report of 1813 on the death at Scorrybreck at the age of 86 of 'Malcolm Nicolson, Esq., who, with his predecessors, lineally and without interruption, possessed that farm for many centuries back'. A later chief emigrated to the Antipodes, and his origins were commemorated in an Australian sheep station named Scorrybreck. A Lowland family, the Nicolsons of Lasswade, have become chiefs of the name although it is not clear why this honour should not still belong to the family of Scorrybreck.

Ogilvie

The Ogilvies are one of the most distinguished families in Scotland, descended from the ancient earls of Angus (the old Gaelic title, *Mormaer*, carried more weight than 'earl'). Continual historical records take us back as far as Dubhucan, Earl of Angus in the early 12th century, whose son Earl Gillebride, or Gilbert, is regarded as the founder of the Ogilvies. He bestowed the lands of Ogilvie and Easter Powrie on his younger son, also Gilbert, and for half a millenium those lands passed down in unbroken male descent in the same family, the Ogilvies of that ilk. The territorial name is said to derive from the Ancient British *ocel fa* (high plain).

Another branch, ultimately more important, were the Ogilvies of Auchterhouse, who were hereditary sheriffs of Angus in the 14th century. One of them fought with Joan of Arc against the English; another, Sir Walter Ogilvie of Auchterhouse, died at the battle of Harlaw in 1411. He had two sons: from the elder sprang the house of Inchmartine and from the younger the house of Airlie (originally Eroly). The latter was Sir Walter Ogilvie, Lord High Treasurer, who married the heiress of Lintrathan and built the

tower of Airlie. His grandson became Lord Ogilvie of Airlie in 1491, and the eighth Lord Ogilvie was created Earl of Airlie in 1639. He was recognised as overall chief of the Ogilvies and the present chief is his descendant.

Throughout the series of crises, civil wars and rebellions between 1639 and 1745 the Ogilvies were staunch supporters of the Stewart dynasty, an allegiance which entailed much grief for them.

Like other clans, the Ogilvies had their feuds, which had the effect of bringing the many branches of the clan together. There was a tremendous battle with the Lindsays, their immediate neighbours to the north, in 1446, when (it is said) 500 Ogilvies were killed, and there was a later feud with the Campbells resulting from Campbell encroachments on Ogilvie lands in the late 16th century.

The later civil disturbances offered unparalleled opportunities for conducting private quarrels in the

Ogilvie

guise of public duty, which the Earl of Argyll was foremost in exploiting.

In 1640 Argyll was commissioned to proceed against the clans of Atholl and Angus who had risen to resist the Covenant. He commanded 4,000 Highlanders, 'well-timbered men', who carried out their commission of fire and sword with customary zeal, not sparing women and children. To this campaign belongs the famous destruction of the 'bonnie House of Airlie', memorably related in ballad. However, the ballad's attribution to Argyll of lecherous designs on the Countess of Airlie is probably false: neither she nor the earl was at home at the time. Their absence was fortunate, for Argyll did indeed leave scarcely 'a standing stone in Airlie' (nor a standing Ogilvie). It was this campaign which turned Montrose against Argyll for good and all.

Cortachy Castle, the seat of the Earl of Airlie.

James, second Earl of Airlie, was captured at the battle of Philiphaugh (1645), which put an end to Montrose's great campaign. He was incarcerated in St Andrew's Castle under sentence of death but, shortly before the execution was due, escaped disguised as a woman in clothes provided by his sister. (The number of times this unlikely ploy succeeded does make one wonder about the honour of prison guards.)

The Ogilvies were 'out' in all the Jacobite risings of the 18th century. At Culloden an Angus regiment was led by Lord Ogilvie, son of the fifth Earl of Airlie, 'a boy of twenty with a long straight nose, a heavy jaw and a calm eye', wrote John Prebble, who had probably been looking at the portrait in Winton Castle. He escaped and years later received a free pardon on the grounds of his youth at the time of his offence; the title was restored to his descendants.

The eighth Earl of Airlie was killed in the Boer War in 1900 during a courageous action at Diamond Hill, his last words being a reminder to the distraught NCO bending over him to mind his language. In Scotland Lady Airlie heard the drumming of the ghostly drummer boy which always announces the death of an earl of Airlie.

Another branch of the Ogilvies became earls of Findlater (1638) and of Seafield (1701). The latter title still continues, having passed via the Laird of Grant to Nina, the late countess who was such a notable figure in Highland society and to her son, the present Earl of Seafield.

The seat of the Ogilvie chief today is Cortachy, but the Ogilvies still also hold Airlie Castle (rebuilt on the site of the building destroyed during Argyll's famous raid). Having descended (without much doubt though without firm proof) from the royal Pictish house, the family replenished its royal blood this century when Angus Ogilvie married Princess Alexandra.

Oliphant

The founder of this Scottish family is believed to have been an Anglo-Norman, David de Holifard, who came north with King David I along with other founders of famous families. He was a member of a landed family in Northamptonshire and received lands in Roxeburghshire from his friend the king (whose life he is said to have saved in some military engagement). The name was spelt in different ways – a William Olyfat was captured by the English in 1296 – and it has been suggested that the modern spelling derives from the tales brought back by Crusaders of a 'huge earth-shaking beast' named 'Olifaunt' (elephant). It is a nice story at any rate, and some of the holders of the name, quoted by Dr Black in his *Surnames of Scotland*, did change it to Elephantus or Elifant. It was also sometimes changed to Oliver or variants thereof, and there was a story of a Scot named Oliver or Olifard who fought on the Saracens' side at the siege of Acre and was prevailed on to betray them, thus causing the fall of the city.

Sir John Oliphant, a presumed descendant of David de Holifard, held the lands of Aberdalgie in the early 15th century, and his immediate descendants were prominent in Scottish affairs. His son Lawrence became a lord of Parliament, ambassador to France and keeper of Edinburgh Castle (1493). His son, the second Lord Oliphant, was killed at Flodden in 1513 and his grandson fought at Solway Moss (1542), where he was captured and held for ransom.

The fourth Lord Oliphant was a supporter of Bothwell and Mary Queen of Scots, and fought for the queen at Langside (1568). His son was involved in the Raid of Ruthven (1582), when King James VI was kidnapped in a complicated plot subsidised by the English and designed to scotch the Catholic Duke of Lennox. He was afterward banished, and he disappeared from the ship carrying him into exile in mysterious circumstances. Some say he ended up on the slave benches of a Turkish galley.

Thereafter the family declined, eventually losing all their lands. A cadet branch, the Oliphants of Gask, survived, however. They were notable Jacobites, and the house of Gask was plundered – without orders – by English soldiers after Culloden. Carolina Oliphant (later Lady Nairne) was named after the vanquished prince when she was born at Gask in 1766. She became a composer of verse and ballads, including the famous Jacobite songs, 'Charlie is my darling' and 'Will ye no come back again?', and her comic ballads have been described as rivalling those of Burns.

Ramsay

The distinguished family of the Ramsays of Dalhousie were probably not related to all the Ramsays in Scotland, and there is more than one explanation of the origin of the name. It seems to be a place name, probably in East Lothian, but possibly deriving from the town of Ramsey in the English Fens, where there was a great medieval abbey. The first known Ramsay in Scotland was Simon de Ramsay, possibly an Anglo-

Oliphant

Ramsay

Norman who followed King David I to Scotland and held lands in Lothian. Thereafter, the names of various Ramsays appear in charters etc., and they no doubt belonged to a line linking Simon de Ramsay (alive in 1140) with William de Ramsay, who lived about 150 years later and held the lands of 'Dalwolsy' (Dalhousie).

William de Ramsay swore fealty to Edward I for his lands in 1296, but he later became a supporter of Bruce and was one of those participating in the Declaration of Arbroath (1320), which informed the Pope that the Scots would tolerate no king but Bruce. His son Alexander was also active against the English, saving Dunbar Castle for its countess, Black Agnes, when it was besieged in 1338. Legend ascribes to him other notable exploits against the invaders from the south, but his success, rewarded with royal appointments – Sheriff of Teviotdale, Constable of Roxeburgh – incited the animosity of Sir William Douglas, the Knight of Liddesdale, who captured him and shut him up within the grim walls of Hermitage Castle, where he is said to have died of starvation in 1342.

Nevertheless, the house of Dalhousie prospered, and founded several cadet branches, including the Ramsays of Cockpen and Whitehill and of Balmain. George Ramsay was made Lord Ramsay of Melrose in 1618 but swiftly changed the title to Dalhousie. It was raised to an earldom in 1633.

Since then many Ramsays have been notable soldiers and imperial officials, the most successful of all being the tenth Earl, later Marquess, of Dalhousie, who was the last of his line. He was Governor-general of India, appointed in 1848 at the age of 34.

The most accomplished Ramsay family – whose connection with the Ramsays of Dalhousie, if there was one, is unknown – was that of the two Allan Ramsays, the poet (1686-1758), author of 'The Gentle Shepherd', and his son (1713-84), perhaps the finest portrait painter after Raeburn – certainly the most attractive – born north of the Tweed, if not the English Channel.

Robertson

It is now accepted that the Robertsons are descended from the hereditary abbots of Dunkeld, the senior line of the kindred of St Columba and guardians of the Saint's relics. Abbot Crinan of Dunkeld married a royal princess and their son was King Duncan, who was killed by MacBeth in 1040. From a younger son of King Duncan were descended the old earls of Atholl, and from Conan, son of Earl Henry of Atholl, the Robertsons derived their large territories in that magnificent region.

In Gaelic the Robertsons are known as *Clann Donnchaidh* (children of Duncan); this Duncan, *Donnchadh Reamhar*, was the descendant of Conan

Robertson

and chief of the clan in the early 14th century. In 1451 the lands were erected by royal charter into the barony of Struan for Duncan's grandson Robert, and the majority of the clan took their name from him. Others took different names, such as Duncanson, MacConachie, etc. (see Duncan).

Duncan *Reamhar* (the Stout) was a supporter of the Bruce who fought with his men at Bannockburn, and in later times Clan *Donnchaidh* were loyal adherents of the Stewart dynasty (the Robertson crest is a hand supporting a crown). Robert of Struan (then known as Robert Duncanson) received his barony as a belated reward for apprehending Sir Robert Graham, the murderer of King James I. Since the 16th century the Chief of the Robertsons has been known as Struan Robertson.

During the 16th century the Robertsons lost a large part of their lands to the Stewart earl of Atholl, though this did not affect their loyalty to the Stewart king of Scots. With other Athollmen they fought for Montrose in the civil war and were present at every engagement of that extraordinary campaign.

Alexander, seventeenth of Struan, had one of the most remarkable careers of any Jacobite chief. A poet of some renown, he was preparing to take holy orders when he succeeded to the chiefship about the time of the Revolution of 1688. He took up his sword on behalf of King James VII/II and fought under Bonnie

Loch Rannoch in Robertson territory uncomfortably poised between powerful neighbours – Stewarts, Campbells, Murrays.

Dundee at Killiecrankie. He was attainted and the estates forfeited, but pardoned after the accession of Queen Anne. The Hanoverian succession and the ensuing Jacobite rising of 1715 had him reaching for his broadsword again. He was taken prisoner at Sheriffmuir, rescued, recaptured, again escaped, and got away to France, but he was back in plenty of time to rise again in 1745. After the Battle of Prestonpans he rode home in the carriage of the defeated English general Sir John Cope, but he was now in his mid-seventies and a little too old to fight even by Highland standards. At Culloden the clan was led by Robertson of Woodsheal.

What was left of the estates were forfeited but later briefly regained by Alexander's sister. Some territory in Rannoch remained to the Robertson chiefs – who for a time lived in Ruthven barracks, built to house troops to keep them in order – until the last was sold in the present century. In 1949 the chiefship passed to a resident of Jamaica, though his son remained to represent him in Scotland. The Clan *Donnchaidh* museum near Blair Atholl contains many relics of the clan including the magic stone, *Clach na Brataich*, which is said to have played a part in the fortunes of the clan since the time of Stout Duncan.

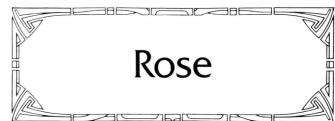

Rose

The Roses of Kilravock in the county of Nairn can be traced back a very long way. Hugh, the first of that name in documentary records, was designated 'of Geddes' in about 1219, in a charter by Sir John Bisset of Lovat, a family with which the Roses were closely connected. The lands of Kilravock were acquired by Hugh's son and namesake on his marriage to a daughter of Sir Andrew de Bosco, whose wife was a Bisset. The connection of Roses, Boscos and Bissets tends to corroborate the theory that the family was of Norman origin and it has been suggested that the Norman forefather of the Roses came over with William the Conqueror's brother, the formidable Bishop Odo of Bayeux, whose territories included the district of Ros, near Caen.

The Chief of Rose, known as the Baron of Kilravock from the 15th century and almost invariably named Hugh, remained in possession of Kilravock for over 600 years, succession proceeding in a direct line, father to son (or occasionally daughter). The castle of Kilravock, scene of a great international reunion of the Roses in recent times, was built by the seventh

Rose

Hunting Rose

Rose of Kilravock in 1460. Much of the original building on the wooded banks of the River Nairn near Cawdor remains, and Sir Thomas Innes wrote that 'there is scarcely a family whose charter chest is more amply stored with documents, not only of private importance, but of great antiquarian interest.' The collection would be richer still had it not been for the destruction of family charters at Elgin when the Wolf of Badenoch set fire to the cathedral in 1390.

The history of the Roses of Kilravock proves that it was perfectly possible for Highland lairds to exist without constant involvement in bloody feuds and conflicts. When King James VI enquired in 1598 how the Black Baron, as the tenth Rose of Kilravock was called, managed to live among such violent neighbours, the baron replied that they were the best neighbours he could have since they made him say his prayers three times a day instead of only once.

Of course, trouble was not always avoided. The Black Baron's successor, for example, was thrown into prison for a time for failing to control some of his clansmen who were feuding with the Dunbars. Earlier, there was a tremendous feud with the Urquharts, and a great raid on the Mackenzies. Then there was the famous incident of the heiress of Cawdor, whose mother was a Rose and whose intended future husband was Kilravock's grandson, abducted by the Campbells in distressful circumstances (see Campbell of Cawdor).

At times of national disturbance, fairly frequent it must be said, the Roses could not always remain on the sidelines even if they wished, and during the wars of independence they fought for Bruce. Moreover, no Rose appears on the famous Ragman's Roll of 1296, which lists those Scottish barons, the great majority of them, who swore fealty to Edward I of England.

In the early 18th century Kilravock opposed the 1707 union with England, but he was not a Jacobite. There were Roses on both sides in 1715 and 1745, but the Baron of Kilravock, though he helped turn the Jacobites out of Inverness in 1715, otherwise concentrated on holding his own. Perhaps the most memorable illustration of the Roses' inclination to remain on friendly, or at least neutral, terms with mutually hostile forces occurred before Culloden, when Kilravock entertained the Jacobite prince and the Hanoverian duke on successive evenings. His sympathies were with Hanover, but Charles was better company.

Ross

The homeland of this clan was the peninsula of Easter Ross north of the Cromarty Firth, a spacious and fertile land which gave them room to expand without immediate collision with hostile neighbours – an uncommon benefit among Highland clans.

In Gaelic the Rosses are known as *Clann Aindreas*, after the alleged progenitor of the old Celtic earls of Ross (and of the Mackenzies of Seaforth). The first of the earls of Ross was Fearchar *Mac-an-t-Sagairt* (son of the priest), founder of the clan whose services to King Alexander II (he defeated the king's enemies in Moray and presented their heads in a bag) gained him the earldom in 1226. As heir of the hereditary abbots of Applecross in Wester Ross Fearchar was already a considerable landholder and a (probable) descendant of the Irish King Niall of the Nine Hostages (died early 5th century).

Ross

The early chiefs were thus the earls of Ross, who wore in battle the sacred shirt of St Duthac. The ruined sanctuary at Tain where this garment was kept can still be seen. It was there that Bruce's queen sought refuge in 1306, only to be hauled out and handed over, albeit unwillingly, by William, third chief and third earl, to the English, who exhibited her in a cage. Subsequently the earl rallied to Bruce, and his son, the fourth earl, married Bruce's sister. The fourth earl was killed at the battle of Halidon Hill in 1333, despite wearing St Duthac's shirt.

The fifth earl died in 1372 leaving no direct male heir, and the earldom passed to his daughter. That resulted ultimately in the struggle for the earldom between the Lord of the Isles and the Regent Albany culminating in the grisly battle of 'Red' Harlaw in 1411.

Meanwhile the chiefship passed to the fifth earl's brother Hugh, who acquired the lands of Balnagowan from his brother-in-law King Robert II in 1374. For over three centuries the Rosses of Balnagowan remained chiefs of the clan.

News of the clan during most of that time is rather hard to come by. Occasional, mostly violent, incidents are reported – the death of one chief in a battle with the Mackays, the death of another in a scuffle at Tain – but clearly they prospered, since by the 17th century the chief could raise one thousand men. A 16th-century chief, Alexander of Balnagowan, was an exceedingly troublesome character whose behaviour so alarmed the many Ross chieftains that they issued a remonstrance urging him to change his ways. This had little effect, and the chief's son was among those who were commissioned to proceed against him with fire and sword.

On the whole the clan played little part in national affairs. Rosses fought in the army that invaded England for Charles II in 1651 only to be resoundingly defeated by Cromwell at Worcester. Later there was more trouble with the Mackenzies, and David, the last Balnagowan chief, who was another bellicose character, was also threatened with the withdrawal of support by his kinsmen in 1676.

After his death Balnagowan and the still extensive Ross estates passed, more or less legally, to another family named Ross, completely unrelated Lowlanders whose name derived from the Anglo-Norman de Roos. The true heir in the male line was Ross of Pitcalnie, a cadet house, and in fact he and his successors appear to have exercised the right of chiefship *de facto*. In the present century they became chiefs in name as well as fact when the last of the usurping line of Ross of Balnagowan died childless, although the chiefship has since passed to another branch, Ross of Shandwick, an early cadet house descended from a younger son of a 15th-century chief.

Ruthven

Ruthven is not a very common name today and in the early 17th century it was scarcely to be found at all – the result of government decree. The story of the Ruthvens in the preceding century is certainly a sensational one. Romantic novelists have had a fine time with it, their imagination fuelled by the obscurity of the facts.

The Ruthvens are said to have been of Norse origin, decended from a Viking warrior who settled in

Ruthven

Holyroodhouse, the royal palace of Edinburgh, scene of one of the many dark deeds in which the Ruthvens were (or, sometimes perhaps, were not) involved.

Scotland. They took their name from the lands of Ruthven in Rannoch, and in 1487 Sir William of Ruthven became a peer.

With Patrick, third Lord Ruthven, who was provost of Perth for many years, things took a nasty turn. He was the leader of the gang of Protestant lords who murdered David Rizzio, the Italian secretary of Mary Queen of Scots, at Holyrood Palace in 1566, at the instigation of the aristocratic delinquent generally known as Lord Darnley, whom the queen in her impetuous way had married. She was six months pregnant at the time and although Darnley's jealousy of Rizzio was probably quite unjustified, she was undeniably fond of the attractive young Italian and his violent death greatly upset her. Well it might, although the oft-repeated statement that he was killed in her presence has been questioned.

Finding Darnley an unreliable protector, Ruthven fled to England and died there soon afterwards, but in spite of the hazard to which he had subjected the prenatal existence of King James VI, his son William, fourth Lord Ruthven, found favour with the young

king and was created Earl of Gowrie in 1581. That did not last long. Three years later he was executed for treason. He had previously been pardoned for his part in the Raid of Ruthven (1582), when the 16-year-old King James VI was seized by a band of Presbyterian earls and held prisoner in Ruthven Castle for nearly a year, a remarkable example of the 'feckless, arrogant conceit' of the Scottish nobles of which the king later complained.

By this time, one might suppose, treason was in the blood, yet the extent of the treason of the third Earl of Gowrie in 1600 is not proven.

The official version of the Gowrie Conspiracy was that the earl and his brother had kidnapped the king in Gowrie House (now Huntingtower) in Perth, telling his courtiers that he had already left while he was in fact confined in an upper room. As the courtiers were hurriedly leaving to catch up with the king, James managed to attract their attention from the window of the room where he was held. They broke in at once and in the ensuing scuffle the Ruthven brothers were killed.

It was suspected at the time, and since, that this was a plot; that the king had in fact engineered the murder of Gowrie and his brother who, as fanatical Presbyterians with an unwholesome record of disloyalty, were undesirable subjects. This does not seem probable, and the fury of James afterwards, abolishing the very name of Ruthven by act of parliament, seems unfeigned. Probably there was some kind of plot again him, and things went wrong.

There were, of course, plenty of honourable Ruthvens, notably the Ruthvens of Freeland, descended from the second Lord Ruthven, who became the senior representatives of the name. Even the Gowrie earldom was revived in this century, for Sir Alexander Hore-Ruthven, Governor-general of Australia, in 1945.

Scott

A Scott is a Scotsman in the way that an Inglis is an Englishman or a Wallace a Welshman. There is no known connection between the Scotts and the original Scots of Dalriada.

The Scotts have been traced back to Uchtred *filius Scoti* in the 12th century whose (assumed) son was Richard le Scot, father of the ancestor of the Scotts of Buccleuch. He acquired considerable estates in Lanarkshire, and they were hugely increased by his descendants, who were to be among the largest landowners in the kingdom. The most eventful period in the history of the 'saucy Scotts' – as wild and unruly on occasion as any other Border clan – was the century or so before the union of the monarchies of England and Scotland brought relative peace to the Borders in 1603.

Sir Walter Scott had a charter to the barony of Kirkud from King Robert II in 1389, and his son Robert acquired the lands of Branxholm, where the Duke of Buccleuch has his seat in the Borders to this day.

The fortunes of the Scotts expanded after the eclipse of the mighty Douglases in 1455. Branxholm was erected into a barony in 1488, although by that time the Scott chiefs had adopted the name 'of Buccleuch'.

Scott of Buccleuch could raise 600 men in the 16th century, though no doubt he wished he could have raised more, for besides the frequent incursions of the English, who set fire to Branxholm Castle on at least

'Scott's View' of the Eildon Hills, from Abbotsford, the mansion Sir Walter Scott purchased in 1811 and largely rebuilt.

Scott

the English may have rejected the scheme out of scepticism about its likely success as much as out of honour. Anyway, Sir Walter fought against them at Pinkie (1547).

His grandson and great-grandson, both also Sir Walter, were men of some distinction. The latter was a formidable guerilla leader who raided Carlisle prison in 1596 to rescue an Armstrong chieftain. He became Lord Scott of Buccleuch in 1606 and later took some of his men to fight the Spaniards in the Netherlands. His son was made Earl of Buccleuch in 1619.

The second Earl of Buccleuch died in 1651 leaving an only daughter, Anna. A highly eligible heiress, she was married to the Duke of Monmouth, an illegitimate son of Charles II, who took the name Scott and became also Duke of Buccleuch. She was made Duchess of Buccleuch in her own right and after her husband's rebellion and execution the title and lands remained intact through her.

The third Duke of Buccleuch married the Douglas heiress, thereby acquiring the huge estates of the duchy of Queensberry, including the Douglas seat at Drumlanrig, and becoming one of the richest men in Britain.

Cadet houses included Balweary, to which belonged Michael Scott, the famous wizard, known to 'loup on a muckle black horse that cam doon frae the cluds' and perform other equally remarkable feats. Another branch was the house of Harden, which produced not only the greatest of Scotts but surely one of the greatest of Scots, Sir Walter (1771-1832) of Abbotsford, who probably did more for his country's image and reputation than any single individual. His novels may be less popular today but his influence is never likely to be expunged.

two occasions, there was fierce rivalry with the Kerrs. Scott and Kerr sometimes split the ward of the Middle March between them, but Sir Walter of Buccleuch, who was sole warden, was killed by the jealous Kerrs in Edinburgh High Street in 1552. This was the man who had, it appears, once offered to turn the infant Mary Queen of Scots over to Henry VIII, a plan described by the Duke of Suffolk as 'not with the King's honour to be practised in such sort', although

A detail of a portrait of Sir Walter Scott (1771–1832) by Raeburn. With Burns, Scott helped to restore national self-confidence.

Seton

The Setons were not a clan, and there is little evidence of the different branches of the family acting in alliance, yet Seton is a famous name which became connected with several of the greatest Scottish families and was closely associated with the Stewart dynasty. The name is said to derive from the village of Sai in Normandy, although other explanations are offered, for instance that it means 'sea-town' and refers to Tranent, between Musselburgh and Haddington (and not much of a 'sea town' today), where the Setons held property at an early date.

Alexander de Seton held lands in East Lothian in the mid-12th century. Several generations later Sir Alexander of Seton was a close adherent of Bruce. Sir Christopher Seton married Bruce's sister and was killed fighting against the English.

The male line failed in the 14th century and the Seton heiress was abducted in 1347 by Alan of Winton, probably a cousin. Brought to justice, his fate was placed in the injured lady's hands: she was given the choice of a wedding ring or the executioner's sword, and chose the ring. Alan of Winton later died on crusade, but their son William took the name of Seton and became a peer. From him descended many of the most notable Seton families. His second son married the Gordon heiress and their son became Earl of Huntly in 1449 (the first earl later settled the title on a younger son who took the Gordon name).

The Setons were great builders, responsible for several of the finest houses in Lothian. Sir George, great-great-grandson of Alan of Winton, built the Chapel of Seton in the mid-15th century. Another George, the fifth Lord Seton, was responsible for the magnificent palace of Seton.

A frequent visitor there was Mary Queen of Scots, who regarded the builder of the palace as her 'truest friend'; his sister was one of the Queen's 'four Maries'. Seton helped the queen to escape from Loch Leven castle in 1568 and, after her defeat at Langside he fled to Holland, where he drove a carrier's waggon and tried to enlist the support of the Duke of Alva for Mary.

Two of his sons, whether or not out of gratitude for

Seton

their father's loyalty to his mother, were favoured by King James VI. The eldest son became Earl of Winton in 1600; a younger son, who was later Chancellor of Scotland, was created Lord Fyvie (1597) and Earl of Dunfermline (1605). He built much of the fine tower house of Fyvie in Aberdeenshire (some of the castle is older but one of the four turreted towers is named after him. The nearby classical garden of Pitmedden (now National Trust for Scotland property) also dates from the 17th century. Lord Pitmedden (died 1719),

The famous formal gardens of Pitmedden, first laid out by Sir Alexander Seton in 1675 and now restored, complete with pavilions, sundials and classical fountains.

the famous judge, was a member of a cadet house of the Seton earls of Dunfermline, descended from a younger brother of the fourth and last earl, who held a subordinate command under Viscount Dundee at Killiecrankie and was forfeited as a result.

Other branches of the family were active in the Jacobite rising of 1715, with generally unfortunate results. George, fifth Earl of Winton, was captured and sentenced to death, but escaped from the Tower of London. Several of his cousins were also attainted.

The Seton family has provided its own historians, the main – somewhat exhausting – work being George Seton's *A History of the Family of Seton during Eight Centuries* (1896).

Shaw

The Shaws, who were described as the best fighters in Mar's forces during the Jacobite rising of 1715, were a sept of the Mackintoshes, and prominent members of Clan Chattan, the confederation of the Cat. The origin of their name is not certain, but it is probably an approximation of the Gaelic name *Sithech*. The question of the relationship between Clan Shaw and the Lowland Shaws of – mainly – Lanarkshire and Ayrshire has also been much debated, the weight of opinion maintaining that they were of wholly different origins.

The home of Clan Shaw was Rothiemurchus, part of the Mackintosh patrimony, and according to legend it was bestowed upon an ancestor of the clan for his services at the famous (though problematical) battle of the clans on the North Inch of Perth in 1396. Grave doubts have been cast on the inscribed gravestone at Rothiemurchus which purports to mark the remains of Farquhar Shaw 'who led . . . this clan who defeated the 30 Davidsons of Invernahavon on the North Insh at Perth in 1390'. The year is wrong and the inscription is relatively modern; no one can be sure what it said originally. There is record, moreover, of the Shaws receiving the lands of Rothiemurchus from the Bishop of Moray in 1226. Later, they were leased to the Comyns, who when the lease expired were reluctant to leave.

James Shaw of Rothiemurchus, son or grandson of Shaw *Corrfhiaclach* (Bucktooth) who is regarded as the first chief, was killed at the battle of Harlaw in 1411. His son Alasdair *Ciar* recovered Rothiemurchus, but in the 16th century the lands were lost to the Grants. The young Shaw chief murdered his

Shaw

stepfather in a moment of rage and his lands were forfeited to the Crown and sold to the Laird of Grant who bestowed them on his younger son Patrick. Despite efforts ranging from gentle persuasion through legal writ to armed force by Clan Chattan to regain them, Rothiemurchus has remained in Grant hands to this day.

The Shaws of Tordarroch descended from a younger brother of Alasdair *Ciar*, whose name was Adam or *Aodh* (Hugh), and were known as Clan Ay. This name is generally said to be derived from the founder, but Sir Iain Moncreiffe speculated that it is actually the genitive of Shaw, 'Clay Ay' meaning 'children of Shaw'. The significance of this is that it tends to confirm that after the collapse of the house of Rothiemurchus the Shaws of Tordarroch were recognised as chiefs of the name. They certainly signed the Clan Chattan bonds of union in the 17th century.

Tordarroch was held on a wadset (mortgage) from the Mackintosh, who reclaimed the property in the late 18th century, but it has since been regained by the chiefs of Clan Ay.

Sinclair

The name Sinclair (Saint-Clair) is of Norman origin. In the mid-12th century Henry de St Clair held the lands of Herdmanston near Haddington, lands which remained in Sinclair hands for many centuries. His presumed descendant was Sir William Sinclair, a prominent figure in national affairs, guardian to the

Sinclair

heir of King Alexander III, who gained the barony of Rosslyn, Lothian, in 1280. His son fought with Bruce at Bannockburn and his grandson, also Sir William, died fighting with Douglas in Spain against the Moors on their way to deposit Bruce's heart in the Holy Land.

The marriage of this crusader's son was to transport the Sinclairs to the far north, where some still remain. His wife was the heiress of Orkney and Caithness, and their son Henry became in 1379 Earl (*jarl*) of Orkney, the premier title of the Norwegian nobility. Through his mother he was descended from the ancient Norse royal family whose decidedly unroyal nicknames (Halfdan the Stingy, Eystein the Fart – in Sir Iain Moncreiffe's preferred translations) recede far into the mists of Scandinavian myth.

Viking blood seems to have had a powerful effect in the Sinclairs (unless one believes modern accounts which tell us the Vikings were just peace-loving farmers looking for a few spare fields to settle down). In 1395 the Sinclair Earl of Orkney went on the controversial voyage of the Zenos and may have touched on North America. Zeno's account also tells us that he commanded a large fleet on behalf of the Earl of Orkney, the main business of which was piracy.

The grandson of the Norwegian earl was the last of Orkney but the old family title of Earl of Caithness was restored to him in 1544. He was the builder of Rosslyn Chapel, a famous architectural gem. Its fine tracery is in marked contrast to the northern stronghold of the Sinclairs, the gaunt and impregnable Girnigo Castle, on a rocky promontory north of Wick overlooking Sinclair's Bay.

There was much in the history of the family that was appropriately grim for this setting; violent deaths were not uncommon. The first Earl of Caithness's heir

was retarded, so his second son received the old barony of Rosslyn and the third, William, became second Earl of Caithness. He was killed at Flodden, and the third earl died in a Sinclair civil war in the Orkneys. The fourth earl's eldest son, the Master (a common title for elder sons) of Caithness, was apparently more pacific than most of his line, and incurred his father's displeasure by making peace with the Murrays, parties to one of the Sinclairs' many feuds. For this he was thrown into a cell in Girnigo Castle and kept in chains until he died, seven years later, of deliberate ill treatment (to hasten his end, it is said, he was given salted meat and denied water). But the unfortunate Master had his moment of violence too when, goaded by his younger brother, William of Mey, he managed to half-throttle his tormentor with the chains that held him. William died from his injuries and, having no legitimate children, the inheritance he had gloatingly anticipated passed to a third brother.

Raeburn's striking portrait of Sir John Sinclair of Ulbster as Colonel of the Rothesay and Caithness Fencibles. Sir John insisted on trews rather than kilt, believing them to be the older form of dress.

He did, however, have two illegitimate sons, from the younger of whom the Sinclairs of Ulbster descended. The outstanding member of this family (at any rate until Viscount Thurso, who served in Winston Churchill's war cabinet) was Sir John Sinclair of Ulbster (1754-1835), well known as an agricultural reformer, chiefly responsible for the creation of the Board of Agriculture in 1793, and a considerable authority on Highland custom. His magnificent portrait by Raeburn is one of the splendours of the Scottish National Portrait Gallery.

In the north the Sinclairs came under pressure from various rivals, notably the Gordons, and eventually lost most of their lands. The title has passed through a large number of cadet houses, but there is still a Sinclair Earl of Caithness who owned the long-ruined Castle of Girnigo until 1986.

Skene

Skene

The Skenes were an early sept of Clan *Donnchaidh*, most of whom later took the name Robertson, and they appear to have adopted the name Skene before they came into possession of the barony of Skene, west of Aberdeen. The inference is that the lands were named after them rather than vice-versa.

Their origins are explained in a picturesque legend which would be more easily believed were it not so familiar in variant forms in other families. It is the one about the young chief saving the king from a wild beast. In this case, the hero was Thomas of (?)Rannoch, the younger son of a proto-Struan-Robertson, and the king was presumably Malcolm *Ceann Mór*. He was attacked by a large wolf which the progenitor of the Skenes fended off with an arm wrapped in his plaid and then stabbed with his knife (*sgian*, or 'skene'). (One writer has objected on the grounds that an Athollman would have been more likely to have stabbed Malcolm than the wolf.) As a reward the king offered the brave lad as much territory as would be covered by a hawk in flight, and the obliging bird encompassed what became the barony of Skene.

More prosaically, the lands of Skene were erected into a barony by a charter of King Robert Bruce in 1318 for Robert, grandson of John de Skene whose name was among those swearing fealty to Edward I of England in 1296.

In the course of the next century or two many Skenes crop up in the records, suggesting that the clan

Achievement of Skene of that ilk

Above: Provost Skene's house in Aberdeen. Originally built in the mid-16th century, it was much enlarged in the late 17th after it was bought by George Skene. It is now a museum.

Left: The coat of arms of Skene of Skene. The three dirks, or skenes, piercing wolves' heads recall the legend of the founding of the Skene barony.

was prospering. A laird of Skene was killed at Harlaw (1411), fighting almost in his own territory. Another fell at Flodden (1513), but in 1516 the laird was excused attendance in the host that was later vanquished at Pinkie (1547) on the grounds of illness, though it could not have been too serious as he lived another 57 years. In his place he sent his uncle, who did not survive the battle.

The lairds of Skene held on to their lands throughout the troubles of the 17th and 18th centuries, and the last of the line, who was deaf and dumb as well as childless, died in 1827. The property was entailed to a nephew, the Earl of Fife, and the chiefship would appear to have passed eventually to a cadet branch settled in Austria who, however, seems to have shown little interest.

Among notable bearers of the name was William Forbes Skene (1809-92), the great Victorian authority on the history of Celtic Scotland. He belonged to the Skenes of Rubislaw, owners of the Rubislaw quarry which, besides Aberdeen granite, once yielded a type of non-gem beryl known as Davidsonite.

Smith

In pre-industrial societies in many parts of the world, the trade of smith bestowed a certain status, higher than that of other crafts. (Hephaestos was the only Greek god who did an honest day's work.) Perhaps this explains why the name became so common – smiths being possibly more inclined to commemorate their trade than humbler craftsmen.

Early Scottish examples included Alexander Smyth, who was the resident blacksmith at the abbey of Coupar-Angus in 1497 (where there was also a wheelwright called Wrycht, a mason called Mason and a porter called Porter), and James Smyth, smith to the Bishop of Dunkeld in 1506. In Latin charters the name sometimes appears as Ferro or Faber.

Surnames based on a trade or craft are comparatively uncommon in Gaelic, which some have seen as evidence that Highlanders were not much inclined to industrial pursuits though other reasons, such as the predominance of patronymics until a very late date, seem more probable. The Gaelic name for a smith, meaning not only a man who made ploughshares and horseshoes but also an armourer – certainly a vital

Smith

craft among the clans – is *Gobha*, which is the origin of the names Gow and MacGowan (see Gow). However, even in the Gaelic-speaking Highlands the name appears to have been sometimes anglicised as Smith, and there are many Smiths in Lewis, where Gaelic is still generally spoken even now. A notable contemporary example is the bilingual poet and novelist Iain Crichton Smith (*Iain Mac a'Ghobhainn*), who was born in Lewis. There was, however, never such an association as a Clan Smith.

The Gaelic *ceard*, which came to mean principally a tinker, originally also described a craftsman in metal, perhaps brass in particular. This is the origin of the name Caird, or Kerd (not to be confused with Cairns, which has a territorial origin). Some cairds took the name Tinker or Tinkler, and some, in the west, took the name Sinclair. Possibly others became Smiths.

Stewart

Sentiment ascribes a Celtic origin to the royal house of Stewart, but the Banquo of Shakespeare's *Macbeth*, the ghostly procession of whose heirs somewhat interrupts the action, was not a historical character – at least, there is no trace of him except in Holinshed's chronicle where Shakespeare found him. The ancestors of the Stewarts were, inescapably, of French origin. However, sentiment is not yet confounded, for these ancestors were not Normans but Bretons (probably connected with the counts of Dol and Dinant) and, the Bretons being of Celtic origin, the Stewarts were most likely of Celtic descent after all.

The ancestor of the Stewarts came to England in the wake of the Norman conquest and acquired estates in Shropshire and Norfolk, among other parts. A younger son, Walter fitzAlan, was among the

'Queen's View', at the eastern end of Loch Tummel, in Atholl.

entourage of King David I when he left the English court for his Scottish throne. He became High Steward (seneschal) of Scotland, the greatest office in the kingdom, which became hereditary in his family in the next reign and thus gave them their surname, (from the time of the French-raised Mary Queen of Scots it was often spelt Stuart).

The sixth High Steward, Walter, married Bruce's daughter Marjorie and when King David II died without children in 1371 their son, the first Stewart monarch, became king as Robert II.

The Stewarts were kings (and queen) of Scots for over three centuries and it is therefore difficult, though tempting, to generalise about them. To remain in possession of the crown for so long was in itself success of a kind, and on the whole the Stewart monarchs were both intelligent and ruthless, useful qualities in a sovereign, though also capable of extraordinary pig-headedness and blindness.

To their feudal subjects – anyway, to those that mattered politically – the Stewarts were merely one of many noble houses who happened, more or less by

Royal Stewart

lucky chance, to have gained the throne. To assert the authority of the Crown was the constant endeavour of the king, and to this end the Stewarts were prepared to employ almost any means. The experiences of the young King James VI, treated as a pawn in the power struggles of aristocratic factions, resulted in his belief that monarchy in England, where the Crown had already emerged victorious from a similar contest with overmighty subjects, was a much more pleasant occupation than it was in his native land.

Perhaps the gravest criticism of the Stewart monarchy as a whole is that, far from uniting Highlands and

Falkland Palace, a royal hunting lodge built in the early 16th century, expanded by James V on a lavish scale, and often visited by Mary Queen of Scots. After the death of James VI in 1625 it fell into disuse and part was destroyed by fire.

Dress Stewart

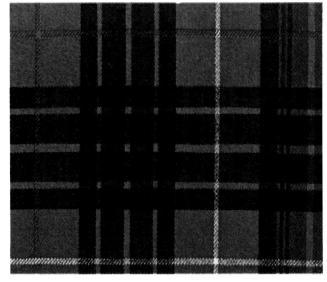

Hunting Stewart

Lowlands, it perpetuated and aggravated the division between the Gaelic-speaking north and the English-speaking south. Conciliation was tried occasionally, usually (though not always) when force was impracticable, but the culmination of the Crown's efforts to bring the whole country under its authority was the deliberate, often brutal, suppression of Gaelic culture.

It is this that gives Jacobitism its bitter-sweet flavour. For the Stewart monarchy, historically no friend to the clans, turned to them in its hour of need when, largely through its own ineptitude, it had forfeited the loyalty of its English subjects, and it did not turn to them in vain. The final episode was the rising of 1745 and its aftermath, one of the most dreadful episodes – the worse for being so unnecessary – in modern British history, which resulted not

The gates of Traquair House near Peebles (the house, very ancient, is said to have housed 27 Scottish and English monarchs), which have not been opened since Prince Charles Edward departed in 1745.

only in the final eclipse of the dynasty but also in the virtual extinction of the old clan system and the destruction of Highland society.

The last of the direct male line of the royal Stewarts was Henry, Cardinal Duke of York, brother of Prince Charles Edward, who lived until 1807 (Bonnie Prince Charlie died, a sad old drunk, in 1788). Ironically but quite legitimately, representation of the royal Stewart line passed to the Hanoverian monarch George III, by virtue of his descent from King James VI/I's daughter. The Cardinal acknowledged this by leaving the Scottish royal jewels that he possessed to George III and his descendants. One of the titles of the present Prince of Wales is Great Steward of Scotland.

Since 1807 the senior representatives of the male line have been the earls of Galloway, descended from the prolific Sir John Stewart of Bonkyl (see below).

The tartan known as the Royal Stewart appears to have little connection with the royal Stewarts. Its origins are discussed in an earlier section.

Stewart of Atholl

Stewart of Atholl

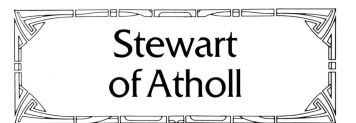

The ramifications of the Stewarts were considerable, and at one time Stewarts have held no fewer than seventeen earldoms, besides several dukedoms and many lesser titles. There is a saying that not all Stewarts are kin to the king; nevertheless, a great number of them were. Lines descending from Sir John Stewart of Bonkyl, a younger son of the fourth Steward (who was great-grandfather of King Robert II and married a granddaughter of the great Somerled of Argyll), were especially fruitful.

The heavy Stewart settlement in Atholl dates from the time of Alexander Stewart, Earl of Buchan, second son of King Robert II and best known by his nickname, the Wolf of Badenoch (c. 1343-1405). The depredations of this man, ostensibly a pillar of official justice, were remarkable even by the standards of 14th-century Scotland. Having been censured by the Bishop of Moray for his treatment of his wife, he set fire to Forres and Elgin in revenge (1390). The Wolf's cubs were scarcely less savage than their sire: one of his illegitimate sons became Earl of Mar by the straightforward means of murdering the Douglas earl and forcing his widow to marry him.

On the death of the Wolf the earldom of Buchan passed to his brother Robert, Duke of Albany, from whose younger son James the Stewarts of Ardvorlich descended (Albany was also the direct male ancestor

of the present Earl of Moray). Another illegitimate son of the Wolf, James, was the ancestor of the Stewarts of Garth, perhaps the most famous branch of the Atholl Stewarts, who included the 19th-century historian of the Highlands, General David Stewart of Garth. Other branches included the Steuarts (their preferred spelling) of Cardney as well as the Earls of Buchan.

After King James I was murdered in 1437 his widow Joan Beaufort married another Stewart, Sir James, known as the Black Knight of Lorne, who was descended from another son of Sir John Stewart of Bonkyl. Their son Sir John Stewart of Balveny (died 1512) was created Earl of Atholl by his half-brother, King James II (the title had been held previously by several Stewarts of the royal line, including the unfortunate grandson of King Robert II, the Duke of Rothesay, who was starved to death in Falkland Castle by his ambitious uncle, Albany).

The most notable member of this line was the fourth earl (great-grandson of Sir John Stewart of Balveny), a leading Catholic noble in the reign of Mary Queen of Scots. After her defeat and flight he supported her restoration against the party of the young King James VI, and there was a strong suspicion that his death in 1578 was the result of poison.

After the death of the fifth earl in 1595 the earldom reverted to the Crown, but following the marriage of the heiress Lady Dorothea Stewart to the Murray Earl of Tullibardine, the title and about 200,000 acres of Atholl passed to that family (1629).

The Stewarts of Atholl were naturally zealous in the cause of the Stewart dynasty, and the leadership of their Murray overlords being doubtful in that cause they served under others. In Dundee's campaign against William III they were led by Stewart of

Ballechin, whose family descended from an illegitimate son of King James II. There were said to be 1,500 of them at that time.

Stewart of Appin

Stewart of Appin

The royal Stewarts could not be regarded as a clan in the usual sense of the word – the king was their 'chief' and the entire nation his 'clansmen' – but the Stewarts of Appin were effectively a West Highland clan in themselves.

Most of the main Stewart lines, including the Stewart earls of Atholl, descended from the fourth High Steward, whose younger son John married the heiress of Bonkyl, fought with Wallace, and produced seven sons. Three of these sons were the founders of noble families, the youngest of the three, Sir James Stewart of Pirston (Pearston) in Ayrshire, who died at Hallidon Hill in 1333, being the ancestor of the Stewarts of Appin. (The other two were Sir Alexander, whence the pre-Douglas earls of Angus, and Sir Alan of Dreghorn, whence the dukes of Lennox: see below.)

A younger son of Sir James of Pierston had two sons, of Innermeath and of Durrisdeer, each of whom married an heiress of the MacDougall lords of Lorne. From Sir John of Innermeath (died 1421) a number of famous Highland families descended, including the Stewarts of Appin (and, from younger sons, the earls of Atholl via the Black Knight of Lorne, and the Steuarts of Grandtully). The lordship of Lorne was held by the Stewarts for less than a century (1388-1470), afterwards passing to the Campbells.

Dugald, the great-grandson of Sir John of Innermeath, was the first Stewart of Appin, and his family held those lands for about 400 years. From his grandson Alan, third Stewart of Appin, numerous cadets stemmed – Achnacone (this family still holds land in Appin), Fasnacloich and Invernahyle. Another, later cadet house of the Stewarts of Appin was Ardshiel, who provided their leader during Dundee's campaign in 1689 and again at the battle of Culloden (1746), the Appin chief being a minor on both occasions.

The Stewarts of Appin were at one with other branches of the family in loyalty to their royal kinsfolk, and a bond of association was signed by the Stewarts of Appin, Atholl and Balquhdder in 1645, following action with Montrose during the civil war.

The Appin regiment suffered heavy casualties at Culloden and their families suffered no less in the harrying of the clans which followed that defeat. The Appin Murder in this period has gained popular notoriety largely through the account of it in Robert Louis Stevenson's *Kidnapped*. Colin Campbell, whom Stevenson called the Red Fox of Glenure, a factor in charge of the forfeited estate of Ardshiel, was shot dead near Ballachulish in 1752. The suspected murderer, Allan Breck Stewart, escaped but James Stewart, brother of the chief, was arrested, charged with the murder in a Campbell court at Inveraray presided over by the Duke of Argyll himself, convicted and hanged.

Sir Alan Stewart of Dreghorn, son of Sir John of Bonkyl and brother of the ancestor of the Stewarts of Appin, was the forefather of the dukes of Lennox and thus also an ancestor of the later Stewart kings. His descendant, Sir John Stewart of Darnley (died 1429), who was also seigneur of Aubigny, married a daughter of Duncan, Earl of Lennox, and their grandson became the first Stewart Earl.

The second earl died at Flodden (1513) and his grandson, the fourth earl (died 1571), having failed to acquire supreme power for himself by various machinations, secured the marriage of his son, usually known as Lord Darnley, to Mary Queen of Scots (Darnley's cousin). He thus became, eventually, grandfather of King James VI/I.

Darnley was soon disposed of, a mysterious explosion failing to conceal the fact that he had been strangled before he was blown up, and the Earl of Lennox became one of the queen's chief opponents. He died in battle and was succeeded by his second son, the fifth earl, whose daughter Lady Arabella Stuart was the miserable lynchpin of numerous plots over the succession and died insane in the Tower of London in 1615.

Sutherland

Sunset over Loch Linnhe. The country of the Stewarts of Appin, 'the unconquered foe of the Campbells' (and there weren't many of those), lay on the east bank of this beautiful sea loch.

Esmé Stewart, a nephew of the fourth earl, was a great favourite of King James VI, who made him Duke of Lennox in 1581. His son, the second duke, became also Duke of Richmond and an Englishman.

'La Belle Stuart', who modelled for the figure of Britannia on the old penny, was the wife of the sixth Duke of Lennox, and herself a Stuart by birth. Whether she was also the mistress of yet another Stuart, Charles II, has been disputed.

Sutherland

Sutherland comes from the Norse *Sudrland*, which was how the Norsemen described the most southerly of their dominions. The earldom of Sutherland, one of the oldest continuous earldoms in Britain, was created in the early 13th century for the lord of Sutherland, a descendant of William de Moravia (of Moray) who was also the ancestor of the Murrays. The Sutherland clan, unlike most clans, did not generally adopt the name of their chief in the days when surnames became common and many of them were in fact named Murray.

The second Earl of Sutherland fought for Bruce, and the fourth fell at Hallidon Hill fighting the English in 1333. The fifth earl continued the tradition, marrying a daughter of Bruce and providing a large company for the army which was defeated at the battle of Neville's Cross (1346). His son by the Bruce princess might have become heir to the throne, avoiding the Stewart succession, had he not died young. A son by the fifth earl's second wife became the next Earl of Sutherland, while another founded the notable cadet house of the Sutherlands of Forse. The fifth earl himself died in 1370, possibly a victim of the Mackays, who were at feud with the Sutherlands for centuries.

Robert, sixth earl, who married a daughter of the Wolf of Badenoch (son of King Robert II), was the builder of Dunrobin (i.e. Robin's castle), overlooking the sea near Golspie. Needless to say it had little in common with the present romantic edifice, which is largely the work of Sir Charles Barry, architect of the Westminster Houses of Parliament in the 19th century (though Dunrobin was altered again early in this century after a fire had destroyed part of it).

Both the eighth and ninth earls were afflicted by mental trouble. The latter's daughter Elizabeth was married to Adam Gordon of Aboyne, brother of the Earl of Huntly, and when the ninth Earl of Sutherland

Above: Dunrobin Castle, former home of the dukes of Sutherland, overlooking the Moray Firth. Although parts date back to the Middle Ages, most of it is 18th- and 19th-century.

Below right: Kenneth Sutherland, third Lord Duffus, painted by Richard Waitt in the early 18th century.

died Gordon took possession of the earldom, an act without legal justification which was resisted by Alexander Sutherland, half-brother of Elizabeth and the rightful heir. He enjoyed considerable support locally and twice recaptured Dunrobin, but was killed in a skirmish, leaving the Gordons in possession.

Subsequent earls retained the name Gordon, presumably because the Earl of Huntly wished to retain them as a sept of his own clan. To protect themselves against Sutherland claimants the Gordons in 1601 obtained a grant from King James VI that if the direct line from Adam Gordon of Aboyne failed the earldom of Sutherland should pass to the Gordons of Huntly. The sixteenth earl did assume the name Sutherland at the end of the 17th century, but when his descendant died in 1766 leaving only a daughter, a great legal argument broke out over the succession. The Sutherlands lost again, and the title was bestowed on the late earl's daughter who became Countess of Sutherland in her own right (1771). However, she and her wealthy husband George Leveson-Gower, Marquess of Stafford, later became Duke and Duchess of Sutherland.

The duke and duchess are for ever associated with the notorious Sutherland Clearances of the late 18th century, which destroyed the ancient clan. It should be said that the duke's motives were entirely charitable and in forcing his tenants to move down to the coast where their poverty would be relieved – not for long as things turned out – by the booming kelp industry, he spent a good deal of his money, though he could certainly afford it. He was in a way the archetypal do-gooder, zealous in his pursuit of progress, oblivious to individual preference, ignorant of local culture.

The third Duke of Sutherland was a similar sort. He invested a huge sum of money to build the Highland Railway but insisted that it pursued a roundabout route which would not disturb the shooting.

With the death of the fifth duke in 1962 the ducal title passed to another family, and his niece Elizabeth became countess of the old Scottish earldom and chief of the clan.

Besides the Sutherlands of Forse, the Sutherlands of Duffus in Moray were a famous house. They were descended from the second son of the fourth earl and also had to withstand Gordon attempts at their deprivation. Kenneth, Lord Duffus, was 'out' in the Jacobite rising of 1715 (the earls of Sutherland supported the Hanoverians). His portrait showing portly knees below his belted plaid (in no recognisable tartan) is in the Scottish National Portrait Gallery. His estates being forfeit, he fled abroad, served in the Russian navy and married into an aristocratic Swedish family. The estates were restored to his grandson, but the line became extinct in a later generation.

Thomson (MacThomas)

Thomson is a fairly common surname in Scotland, usually spelt without the P that is common in England. In the Gaelic-speaking Highlands the name is *Mac Thómais*. It was often anglicised as MacTavish, a common name in Argyll where Clan Tavish was a minor sept of the Campbells, descended from an illegitimate son of the Lord of Lochow in the 13th century. They were possibly connected with the Border family of Thomson of that ilk. Some MacTavishes were called Taweson, as well as Thomson.

There was also a sept of the MacFarlanes known as

Thomson

Thomason, or other variants, whose ancestor was the son of a MacFarlane chief called Thomas. However, the largest group was a sept of Clan Chattan whose name was usually anglicised as MacThomas, although subject to numerous variations including MacCombie, MacComa, etc. They were believed to be descended from an illegitimate son of William, seventh Chief of Mackintosh, and they settled mainly in Glenshee and Glenisla. A charter of 1571 confirmed John McComy-Muir (presumably *Mac Thomaidh Mór*) in the lands of Finzegand, Glenshee, although the MacThomases were named among the 'broken' clans in the late 16th century.

During the civil war the MacThomas chief apparently acted as a parliamentary agent, and in the 17th century the MacThomases (or MacComies) conducted feuds with their Farquharson neighbours, among others.

Captain Patrick MacThomas was recognised by Lyon Court as Chief of Clan MacThomas of Glenshee in 1968.

In the 18th century the name also occurred in Lewis, home of the contemporary Gaelic poet *Ruaraidh MacThómais*, and in other parts of the country. In Shetland the usual form was Thomasson.

Urquhart

The name Urquhart is generally agreed to be of territorial origin. The Urquharts of Loch Ness, where Castle Urquhart enjoys a splendid situation on a promontory commanding the eastern end of the loch, probably derived their name from *Urchardau* meaning 'wood-side', but another likely derivation is from *urchar*, a cast or a shot. Professor Watson (in *The Celtic Place-Names of Scotland*) also suggested it may refer to 'a spur or offshoot of rising ground'.

According to family tradition, the Urquharts, who at one time owned much of the Black Isle, were originally linked with Clan Forbes and to the lords of Aird. In the 17th century Sir Thomas Urquhart traced his ancestry back to the third millenium BC, but history confirms no one earlier than the 14th century, when the Urquharts became hereditary sheriffs of Cromarty, originally as a result of marriage to a daughter of the Earl of Ross. The family prospered and established branches in Moray and Aberdeenshire.

A 16th-century laird is said to have been the father of 25 sons, of whom seven were killed at the battle of Pinkie (1547). His successor, Alexander Urquhart, seventh Sheriff of Cromarty, had two sons of whom the younger, John, was the founder of the house of Craigfintry. This was the tutor of Cromarty (an office which implies guardianship of both the person and the estate of an under-age chief), who administered the lands with 'great dexterity in acquiring of many lands and possessions, with all men's applause' – well, almost all.

The strain of eccentricity which reached full flower in Sir Thomas Urquhart of Cromarty in the 17th century was already apparent in his great-grandfather a century earlier. This man, also Sir Thomas, had himself hoisted to the battlements on a couch every evening in memory of Christ's Resurrection.

His grandson (again, Sir Thomas, 1582-1642) was knighted by King James VI whose scholarly if undisciplined interests he shared. He was not, according to his son, much of a businessman and proved a soft touch for 'many cunning sharks'.

His son, the famous Sir Thomas Urquhart (?1611-60), inherited his intellectual interests. He took part in the rising on behalf of Charles II in 1649 and was captured at Worcester. Unfortunately, he could not bear to be parted from his manuscripts and had taken them with him on campaign. Cromwell's soldiers, displaying the traditional contempt of the sword for the pen, used them as lavatory paper. Sir Thomas was imprisoned for two years in the Tower of London and it was probably then that he began the translation of Rabelais in which his literary fame chiefly resides.

One of the largest of Scottish castles, it fell into Grant hands in the 16th century.

Urquhart

Wallace

Sir Thomas died in 1660, the joyous hilarity occasioned by news of the Restoration of the monarchy apparently inducing a fatal stroke, and the Cromarty estates passed to his cousin, John Urquhart of Craigston, descended from the Tutor of Cromarty, who sold them. Another branch of the family regained them briefly in the 18th century. In recent years the chiefship was re-established in the person of an American citizen. The attractive ruins of Castle Craig on the Cromarty Firth are today held by the Urquharts of Craigston.

The name Wallace appears in old charters as Wallensis, meaning a Welshman, but in Scotland the name referred not to Wales but to the Ancient Britons' kingdom of Strathclyde. The first known Wallace was Richard Wallensis of Richardston (now Riccarton) in Ayrshire, formerly part of the kingdom of Strathclyde. He was a vassal of Walter FitzAlan the Steward, ancestor of the Stewart dynasty.

His grandson, Adam Wallace of Riccarton, had two sons, the younger of whom, Malcolm, received lands in Elderslie, Renfrewshire, where William Wallace,

Scotland's great national hero, was born about 1275.

After a succession of generally strong and successful monarchs, Scotland was thrown into crisis by the early death of King Alexander III, leaving the infant daughter of the King of Norway as heir to the throne. The Maid of Norway's death soon afterwards meant that the royal line was at an end. There were many claimants, the strongest being Robert Bruce and John Balliol, and the Scots took the decision, potentially hazardous but better than the certain alternative of civil war, to invite Edward I of England to adjudicate. He chose Balliol. That was the constitutionally correct choice, but it soon became clear that Edward, whose predecessors had claimed overlordship of the Scots with varying degrees of conviction, regarded himself as the true ruler. Even Balliol, expected to be compliant, could not stomach Edward's demands, but Edward was already poised to invade, and he made short work of Balliol and the divided Scots. Having conquered Scotland and despatched Balliol to the Tower, Edward regarded the whole episode as satisfactorily terminated.

About six months later, in the spring of 1297, there was a minor scuffle in the marketplace at Lanark between some English soldiers and the young William Wallace, who escaped with the aid of a young woman. The girl, possibly his wife, was later executed by the sheriff of Lanark. The same night Wallace killed the sheriff. He became automatically an outlaw, but in a matter of weeks he was the leader of

Above: Stirling Castle, which has guarded the main route to the Highlands since early times, although much of the present building dates only from the 15th century. It was a magnificent royal palace in the reign of James V.

Right: The tower at Abbey Craig, north of Stirling, is a memorial to Scotland's great hero, William Wallace, who stands, sword raised, at the corner.

widespread national resistance to the English occupation. At Stirling Bridge Wallace and Sir Andrew Moray annihilated a large and well-equipped English army and freed most of Scotland.

However, in 1298 Wallace was heavily defeated by Edward I and for the next seven years he was on the run, limited to guerilla raids while the English soldiers ravaged the kingdom. In 1305 he was captured and after a trial in London executed with grotesque barbarity as a traitor, though as he said at his trial, Wallace had never sworn fealty to Edward, not even, like most Scottish landholders, under duress at Berwick in 1296.

Not much is known for certain about Wallace. That he could achieve the position he did, among the selfish, treacherous and quarrelsome Scottish barons, suggests a character of extraordinary force.

Wallace himself left no descendants, but a great many families of his name trace their descent from the Wallaces of Riccarton.

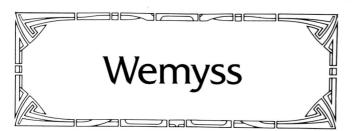

Wemyss

The premier clan of medieval Scotland was Clan MacDuff, whose chiefs, descended from the royal line, were the earls of Fife. A younger son of Gillemichael, Earl of Fife in the first half of the 12th century, obtained the lands of Wemyss, which gave his descendants their surname, from his father. It is said that the name is a corruption of the Gaelic word for a cave, *uamh*, and below what remains of the old castle at East Wemyss known as MacDuff's Castle there are indeed caves, which contain indecipherable drawings dating from Pictish times.

In 1304 Sir Michael of Wemyss reluctantly played host to Edward I of England but he subsequently joined Bruce's rebellion and incurred the special resentment of the 'Hammer of the Scots', who sent instruction 'to burn, destroy and strip' his lands. Later, the family established numerous cadet branches, and Wemyss of Wemyss eventually emerged as the senior line descended from the old MacDuff earls of Fife.

In the 17th century Sir John Wemyss became an earl. When his son, the second earl, died in 1679, he left only a daughter, Margaret, who married a kinsman, Sir James Wemyss of Caskyberry, later Lord Burntisland. Their son David, the fourth earl, married the eldest daughter of the Duke of Queensberry and their son, the fifth earl, was the first to be officially recognised as representative of the family of the MacDuff earls of Fife. An endearing portrait of him, painted about 1715, in the uniform of the Royal

Detail of Allan Ramsay's attractive portrait of the fifth Earl of Wemysss in the uniform of Captain-General of the Royal Company of Archers, about 1715. The Archers are the Queen's bodyguard in Scotland.

Wemyss

Company of Archers is still in the Archers' possession.

During the Jacobite rising of 1745 the earl's eldest son Lord Elcho (a title first bestowed on the first Earl of Wemyss) raised a troop of cavalry for Prince Charles and was subsequently attainted. When he died in exile, the title went to his younger brother who, however, had taken the name of Charteris (deriving from the French *Chartres* and pronounced Charters) on inheriting a fortune from his maternal grandfather, Colonel Francis Charteris (an unsavoury character who allegedly made most of his money by cheating at cards).

A third brother, James, inherited Wemyss, including the fine castle at West Wemyss which overlooks the Firth of Forth opposite Edinburgh. It was originally built in the 15th century but has been much altered in the intervening period.

The present chief, Wemyss of Wemyss, is descended from James, while the present Earl of Wemyss is descended from his elder brother.

253

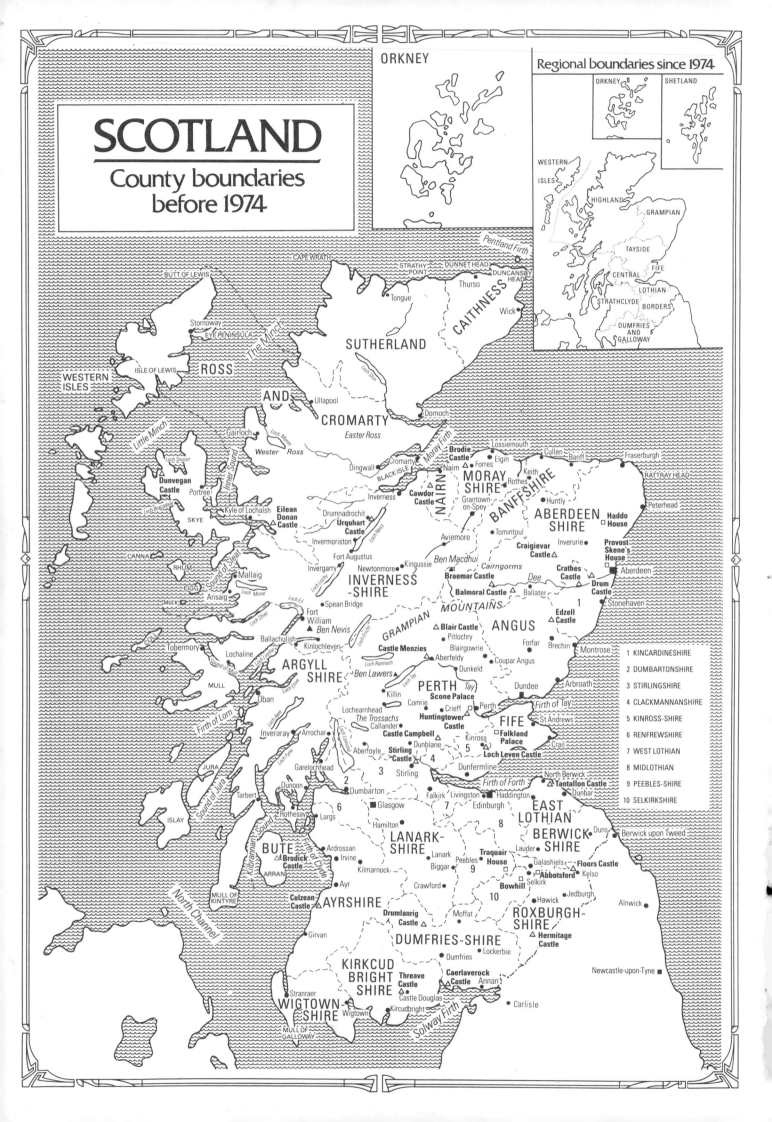

SCOTLAND
County boundaries before 1974

ORKNEY

Regional boundaries since 1974

ORKNEY SHETLAND

WESTERN ISLES

HIGHLAND

GRAMPIAN

TAYSIDE

FIFE

CENTRAL

LOTHIAN

STRATHCLYDE

BORDERS

DUMFRIES AND GALLOWAY

Pentland Firth

CAPE WRATH

BUTT OF LEWIS

STRATHY POINT

DUNNET HEAD

DUNCANSBY HEAD

Thurso

CAITHNESS

Tongue

Wick

SUTHERLAND

Stornoway

EYE PENINSULA

ISLE OF LEWIS

WESTERN ISLES

ROSS

Loch Shin

AND

Ullapool

Dornoch

CROMARTY

Gairloch

Easter Ross

Little Minch

Loch Maree

Wester Ross

Moray Firth

Lossiemouth

Loch Snizort

Cromarty

Cullen Banff

Fraserburgh

Dingwall

BLACK ISLE

Brodie Castle

Elgin

Dunvegan Castle

Portree

Loch Bracadale

Inverness

Nairn △ Forres

Keith

Rothes

RATTRAY HEAD

SKYE

Kyle of Lochalsh

Eilean Donan Castle △

Drumnadrochit

Cawdor Castle

NAIRN

MORAY SHIRE

BANFFSHIRE

Huntly

ABERDEEN SHIRE

Haddo House □

Peterhead

CANNA

Urquhart Castle

Invermoriston

Loch Ness

Grantown-on-Spey

Aviemore

Tomintoul

Inverurie

Craigievar Castle △

Provost Skene's House

RHUM

Fort Augustus

Newtonmore Kingussie

Ben Macdhui △

Cairngorms

■ Aberdeen

Mallaig

Invergarry

Loch Lochy

INVERNESS-SHIRE

Braemar Castle

Dee

Crathes Castle

Drum Castle

MUCK

EIGG

Arisaig

Loch Morar

Loch Eil

Spean Bridge

Balmoral Castle △

Ballater

1

Stonehaven

Sound of Sleat

COLL

Tobermory

Fort William

▲ Ben Nevis

Loch Shiel

GRAMPIAN

Blair Castle △

MOUNTAINS

ANGUS

Edzell Castle △

Lochaline

Kinlochleven

Loch Leven

Pitlochry

Forfar

Brechin

Montrose

Sound of Mull

MULL

Castle Menzies

Blairgowrie

1 KINCARDINESHIRE

ARGYLL SHIRE

Ben Lawers △

Loch Rannoch

△ Aberfeldy

Dunkeld

Coupar Angus

2 DUMBARTONSHIRE

Oban

Loch Etive

Loch Tay

Killin

PERTH

Tay

Dundee

Arbroath

3 STIRLINGSHIRE

Firth of Lorn

Lochearnhead

Comrie

Crieff

Scone Palace

□ Perth

Firth of Tay

4 CLACKMANNANSHIRE

Loch Awe

The Trossachs

Callander

Huntingtower Castle

St Andrews

5 KINROSS-SHIRE

Inveraray

Arrochar

Loch Lomond

Castle Campbell △

Dunblane

Kinross

FIFE

Falkland Palace □

Crail

6 RENFREWSHIRE

JURA

Garelochhead

Aberfoyle

Stirling Castle △

5

Loch Leven Castle

7 WEST LOTHIAN

Sound of Jura

Dunoon

2

Stirling

4

Dunfermline

8 MIDLOTHIAN

Tarbert

3

North Berwick

9 PEEBLES-SHIRE

Dumbarton

Firth of Forth

△ Tantallon Castle

10 SELKIRKSHIRE

Rothesay

Largs

6

■ Glasgow

7

Falkirk Livingston

□ Haddington

Dunbar

ISLAY

Kilbrannan Sound

Hamilton

Edinburgh

EAST LOTHIAN

BUTE

ARRAN

Ardrossan

Irvine

LANARK-SHIRE

8

BERWICK-SHIRE

Duns

Berwick upon Tweed

Brodick Castle △

Kilmarnock

Lanark

Lauder

Floors Castle

Firth of Clyde

Biggar

Peebles

Traquair House

Galashiels □

Kelso

MULL OF KINTYRE

Ayr

9

□

Abbotsford

Selkirk

Culzean Castle △

AYRSHIRE

Crawford

Bowhill

Hawick

Jedburgh

Alnwick

10

ROXBURGH-SHIRE

North Channel

Girvan

Drumlanrig Castle △

Moffat

Hermitage Castle ▲

DUMFRIES-SHIRE

Lockerbie

MULL OF GALLOWAY

KIRKCUD BRIGHT SHIRE

Threave Castle △

Caerlaverock Castle ■

Annan

Dumfries

Newcastle-upon-Tyne ■

Stranraer

Castle Douglas

WIGTOWN-SHIRE

Wigtown

Kircudbright

Solway Firth

Carlisle